D1637292

THE CAREER LATTICE

·················

Combat Brain Drain, Improve Company
Culture, and Attract Top Talent

JOANNE CLEAVER

New York   Chicago   San Francisco   Lisbon   London   Madrid   Mexico City
Milan   New Delhi   San Juan   Seoul   Singapore   Sydney   Toronto

The **McGraw·Hill** Companies

1 2 3 4 5 6 7 8 9 0   QFR/QFR   1 0 9 8 7 6 5 4 3 2

ISBN: 978-0-07-179169-4
MHID: 0-07-179169-8

e-book ISBN: 978-0-07-179170-0
e-book MHID: 0-07-179170-1

This publication is designed to provide accurate and authoritative information in regard to the subject matter covered. It is sold with the understanding that neither the author nor the publisher is engaged in rendering legal, accounting, or other professional service. If legal advice or other expert assistance is required, the services of a competent professional person should be sought.

> —*From a Declaration of Principles jointly adopted*
> *by a Committee of the American Bar*
> *Association and a Committee of Publishers*

McGraw-Hill books are available at special quantity discounts to use as premiums and sales promotions, or for use in corporate training programs. To contact a representative, please e-mail us at bulksales@mcgraw-hill.com.

This book is printed on acid-free paper.

To Mark: Up, down, and sideways, the best partner I could hope to have,
and far better than I deserve

CONTENTS

FOREWORD

Eric Winegardner
VICE PRESIDENT, MONSTER WORLDWIDE

THE CORPORATE LADDER. Remember when it was the only way to the top? Only a few were chosen to advance. And even fewer made it.

The corporate ladder is no more.

Today's workers are their own advocates. They want work that is meaningful. They want to follow their curiosity, their interests, their skills and most importantly, their passions, to continuously grow and evolve. To succeed not because they got to the top, but because they are part of a winning team.

Over 4 million people search Monster every day to find their next job. They are looking for a better chance, a better job, a better opportunity. Finding better is the beacon that pulls us all forward. We know it is out there. It is in all of us. It is less about a giant leap. It is about small steps to better. Employers are looking to find better talent. People are looking for better jobs.

Some people believe finding better is difficult. There is a skills gap in our economy. In *The Career Lattice*, Joanne reflects that today there are jobs without people and people without jobs. Unemployment is high but jobs still go unfulfilled. So how do you find better, as an employer and as a worker?

Employers want people who are adaptable, ready and willing to take on new skills. Flexibility is the key to success. Those who are experts today, may be left behind tomorrow.

The lattice embodies the concept of continuous learning. Moving across, up, even down can help today's workers find their next job, their next career. Today's managers must not only understand the lattice, they must live it. They must be pathfinders, showing their workers the way to better—the path to their next skill, their next job, even their next career.

Finding better is within you, whether you are the person who is looking for the next job or the manager who is responsible for helping others achieve their goals.

Don't be fearful of the lattice. The lateral move, the change to a new industry, the leap to a new role. Read on. Find the path to your success and the success of your team. The road is no longer straight. But the journey is worth it.

ACKNOWLEDGMENTS

Every book has many authors in addition to the one whose name is on the cover. In the parlance of *The Career Lattice* (Chapter 2), my crew came through. Sincere thanks and everlasting gratitude to:

My lookouts: Holly Root of the Waxman Agency; Pam Tate of the Council for Adult and Experiential Learning; Parthavi Das of Women in Cable Telecommunications; Zach Gajewski and Daina Penikas of McGraw-Hill; and David Moldawer, now of Amazon.

My wingpeople: Kristen McGuire, who kept this project on track and kept me away from many ditches, detours, and distractions. I could not ask for a better collaborator or friend. Stephanie Cleaver masterminded the lattice diagrams and collaborated on the graphic elements. I am grateful to have reared a talented and thoughtful designer.

My spotters: Beth Doyle, Dorothy Wax, and Shawn Hulsizer of the Council for Adult and Experiential Learning; and each employer and latticer who shared his experiences so that others could have career success, especially those involved in San Antonio's Mission Verde.

It is impossible to put my husband, Mark, in any category, lattice or otherwise. He understands that the creative process sometimes happens while one is quilting, shopping, baking, swimming, walking, or watching *Real Housewives* marathons. Without his constant encouragement and practical support, *The Career Lattice* would still be only a good idea.

The goodwill and good work of these people should not be tarnished by any inadvertent errors, for which I am wholly responsible.

INTRODUCTION

The Atwood Cafe is an oasis of Victorian comfort right in the middle of Chicago's hyperkinetic Loop. When Pam Tate and I meet there to talk through the next stage of our collaboration on *The Career Lattice*, we settle in on loveseats for rich coffee served on a polished mahogany table. By the time our oatmeal (Pam) and omelet (me) arrive, we are deep into our ongoing conversation about how career paths for everyday Americans are being rerouted.

For three decades, Pam and I had parallel career paths. As president of the Council for Adult and Experiential Learning (CAEL)*, Pam has been the lead architect for the redesign of American career paths. CAEL helps workers manage their careers to enable lifelong economic self-sufficiency through workplace and college training and counseling. Meanwhile, I spent the same three decades researching and reporting on the same trends as they play out for workplaces and individuals. When we met in September 2010, we immediately realized

---

*The Council for Adult and Experiential Learning (http://www.cael.org/) is a national nonprofit that collaborates with hundreds of major employers and thousands of colleges to introduce new career pathways for working adults. Its programs equip adults to identify and pursue new careers that blend their existing knowledge with fresh skills and strategies for professional and personal advancement. *The Career Lattice* is based both on case studies and materials adapted with permission from CAEL, and on the author's own research.

that CAEL's expertise was a perfect match with my desire to help Americans reclaim their career aspirations through latticing.

Pam has spent nearly all her career at CAEL. Founded in 1974, the nonprofit had nearly lost its way in 1989. A dispirited board of directors told Pam that if she really thought she could revive CAEL, she could have at it. She moved to Chicago, put some of her own resources on the line, and started building alliances with national employers, unions, colleges, and policy makers. Pam's own influence grew along with CAEL's as CAEL became the national authority for designing training programs that set Americans on fresh career paths.

Meanwhile, 15 miles north of CAEL's headquarters in the Chicago Loop, and only vaguely aware of CAEL, I started fresh out of grad school as a freelance business journalist. I sewed my own bootstraps and hoisted myself up, and by 2000 I was writing articles and books and managing research projects about women in business, careers, entrepreneurship, and family travel. With my three daughters in high school and college, I cycled through staff editing positions at the *Milwaukee Journal Sentinel* and the Tribune Company, gaining management and digital publishing experience, and managing major research projects for associations and publications. By the time I met Pam, it was dawning on me that my zigzag career path was actually a more reliable route to economic stability than the once safe, now sinking staff journalism jobs that I had once coveted.

The traditional up-or-out career path has been crumbling for two decades, buffeted by the relentless forces of a global labor force, the automation of professional job functions, and the flattening of workplace organizations. Lattices are the emerging model, either by design (the rise of teams, matrixed relationships, and new leadership designs) or by default (layoffs and shrinking industries). The Great Recession knocked millions of people off the career ladder and tore rungs from the grasp of millions more. When Pam and I met to see how CAEL's expertise and my journalistic expertise could bring hope and a new vision of lifelong advancement to working Americans, we realized that the career lattice could be a powerful force for recovery.

When an earthquake breaks up a highway, some people insist on fixing the road. Others see an opportunity to rethink the purpose of that stretch of highway: to get people from one city to the next, with rest stops, refueling points, and scenic detours along the way. Must the fractured pavement and shattered ramps simply be rebuilt or patched? Doesn't a seismic event invite a remapping of how travelers navigate from one major destination to the next?

The career lattice is both more stable and more dynamic than the linear career ladder. By latticing, working Americans in all industries, of all ages, and in all career stages can be positioned to move quickly into emerging jobs. *The Career Lattice* brings to all workplaces and all workers CAEL's expertise and encouragement in remixing current abilities with new skills and experiences to move ahead steadily.

The lattice is about evolution. It's about adding new skills, experience, abilities, and networks to those that already exist. It's about letting go of the bits that are no longer relevant in the workforce while blending in new elements that anticipate and encourage the growth of individuals and organizations.

The Career Lattice draws on the experience and wisdom of CAEL's experts, staff members and clients alike, as well as other individuals and employers, from Accenture to Xerox, who have mastered the career lattice in part or as a whole.

America's workers need and deserve career paths that make the most of everything they bring to work. *Your* workplace needs employees who bring all of their talents, experiences, and ambitions to achieve the daily goals that add up to growth. Lattice your own career—and show your colleagues how it's done.

CHAPTER 1

THE CAREER LATTICE:
Sustainable Growth for Employees, Organizations, and the Local Economy

Andrew Madison's career had come to a dead end. For 16 years, he had been a field service engineer, helping customers of his employer, a semiconductor manufacturer, get their projects up and running. He was already weary of the travel, and of fixing glitches but never seeing the overall results of his work, when the Great Recession hit in 2008. His employer offered him a buyout. He took it.

But where could he go? He had an associate's degree in electrical engineering enhanced by additional certifications, but he knew he didn't want to just take another job based on his technical qualifications. He wanted to move into a growth industry, but he also wanted a job that would expand his professional horizons in a more satisfying direction. He thought he would make a good project manager, but so far he hadn't the opportunity to try that.

Paving a new career path one step at a time, Madison traded on his most reliable aptitude: his ability to master new technical skills quickly. After six months in a specialized solar training program, he became qualified to design and supervise the installation of photovoltaic panels and thermal solar water heaters. "I didn't know what I wanted to do in solar, but I knew I didn't want to be on the roof, doing installations," he says. Madison realized that he'd underestimated the value of his long track record of collaborating with customers. He had put himself through college doing phone sales for a telecommunications company. And he liked figuring out how to solve customers' problems.

Solar sales and design was the perfect intersection of what he was trained to do, what he was good at, and where he wanted to go. So, he took his passion for solar energy to Novastar Energy, a San Antonio company that designs and installs solar energy systems for homes and businesses. His job was to scope out the project, draw the conceptual design, and make sure that customers got the results they anticipated. "Once they have their systems installed, and their electric meters are running backwards, they're giddy," he says of homeowners.

Madison sees a bright future for his career, even if solar economic development slows. "At first, my move to solar was not about the money; it was about doing something I was passionate about. Now, I see that my skill set is in demand in many different ways and even different industries. I have confidence in my opportunities, even in this economy," he says. And based on his newfound appreciation of his people skills, he envisions himself as a team leader, or even a regional sales manager. Because he is now on a career lattice, Andrew Madison will never again have to back out of a career cul-de-sac.[1]

UNTIL NOW, THE prevailing Western career metaphor has been the ladder, straightforward and steep. The ladder's message is that the main way up is either to wait until everyone ahead has moved up a rung, opening a logical and obvious, if incremental, spot . . . or, if you have the stomach for it, to claw over the backs of those between you and a promotion. The ladder has worked for a few people. They are called CEOs. But in an era of team-centric, flattened organizations, with technology changing whom we work with and how, the ladder is rotting away.

The emerging model is the lattice. A career lattice is a diagonal framework that braids lateral experiences, adjacent skill acquisition, and peer networking to move employees to any of a variety of positions for which they have become qualified. About a third of U.S. employers have adopted some sort of structured lateral career path for at least some of their employees.[2] The ladder stifles the creativity and flexibility that workers need if they are to meet the challenges of a global economy. The career lattice is win-win-win, short term and long term, for employees, managers, organizations, and even economic growth.

The Career Lattice explores the advantages and flexibility of career lattices for individuals, for managers, and for talent planners such as human resources staff and executives. It draws on the deep expertise of the Council for Adult and Experiential Learning (CAEL), which invented the lattice model that has been widely adopted in healthcare and businesses. CAEL's programs have also popularized strategic lateral career paths. In addition, *The Career Lattice* mines the author's understanding of workplace cultures and programs, developed through the research projects designed and managed by her firm, Wilson-Taylor Associates, Inc.

Grounded in proven practices, the strategies outlined in *The Career Lattice* will show you how to adopt strategic lateral career paths for your organization, your staff, and yourself. *The ability to lattice to adjacent positions will be the defining career skill of the next two decades.*

Figure 1-1
How Latticing Reinforces Economic Development in San Antonio Through Interlocked Programs

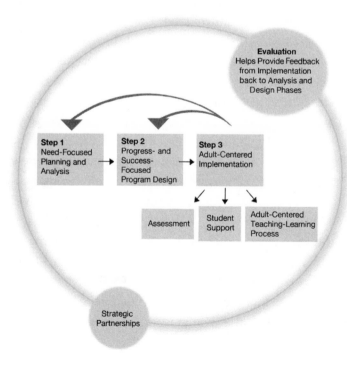

How Lattices Work for All

Politics aside, it's clear that the old economic growth drivers must be reinvented. Career lattices are a flexible model for entire industries— even for entire regions. Lattices deliver immediate results while reorienting workplaces for long-term growth, which explains why they are being woven into progressive industries and economic growth coalitions.

Andrew Madison's story is being replicated across San Antonio as its employers and policy makers align behind Mission Verde, the region's plan to drive sustainable economic growth through sustainable energy industries. CAEL designed green career lattices for Mission Verde (see Figure 1-1). Now, Alamo Colleges, a system of five community colleges in the metro San Antonio area, is building on that design with "green" training curricula. As employers, economic development leaders, academics, and trainers absorbed the profound shift in perspective inherent in the career lattice, many of them came to realize that their own career paths had shifted from the ladder to the lattice. Mission Verde is on the leading edge of a trend that will transform American workplaces, workforces, and the definition of career success. This realization has made lattice advocates of the Mission Verde collaborators. Their stories are told throughout this chapter. As you see how many of the Mission Verde leaders are integrating the lattice into workplaces and their own lives, you will see how you can use career lattices to foster economic growth that is broad-scale and, just as important, self-fueling.

San Antonio is using a macro-lattice model to anticipate the skills that green energy employers will need. The Mission Verde project trains workers for green energy jobs while simultaneously building demand for energy projects, so that green energy companies will need those newly trained workers. The career lattice plays out for organizations in the same way: it is a fresh approach to ensuring that the right talent is available at the right time for new jobs and hard-to-fill jobs. And for individuals, the career lattice provides direction for constant, consistent growth so that they are qualified for a range of positions, not just the single step up that is available on the ladder.

Career Lattices Solve the Skills Gap

Millions of people are caught in a perpetual career catch-up. They gain a certain degree of experience and expertise in a seemingly safe job category ("They'll never outsource this!"), only to find that, in fact, they can outsource this, and their final weeks are spent training their overseas replacements. "As I speak around the country, I especially find professionals who have never had to look for a job having a hard time accepting this. They have their degrees, they advanced their careers, they are doing everything right, and then they can't find a job," says Henry DeVries, assistant dean for external affairs for the University of California–San Diego Extension and coauthor of *Closing America's Job Gap*.[3] The worst hit, DeVries observes, are people in technical fields— people who have always relied on knowing a great deal about how to carry out specific tasks, from engineering to editing—because they lack the necessary career navigation skills to surf roiling industry changes and keep their careers afloat.

Jobs Are Not Where They Used to Be

Federal policies notwithstanding, the United States seems to be mired in a pattern of jobless "recovery" from recessions. Hardly a week goes by without news stories relaying the distress of the unemployed, the barely employed, and the chronically underemployed. The same news outlets also report the frustration of employers looking for skilled welders, innovative software developers, and multitasking website product managers. There's a chasm, not a gap, between those who need work and those who need to hire.

The Georgetown University Center on Education and the Workforce projects that, "By 2018, the economy will create 46.8 million openings—13.8 million brand-new jobs and 33 million 'replacement jobs,' positions vacated by workers who have retired or permanently left their occupations. Nearly two-thirds of these 46.8 million jobs—some 63 percent—will require workers with at least some college education. About 33 percent will require a bachelor's degree or better, while 30 percent will require some college or a two-year associate's degree. Only 36 percent will require workers with just a high school diploma or less."[4]

Researchers and recruiters tend to focus on the educational and technical skills gaps. Those qualifications are the easiest to quantify because they describe the tasks that are essential to the job. Employers are chronically short of candidates for engineering, computer science, information technology, and highly skilled manufacturing positions. New types of jobs, with new types of required skills, are invented along with new technologies. Latticing provides context and direction that minimizes "brain drain" and maximizes retention of highly skilled professionals. At the same time, on the low-tech end of the career spectrum, millions of people are stuck in jobs that appear to be dead ends. Lattices can fill chronic skills shortages, position employees to seize new types of positions, and create the hope and the means for entry-level employees to advance their job prospects and their incomes.

The McKinsey Global Institute projects a shortage of up to 1.5 million workers with bachelor's degrees by 2020—even as upwards of six million Americans who lack high school diplomas are unable to stay employed.[5] DeVries notes that math and science are required for about 75 percent of the new jobs that will be created in the next decade. The technical skills gap is starkly outlined in the current Bureau of Labor Statistics Employment Projection, shown in Table 1-1.

Table 1-1

Thirty Occupations with the Largest Projected Job Growth, 2010–2020

% Growth	Job	Lower Skill	Mid-Skill	Higher Skill
70.5	Personal Care Aides	X		
69.4	Home Health Aides		X	
61.7	Biomedical Engineers			X
60.1	Helpers—Brickmasons, Blockmasons, Stonemasons, and Tile and Marble Setters	X		
55.7	Helpers-Carpenters	X		
52.0	Veterinary Technologists and Technicians		X	

% Growth	Job	Lower Skill	Mid-Skill	Higher Skill
48.6	Reinforcing Iron and Rebar Workers	X		
45.7	Physical Therapist Assistants		X	
45.4	Helpers—Pipelayers, Plumbers, Pipefitters, and Steamfitters	X		
43.7	Meeting, Convention, and Event Planners			X
43.5	Diagnostic Medical Sonographers		X	
43.3	Occupational Therapy Assistants		X	
43.1	Physical Therapist Aides	X		
42.4	Glaziers	X		
42.2	Interpreters and Translators			X
41.3	Medical Secretaries	X		
41.2	Market Research Analysts and Marketing Specialists			X
41.2	Marriage and Family Therapists			X
40.5	Brickmasons and Blockmasons	X		
39.0	Physical Therapists			X
37.7	Dental Hygienists		X	
37.6	Bicycle Repairers	X		
36.8	Audiologists			X
36.5	Health Educators			X
36.5	Stonemasons	X		
36.4	Cost Estimators			X
36.4	Medical Scientists			X
36.3	Mental Health Counselors			X
36.0	Pile-Driver Operators	X		
35.9	Veterinarians			X

Source: Bureau of Labor Statistics, Employment Projections Program, 2010.

An associate's degree certainly can be the start toward lifelong economic self-sufficiency, but nobody can afford to rest on his baccalaureate laurels. First, how do the veterinary technicians and home health aides find their way to a bachelor's degree while working to support themselves and their families? And even those who have bachelor's degrees cannot go on automatic pilot. Their first postgraduate jobs do not define their career paths; they must evolve their skills. The Georgetown University Center on Education and the Workforce found that college-educated employees continued to get more training over the course of their working lives than colleagues who started out with less higher education (see Figure 1-2).

Technical training is of no use if it perpetuates a dead-end career path. Career lattices are the proven framework for lifelong career growth for everyone from childcare workers who hope to achieve their general equivalency diploma to postgraduate-degree-collecting professionals.

Setting aside the escalating—and important—issue of earnings inequality, it's fair to say that widespread economic growth and stability will happen only if lower- and moderate-earning workers are able to increase their base wages, most likely by advancing their skills so that they can move to better-paying jobs. In fact, high-growth jobs are polarized on the wage scale. Many of these jobs, especially the aide and assistant jobs, start at the very lowest level of any structure, lattice or ladder. How will people on the lowest rungs get ahead, especially if they do not have the luxury of taking a sabbatical from full-time work to immerse themselves in a traditional four-year college course of study?

Figure 1-2

Workers with the Most Education Receive the Most Training

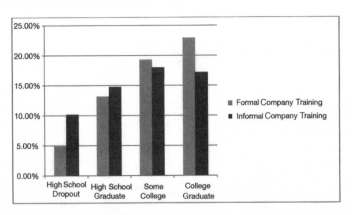

Source: *Help Wanted: Projections of Jobs and Education Requirements Through 2018* (Georgetown University Center on Education and the Workforce, June 2010), p. 13.

Career lattices have already enabled thousands of childcare workers to become program directors, teachers, social workers, and professionals. Similarly, career lattices have already enabled thousands of hospital nursing assistants to become technicians, licensed practical nurses, registered nurses, pharmacy technicians, and a host of other specialized healthcare paraprofessionals and professionals. Now, career lattices are catalyzing widespread change in all industries. If a high school dropout can navigate her career lattice to rise from an assistant at a childcare center to a center director with a bachelor's degree in education, without interrupting her income, then so can a drywaller, a former mortgage loan officer, or a middle manager.

Those who front-load their educations and enter the workforce with sophisticated skills and healthy initial paychecks cannot afford to allow their expensive skills to become obsolete. One need only read the latest issue of any lifestyle or business magazine aimed at affluent audiences to come across the story du jour of career reinvention. These stories inevitably involve highly paid, highly skilled professionals who burn out after 20 years—for many, just a few years after they finished repaying their student loans. They, too, need career lattices if they are to remain relevant, challenged, and engaged.

No matter where they start on the education and earnings lattice— at the bottom, in the middle, or near the top—most workers expect to grow in their careers. Those who assume that a pricey education will buy them decades of luxuriating in the velvet coffin of a workplace untouched by restructuring, outsourcing, and layoffs won't even get a short nap. Even the last bastion of workplace protectionism is crumbling under economic realities: in May 2011, the *Chronicle of Higher Education* and the Pew Research Center found that 69 percent of college administrative leaders would rather have faculty work under annual or long-term contracts than grant them tenure.[6]

Thomas Friedman, the *New York Times* economic columnist, terms workers with the killer combination of high skills, excellent critical thinking ability, and the habit of continually morphing to the next opportunity "the new untouchables."[7] Nobody who waits for work to come down an assembly line, whether that's the assembly line of bankruptcy cases at a law firm, the assembly line of daily assignments at a news organization, or the assembly line of parts at a factory, will be employed long-term.

Jobs Are Not What They Used to Be

The skills gap encompasses more than technical qualifications. There is just as wide a mismatch in the flexibility of workers, as those with chronic inflexibility are unable to make the transition to higher-skilled, higher-paying jobs. On the career ladder, there is one way to get ahead: replicate the skills and experience of the person on the next rung and hope that he will soon move up, opening up that spot for you. The ladder assumes static business conditions and market demand. The reality is that great opportunities open up in new projects, new departments, and new ventures that require some of what employees can already do. However, to qualify for these positions, they have to bridge the gap and acquire the missing skills and experience.

What Latticing Is Made Of

Constantly changing conditions require new skills, including the new skill of navigating lateral moves. Business skills such as financial management, web marketing analytics, and project management skills are essential for moving ahead, but employees often don't know which sets of skills lead to which new opportunities. Relational and creative skills, such as the ability to collaborate, business development, and communication, are even less likely to be spelled out for employees. However, relational and creative abilities are the hard-to-define "cultural fit" that can spell the difference between success and disappointment for two employees with identical technical qualifications.

Business Skills

Everyone is an entrepreneur, we are told, typically by those employed full time as researchers at think tanks, academics at universities, and reporters at national news outlets. What they mean is that each worker, from barista to barrister, needs to think of herself as a freestanding "brand," thinking strategically about her career direction and how to advance. Much ink has been spilled on this idea, but less attention has been devoted to exactly how to engineer this framework. This is why doctors find themselves flummoxed about running their practices and why millions of Americans are stranded within organizational "silos" with no apparent way to daisy-chain to similar positions in different silos, or even to adjacent positions within their own silos.

Often, the missing link is business skills. Promising employees are promoted on the basis of their performance and potential, only to find that they are missing skills that are essential if they are to continue to get ahead. A bank teller rises to branch manager and finds that he must now quickly get up to speed on labor law and how to navigate performance reviews, hiring, and firing. A gifted Internet developer is put in charge of a key project and suddenly must vet budgets. A few organizations have created professional tracks for technical and content wizards, such as ace programmers and superstar academics. Professional tracks enable them to earn more and gain some incremental title recognition—"senior"—as they continue to gain technical or content prowess. They might have to mentor up-and-comers, serve on committees, and represent their organizations at conferences, but they are largely sheltered from wading in tedious pools of business functions.

Professional plateaus work for some, but most employees want to grow and advance. According to the 2011 Skills Gap survey conducted by consulting firm Accenture, 68 percent of employees believe it's up to them to assemble the skills they will need to grow in their current positions and qualify for promotions.[8] Career lattices enable employees to identify and pursue business skills that they will need if they are to move to positions that are within reach. It's easier to get motivated to learn, say, basic accounting or meeting facilitation when you can observe firsthand how your teammates make the most of those skills to get things done. As employees learn how to "read" the economic trends in their industries, they can anticipate the business skills they will need in order to link their current positions to emerging jobs. Often overlooked are skills and abilities developed outside employees' official job descriptions and daily duties. These skills can position employees to quickly rappel to a new position because they already know how to do that other job. Chapter 2 parses CAEL's Learning Counts program, which shows employers how to excavate this overlooked vein of employee talent.

Ideally, workplaces would offer business skills training in bite sizes, as needed. However, training and development budgets were hit hard by the recession and are likely to return only with sustained economic growth. Most employers think that they offer plenty of room to grow: 87 percent of the respondents in the Society for Human Resources Management 2011 Employee Benefits survey say that they offer "professional development opportunities."[9] And, in classic ladder fashion, that translates mainly to technical skills. In addition, 71 percent of the respondents cover certification fees. However, piling up certifications does not add up to a career path.

The vast majority of employees are on their own. Fewer than half of employers offer cross-training for skills that are not related to a current job, and only 11 percent of the employers in the SHRM survey offered career counseling. Employees who can diagnose their business skills gaps on their own, or with the help of managers, coaches, mentors, and this book, can pursue those skills through online courses, community colleges, or industry-sponsored programs like those designed by CAEL. Equipped with those new skills, employees are positioned to bridge to teams or jobs where they can apply their new abilities immediately.

Relational and Creative Skills

How many times have you read a Q&A with a senior executive and heard him describe the ideal employee as a veritable corporate da Vinci: creative, flexible, a problem solver, insightful, and proactive. Relational and creative skills like these are listed in job descriptions, but in real life, they remain in the realm of "I know it when I see it." Career lattices integrate these sometimes hard-to-define skills, along with experience and knowledge that employees bring from outside work.

Career lattices organize these amorphous skills and clearly show how they qualify employees for advancement. Millennials expect relational and creative skills to be woven into their jobs from the start, as explained in depth in Chapter 5. Their demands are already focusing the attention of some talent development staff members on how they can take a more holistic approach to employee development. Navigating the many demands of midlife requires a keen sense of career direction, as illustrated by the case studies in Chapter 8. The emergence of the "contractor class"—neither freelance nor staff—requires yet another set of relational skills. Managers have to know how to motivate contract workers to do their best on a temporary assignment. Contract workers may want to segue back into traditional employment (as explained in Chapter 9), and if so, they need a lattice to show them how to do this. Or, contractors might see themselves on a continuum closer to full-fledged entrepreneurship, and so want to populate the next stepping points of their lattice with client management skills, still staying on the lattice.

Employers foresee a more flexible and virtual labor force:

57.8 percent—More part-time, temporary, or contract workers

25.5 percent—More telecommuting

21.5 percent—More offshored or outsourced workers

19.9 percent—More older workers (age 55+)

Source: McKinsey Global Institute US Jobs Survey, 2011.

Of course, the diagonal lattice travels up as well as over—the subject of Chapter 7. As leaders rise, their relational and creative skills become exponentially more important than their technical skills. Lowell Bryan, of consulting hothouse McKinsey, believes that the hierarchy (that is, the ladder) is the enemy of flexibility. Fast, flexible collaboration is essential for leaders if they are to anticipate and respond to rapidly changing business conditions—and change *will* continue to be rapid. Bryan's list of emerging skills for top leaders includes managing ambiguity, mutual accountability ("Do I help you? Do you help me?"), and knowing how to identify critical issues that are bubbling up and flag them with the appropriate level of urgency. His term for in-the-moment collaborative problem solving is "the power of collective insight"—in other words, together we can see what any one of us alone cannot.[10]

Georgetown researchers point out that teams accomplish their goals by striving together to achieve a certain performance standard.[11] In a hospital, that might mean achieving a larger percentage of positive patient outcomes, accomplished by new ways of organizing specialists and nurses around each patient. At an e-commerce company, that might be a product manager rallying a team of developers, user experience designers, marketing managers, and business analysts to redesign a website so that it is easier for customers to find what they want and buy it—boosting revenues. Team-centric workplaces must have highly qualified team members who can collaborate to achieve interim and ultimate business goals.

These are skills that are best mastered at lower altitudes where there is less personal and organizational risk. When skills like "managing through ambiguity" are plotted on a career lattice, talent managers can vet mastery of these skills in high-potential candidates.

As they adjust to a slow-growth economy, some organizations are reexamining which talents and skills they have on hand and which they need to acquire or grow. Emerging priorities are heavy on relational and creative skills that are more "caught" than "taught." Employees pick up these skills when they join teams or projects designed to impart certain skills while the actual work is getting done. You will find case studies in Chapter 6 that show how to do this.

The 2010 Global Talent Management and Rewards Survey conducted by WorldatWork and Towers Watson found that one of the biggest challenges facing companies postrecession is "confronting the complexities caused by lack of career advancement opportunities for top talent and employees with critical skills."[12] Translated from management-speak, that means, "How will we keep talented, valuable employees from bolting when they realize they've topped out here?" The solutions proposed by WorldatWork and Towers Watson are decidedly latticey:

▶ Reward employees for improving processes, saving money, developing new products, or contributing to the bottom line.
▶ Create a "multiyear time horizon" with opportunities and retention bonuses (this pays for itself by minimizing turnover).
▶ Show and tell high-potential employees that they are important to senior management by structuring lateral rotations for continued development that align with employees' interests and career aspirations.[13]

Sound familiar?

The Lattice Brings Advancement Within Reach

As the economic crisis recedes, many employees will thaw out their aspirations. Wages eroded during the recession, and training and development budgets were slashed. It might take years for full recovery, but workers are ready to get ahead now. Numerous surveys indicate a major disconnect between the ambitions of employees and the assumptions of leaders, who appear to underestimate the importance of creating structures for continual growth, even in a flattened organization.

The WorldatWork/Towers Watson 2010 survey found that top-performing employees—the kind that employers presumably want to keep—rank "challenging work" and "career development opportunities" as their first and second priorities, even over base pay.[14] (Apparently observing the dramatic cuts in training reported elsewhere in the same report, employees didn't even hope for employer-sponsored training.)

American workers want to stay relevant and engaged. But even as employers lament the lack of job-ready candidates streaming from high schools and colleges, they are not keeping their own employees ready for emerging jobs. The WorldatWork/Towers Watson survey found that American employees can see the skills and experiences they need to keep themselves and their organizations growing—but they can't get at them. The survey found that 62 percent of employees believe that opportunities to develop skills and ability rapidly are important, but only 33 percent of the same respondents thought that this was achievable at their current workplaces. Likewise, 55 percent believed it important to have a wide range of jobs and experiences, but only 37 percent thought that this actually would occur for them where they currently worked.[15]

Broad restlessness at work will propel the most accomplished and ambitious employees to seek growth elsewhere. Employers who swaddle themselves in the delusion that their employees should be grateful to have any job at all will lose money, time, and efficiency as productive, frustrated employees leave. In mid-2011, a third of American workers were seriously considering leaving their jobs, up from about a quarter in 2005, according to Mercer Consulting's global workforce survey. Even more chilling—for bosses, anyway—*another* fifth of U.S. employees are "unengaged."[16] They simply don't care any more about how well they do or how well their organizations are doing. That's over half of U.S. workers who are either trying to leave or so apathetic that they can't even muster the energy to get another job. Structured lateral moves are a proven method of keeping employees engaged, productive, and growing, despite a scarcity of full-fledged promotions.

What Career Lattices Are Not

Lateral moves have picked up some cultural baggage over the years. Traditionally, "high-potential" employees were tapped for the fast track, which usually involved several sprints through lateral rotations. Meanwhile, many of their colleagues plateaued at lower levels, sometimes feeling stuck, sometimes pacified by lateral moves that were granted just to mix it up a bit for them.

Career lattices are not holding patterns. On a career lattice, employees continually add relevant skills and experiences so that they are qualified for emerging jobs and business challenges. Very traditional organizations might still cling to the idea that lateral moves are side steps to oblivion. This book dismantles that notion.

A career lattice is not doing the same job for a different employer. Getting a new job doing the same old thing does not constitute a strategic lateral move—although moving to a lattice-minded organization certainly could pave the way for latticing.

Career lattices are not a panacea for work-life conflict. Though CAEL collaborated in 2002 with clients to introduce the term *lattice* for talent development and career pathing, a few organizations have adopted the term primarily as a work-life tool. Like flexwork, lattices designed primarily in the context of work-life balance have become "defined down" as a reluctant concession to what parents must endure to get through the demands of parenting young children.

The silver lining of the Great Recession is that it has repositioned career lattices as a powerful and sustainable mode of career advancement for everyone. After all, it's a lot easier to stay on a lattice than it is to fall off a lattice or a ladder—and then try to get back on.

The Lattice Is Already Displacing the Ladder

The term *the career lattice* was coined in 1975 for the Career Opportunities Program crafted by the City University of New York.[17] The program's mission was to create many points of career advancement for educators who entered the field at a variety of starting points with a spectrum of credentials. The short, steep ladder of teacher to principal to superintendent did not accommodate aides, paraprofessionals, and specialists. How could a confident, smart, and ambitious aide become a teacher? How could a teacher parlay her strengths to become a curriculum specialist for the district? Pioneered at CUNY, education career lattices are now used in Illinois, Vermont, California, and many other states.

Early childhood education lattices in Tennessee and Los Angeles have created long-term career paths for people (mainly women) who start as childcare workers, positions that are often considered the very bottom of the career path. Good character and endless patience are the essential prerequisites for those who care for babies and toddlers. Precisely because there are almost no barriers to entry, childcare has become a wide funnel for women who lack even high school diplomas. No matter where they start, however, they do not have to stay in diaper-changing mode indefinitely. Early childhood career lattices show childcare staffers the array of additional opportunities that open up as they gain each critical new level of achievement. If they gain a GED, they qualify not only to become a shift leader, but learn about several career paths that branch from gaining an associate's degree. If they get an associate's degree, they gain the platform for certification in nutrition or to pursue certification in training other childcare workers, perhaps even opening their own business. Or, they can supersize that associate's degree and complete a bachelor's degree in education, social work, psychology, or business. At each step, earnings and additional opportunities increase.

Educational lattices have evolved considerably since the 1970s. Here is how the Montgomery County Public School System, in Maryland, outlines its education career lattice.[18]

Lead teacher status is the starting point for a spectrum of teacher leadership roles, which then branch into specialty and administrative roles. To become a "lead teacher," a teacher must demonstrate a spectrum of technical, teaching, and relational/creative skills, as shown in Table 1-2.

Once they are identified as leads, teachers can pursue a variety of teaching roles that draw on their existing credentials or require new credentials. Options include:

- ► Resource Teacher
- ► Consulting Teacher
- ► Instructional Specialist
- ► Math Content Specialist
- ► Academy Coordinator
- ► Staff Development Teacher
- ► Staff Development Specialist
- ► Literacy Coach
- ► Special Project Designer/Leader

Table 1-2

Career Lattice for Montgomery County Teachers

Technical	Teaching	Relational/Creative
Create processes and programs that improve teaching and learning.	Demonstrate a commitment to lifelong learning.	Work with other adults to improve instructional practice.
Create organizational improvement.	Collaborate with parents, staff, and community to achieve success for all students.	Nurture expectations for staff growth.
		Inspire other teachers to reflect on their own instruction.
	Initiate programs to close achievement gaps.	Demonstrate cultural competence.

Source: Montgomery County Public Schools in conjunction with the Maryland County Education Association, "Career Lattice Design Team Report," Montgomery County, Maryland, 2007, pp. 3–4.

Lead teachers are first in line for relational/creative opportunities, such as:

- Professional Learning Communities Coach
- School Improvement Coach
- Serving on the Peer Assistance & Review Program Panel
- Serving on the Career Lattice Program Panel
- Professional Development Trainer
- Mentor Teacher

Realigning Retraining

With career lattices sprouting in school and early childhood systems, it wasn't long before another industry with similar needs caught on. Like education, healthcare has a huge funnel for entry-level jobs. A chronic shortage of registered nurses also underscored the need for new ways of retaining nurses. And health-related occupations are among the fastest growing for the foreseeable future.

In 2002, CAEL collaborated with the Evangelical Lutheran Good Samaritan Society and seven other healthcare systems to design the first known healthcare career lattice, as explained in detail in Chapter 3. CAEL integrated learning assessment and a business sensibility into the lattice model, transforming career lattices to give them universal relevance.

Career lattices—personal and organizational—are the route to economic recovery. The sputtering economy and the specter of chronic high unemployment have fixed the American mind on the importance of sustainable career paths. A survey commissioned by job posting supersite CareerBuilder found that 54 percent of workers laid off in the Great Recession found jobs in completely different fields.[19]

But retraining millions of workers and setting them loose in workplaces where they join millions of frustrated, stuck coworkers is not good enough. A 2010 Towers Watson survey found that roughly half of respondents cited "no clear path for advancement" as the biggest impediment to their careers, followed by 43 percent citing "streamlined structure" (in other words, a flat organization with no place to go or grow). Another 31 percent cited "opportunities unclear," and 30 percent cited "fewer people retiring."[20]

Lattices, whether they are called that or not, are already proving their worth as organizations recalibrate for a slow-growth, prolonged recovery. Employers find the best returns from these lattice techniques of developing talent, according to Towers Watson: competency models, career pathing and planning, talent movement and rotations, workforce planning, and team effectiveness and development.[21]

Career-pathing plans—which often include lateral rotations—are now used at 42 percent of global organizations, according to Towers Watson.[22] And Catalyst, which advocates for the advancement of women in leadership, examined the fate of MBAs of both genders during the 2007–2009 recession and found that lateral moves kept 35 percent of them on track: 23 percent "grew in place" with lateral rotations, while another 12 percent got both lateral moves and promotions. Another 22 percent were straight-up promoted.[23]

Organizations that have flattened by default—through layoffs and attrition—are layering more responsibility on the employees who are left. A survey by Spherion Staffing found that more than half of workers have taken on new roles, and only 7 percent of them got more money for the extra work.[24] Organizations that design lattices around these expanded job definitions create paths that will engage and retain employees. Employees who find themselves doing more for the same salary can turn the situation to strategic advantage by plotting diagonal career steps that leverage their expanded responsibilities into new opportunities.

Lifelong Learning on the Lattice

No one disputes that a bachelor's degree increasingly is the ticket to a middle-class lifestyle. But no matter where they start, workers must expect to fuel a lifelong spiral of blending skills and experience in order to advance—or, in many cases, to stay employed in satisfying positions. Career lattices help individuals and organizations reap greater returns on education.

Business leaders admire bachelor's degrees and underestimate the value of associate's degrees and vocational education, according to a report by Corporate Voices for Working Families/Civil Enterprises. Nearly two-thirds of business leaders believe that a bachelor's degree is the most important credential for career success, with only 18 percent believing the same of technical degrees and 14 percent of associate's degrees.[25] The irony is that many students who graduate with bachelor's degrees are going to find themselves at community colleges and technical schools, at least for a few classes, because those are the schools that offer precisely the kind of ongoing education that those with bachelor's, master's, and even some professional degrees will need if they are to stay relevant.

It is popular to point out that mechanics and machine press operators must deploy sophisticated knowledge of calculus to troubleshoot computerized machines. It is equally true, but overlooked, that a corporate communications manager needs to gain budgeting skills to qualify for director, or that a rising brand manager may have to quickly gain operational fluency in Spanish to make it through an essential rotation managing the company's production plant in Mexico. Some quick-serve restaurants are cross-training kitchen staff to serve customers so that they can pitch in during busy spurts. That means that cooks have to be able to communicate, too. Even law schools are getting pragmatic. Counseling, interviewing, project management, even emotional intelligence are creeping into the curricula. Your bachelor's degree may get you in the door, but it's your ability to quickly pick up adjacent responsibilities that will keep you employed and advancing.

Only a subset of employers pays for bachelor's degrees, so some business leaders live in blissful ignorance of the debt that most students incur to get those degrees (unless, of course, those leaders have recently written tuition checks for their own children). In fact, an associate's degree might be a sturdier platform for launching a career than a bachelor's degree—and more cost-effective, too. A 2011 study of the Florida workforce found that recent grads with associate's or community college degrees earned more than those who earned bachelor's degrees from Florida state universities. The difference was startling: those with associate's degrees in science were earning an average of $47,708, or $11,000 more than those with recent bachelor's degrees from state universities.[26] The short explanation is that the associate in science degree delivered the credentials students needed for decent-paying jobs, without distractions like philosophy and creative writing. Starting on a career lattice with an associate's degree is the best of both worlds. Minimally burdened by student loans and earning a good wage to begin with, new grads are perfectly positioned to rappel up the lattice, adding relevant technical, business, and relational problem-solving skills as needed.

Team-Centric, Lattice Dependent

Researcher Alexandra Kalev, now at Tel Aviv University, analyzed the cultural impact of more than 800 team-centric workplaces and found that lattices emerged organically, even at workplaces that did not have career-pathing programs. Both self-directed work teams and actual cross-training "increase the exposure of nonmanagerial workers from different levels to other workers, managers and jobs across the organization." Because these lateral networks cross job functions and departments, they connect workers in ways that ladders cannot. Traditional job-training programs cluster people with those at their same levels, virtually eliminating opportunities to connect naturally with people outside the employer-prescribed group. But work teams by definition must draw together people with a variety of expertise—and that almost always results in a more diverse group. That diversity plays out in tenure, function, gender, and race, Kalev found.[27]

Collaborative teams—and a halo of lateral relationships that support them—open up new connections and new career opportunities for women and minorities. To paraphrase Kalev, collaborative teams help organizations achieve their diversity goals. Managers are more likely to notice the contributions of individuals within cross-functional teams, and that flags top producers regardless of race or gender—precisely the goal of many corporate diversity programs. It gets better. Kalev also found that cross-functional teams support lateral moves for all employees and actually encourage peers to support one another's ambitions for pursuing adjacent positions and credentials.[28]

Forty years later, those new grads will find themselves latticing into retirement. Make that 50 years later, as imploding retirement income plans will inevitably move the finish line for millions of workers. Nearly two-thirds of baby boomers expect to postpone retirement by one to five years, according to the American Institute of Certified Public Accountants, which gets a close look at how much baby boomers actually have saved up for retirement.[29] While these stalled baby boomers seek a satisfying final act—enabled by the lattice—younger workers will have to lattice around them.

Career lattices link individual workers to opportunities just beyond their reach. They enable employers to make more of the talent they already have—and, in the process, to ensure that productive employees stay engaged and growing. When learning institutions collaborate closely with employers and economic development agencies, lattices ensure that qualified employees are channeled to expanding industries, and that those employees know how to expand the skills they bring to those employers.

The Green Economy: Mirage to Miracle

The green economy seems too logical not to pursue: America needs to replace traditional energy sources with renewable energy sources, so why not redirect millions of un- or underemployed workers to make it happen?

With all the economic bad news, few realize the solar industry is steadily ramping up. The online solar career map found at http://www1.eere.energy.gov/solar/careermap can help you explore your options. Funded by the U.S. Department of Energy and designed by CAEL, the solar career map (see Figure 1-3) allows you to explore an expanding universe of solar-energy jobs, chart possible paths between them, and identify the high-quality training necessary to qualify for them.

Retraining programs are not enough to get them from here to there, especially when there is not yet much of a there there. Efforts across the country to support the manufacture of green energy technologies are largely disconnected from retraining programs. Economic development and venture capital sources operate in different orbits from existing businesses that want to segue into green technologies. Consumer demand is spotty and unpredictable, largely because consumers don't know what to demand.

Dusty, adobe San Antonio has figured it out. Though it is not yet on the national radar, as tallied by the Brookings Institute lists

Figure 1-3

Screen Shot of CAEL's Online Solar Career Map

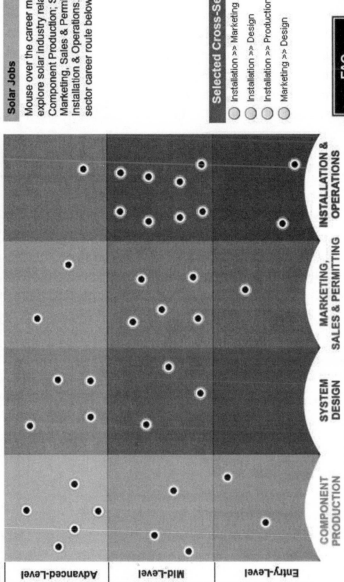

of top metropolitan areas for various elements of the still-sprouting green economy, San Antonio has coordinated green sectors for synchronized growth.[30] Key to its strategy is coordination among job-training programs, investors, business owners, and workers so that green careers are as sustainable as solar power. This chapter illustrates how career lattices are woven into all elements of San Antonio's Mission Verde green economy initiative.

Economic development agencies are supposed to think big. Too often, however, their sweeping plans address jobs but forget workers. The career lattice democratizes economic development. It translates big-picture policies to individuals, who can see a new career unfolding before them in a new way.

That kind of transition requires a lot of open-minded workers who had anticipated lifelong employment using set skills in a set industry. "They have to believe, 'I want to be this, I am this, I want to transition to this,'" says Anson Green, economic and workforce development manager at Alamo Colleges. He plotted a program that would address three types of recruits: millennials who expect to lattice their careers from the outset; currently employed workers who want to lattice into the green economy, using related skills as a starting point; and unemployed or underemployed workers who need to stretch to get onto the green lattice.

A common first step occurs when contractors need to have in-house experts in energy efficiency standards. Once that is cemented, they realize that the certification itself draws customers . . . and that inspires them to channel time and resources to getting more employees on the green career lattice. It doesn't take long before the companies and employees are free from the pinball machine of reacting to economic conditions and are able to get ahead of emerging demand with the right skills at the right time.

Green latticed his way to his current position.[31] His bachelor's and master's degrees in ancient history and classics opened no career doors. Green did what many overqualified postgrads do: he taught. A class of military personnel who were thrilled to improve their English skills as they reentered the civilian workforce made him realize that adult literacy might be a fulfilling career. And it turned out that mastery of Greek and Latin involved some transferable skills after all.

"Studying Greek and Latin, you have to pay close attention to detail. You have to make sense of things when only 30 percent of the information is available. It gave me the skill set to globally assess a situation when there's not a lot of data and make a lot of hypotheses about what the situation is," says Green. In other words, he's good at hearing what students can't say so that he can help them find their direction.

That is how he became a workforce development entrepreneur.

Traditionally, college students go into established fields. Healthcare, education, law, communications, and engineering all have well-defined starting points and, historically at least, high-profile milestones for success. But through Mission Verde programs, students who decide to make the transition into the green economy are entering a new industry with few milestones. Green urges students to never lose sight of how their new industry is evolving, and especially, what that evolution means for their personal career lattices.

"The students in my class know that they should follow CPS Energy [the local utility] to understand their policies and what that means for the green economy, for green companies, and for their own careers," he says.

"Students need to understand that you have a job in solar not because people want to buy solar, but because homeowners have a city incentive to get a break on their energy bill, which made mom and pop more willing to invest in solar in a recession. It's all intertwined, and if students don't know how to follow those breadcrumbs, they are just tagging along, and they can't anticipate the skills they will soon need.

"If I was a student making 15 dollars an hour installing solar panels in 110-degree heat on a rooftop, and I read about SmartGrid [a new electricity infrastructure being tested in San Antonio] rolling out in a year, I would want to get those skills to work installing SmartGrid in thousands of air conditioned attics. That's the end goal, for the student to be his own advocate and job creator."

Driving Demand, Workers to Follow

Here's an experience Lanny Sinkin never wants to repeat. In 2009, Solar San Antonio, a nonprofit promoting solar energy of which he is executive director, piloted a job-training program for solar panel installers . . . and could not place a single trainee in a job.[32]

That failure forced Sinkin to rethink the connections among retraining, career lattices, and economic development. It also made lattice believers of the other members of San Antonio's integrated green economic development project, Mission Verde. "We started driving the demand side to create more jobs," says Sinkin. As home and business owners became more aware of how much they could save on their utility bills by installing solar panels and solar hot water heaters, local businesses saw a steady increase in sales, and new companies started.

Bexar County, in which San Antonio is located, has 600,000 rooftops, estimates Sinkin. At $10,000 per rooftop, "there's a $3 billion industry waiting to be born" if just half of those buildings go solar. In 2007, San Antonio had four rooftop solar installations. In 2011, it was on track for about 300. Unlike the feast-or-famine of major construction projects, solar offers steady growth. The predictable flow of solar work means that construction workers who migrate to solar can take advantage of the career lattice of continual technical advancement to plot their career moves.

General contractors who offer solar installations as a sideline were the first to benefit, and many of them are already adding estimators, designers, and sales support staff. "Eventually full-service companies will emerge who can come to your house and tell you everything you can do, from solar electric to geothermal, and people will get a comprehensive view of what it takes to lower their bills," explains Sinkin. It takes only three years to recapture the cost of replacing an electric water heater with a solar water heater.

Demand is escalating to the degree that new solar manufacturing and assembly plants are starting to look at expanding to San Antonio. "Those 11 guys," says Sinkin, "if we ran that course today, we could place them."

Venture Lattice

Even in San Antonio, entrepreneurs are not cowboys. Not if they want funding, and if they want funding, they come to Randall Goldsmith. As president of the Texas Technology Development Center, he winnows the best bets from the hundreds of wannabe entrepreneurs hoping to be matched with early-stage venture capital.[33]

Goldsmith is looking for more than marketable ideas. He also screens for the intangible qualities that, based on his two decades of experience, indicate that a potential entrepreneur has what it takes to get the company from prototype to market: persistence, patience, good communication skills, and the ability to win buy-in from others.

The ability to influence others in the absence of direct authority over them is critical to working with investors, distributors, partners, and customers. And that ability comes through lateral experiences and relationships, and rarely from being a manager. Passion is important, because it fuels endurance. But passion alone is not enough. "Can you persuade others to get in on your deal?" asks Goldsmith. "There are some things that entrepreneurs can control and some things they can't. For what they cannot control, it comes down to persuasiveness and influence."

As he interviews hopeful entrepreneurs (many of them aiming to get in on the Mission Verde Alliance), he listens between the lines for evidence of having successfully navigated lateral career moves. The determination to understand a concept and a potential market from as many different angles as possible often plays out as a series of lateral moves pivoting around a central concept. That shows Goldsmith—and potential investors—that the budding entrepreneur rerouted her career to circle the start-up idea and, in the process, has probably gained insight from a constellation of coworkers and potential partners.

Goldsmith's own career cycled him through several lateral moves that gave him the perspective needed to lead one of the country's most ambitious venture programs. The first 18 years of his career were spent traditionally, rising through the ranks of his family's fifth-generation commercial construction company. Restless after "building everything

I wanted to build," he took the recommendation of a major client (Texas A&M University) that he pursue urban planning so that he could make plans instead of just working from them.

By 1994, he had gained a PhD in urban planning and segued into a job bringing NASA innovations to market—a trend that started with the artificially orange Tang drink of the space age. Success with that program led to several lateral moves setting up similar programs in various states. With each new position, Goldsmith expanded his network and learned how to bring a different category of laboratory innovations to market. He gained an understanding of the financial returns that investors expect and insight into the personal dynamics that make for a successful entrepreneur.

Those insights are now organized into a structured analysis that he uses to quickly vet potential entrepreneurs before they even get close to a venture capitalist. "I've gone from being an entrepreneur with a fascination for technology and an interest in investment capital, to weave together a career lattice that built my personal professional market value," says Goldsmith.

Building Houses and Lattices

Chartreuse, kelly, seaglass, emerald . . . there are as many shades of green jobs as there are shades of green. Anita Devora, executive director of Build San Antonio Green, sees them all. Build San Antonio Green developed green standards and training programs for builders of single-family houses and developers of multifamily buildings. Cultivating green skills for as many workers as possible is the group's goal.[34]

"People always think about the solar installer or the guy who's putting in the geothermal system. But there are also green jobs for the construction workers who are putting in green systems in houses. They have built on what they already knew how to do," says Devora. "It's not just the skills acquisition and retraining, but learning the solar point of view and processes so that if they want to bridge out of the construction industry, they can take existing business and creative skills and lattice into a new industry."

Though she didn't call it so at the time, Devora latticed her way into her current position. She apprenticed her way into construction, cycling through carpentry, budgeting, administrative work, and bidding and estimating before entering college. As a sociology major, her interests pivoted around "how we could do things differently using existing systems." She segued into a position helping technologies developed at Texas A&M University reach the market. That intersected with the rise of the renewable energy industry in San Antonio and the emergence of the Mission Verde Alliance through Build San Antonio Green.

"I used my passion for construction with my sociological training and my love for renewable energy, and I threw all those things into the hopper and thought, 'Will a builder go from traditional building to full-blown green? No.' We designed our program in levels, from an entry-level energy efficiency to the super-green net-zero-energy home," she says.

Build San Antonio Green aims to bring energy efficiency to all homeowners, "not just the crunchy crowd," by working with local housing authorities, subdivision developers, and multiunit builders. Workers on projects of all sizes, from home remodeling to high-rise construction, can see how their newly acquired green skills are also relevant to other green energy jobs. And for the record, Devora defines a "deep green" job as one that is immersed in alternative energy, such as developing new types of batteries or windmills. A "light green" job blends old and new skills into a position with a solar sensibility.

Not Just Green Jobs—Evergreen Careers

The chicken-and-egg dilemma of growing the green economy is in making sure that its roots can support its shoots. While some agencies prepare workers, others are concentrating on fertilizing demand so that there are enough jobs to keep those workers employed.

W. Laurence Doxsey, director of the City of San Antonio's Office of Environmental Policy, collaborates with the local utility to help ensure that it is contracting with enough alternative energy providers to stimulate demand consistently. In one of its latest projects, the utility added to its qualifications that renewable energy providers be evaluated not just on raw capacity, but also on job creation and training and on educational development programs. In other words, career lattices are becoming an integral requirement for suppliers. In the past, says Doxsey, the city was "open to whoever was hiring and training. Now we are more strategic in looking at the factors. We want the types of jobs that will be here for the long term and reinforce our local priorities."[35]

The lattice of collaborating organizations that support San Antonio's Mission Verde vision is replicated in the coursework and career advising for participants in its programs. "When both business and technology are evolving rapidly, there simply isn't enough time to continually reset workers' careers by retraining from scratch," says Dr. Bruce Leslie, chancellor of the Alamo Colleges, which hosts the Green Job Training Institute. Lattices blend life experience, existing technical, business and "soft" skills, and newly learned skills.[36]

The institute is designed to attract both those who are shifting to green industries from prior careers and students who are purposefully starting their careers in green industries. The Green Job Training Institute offers technical training and lattice career education and coaching in the areas of:

▶ Building Performance and Energy Retrofitting
▶ Renewable Energy
▶ Water Conservation and Management
▶ Environmental Preservation

Green Entrepreneurial Skills is a core course for most of the training programs. The class integrates business and relational/creative skills in the context of specific green careers. Equipping students with the greater context for the green technical skills they are acquiring positions them to interpret green industry trends related to specific steps on their career lattices.

This structure is grounded in recommendations made by CAEL, which provided extensive access to its materials, case studies, and clients for *The Career Lattice*.

CAEL prepared the framework for what is now known as Mission Verde in a 2009 report[37] that outlined how the region could shape a green jobs initiative by linking existing programs through a central coordinating agency. That center is Alamo Colleges' Green Job Training Institute.

CAEL's recommendations were based on its lattice point of view: that helping workers and businesses in construction, engineering, planning, and energy bridge to related jobs in green industries would pave the way for Mission Verde's success. (See Figure 1-4.) When existing companies and workers see a future for themselves from growing laterally into green industries, they become invested in the success of green industries, instead of fearing that they will be displaced by them.

CAEL also detected an opportunity to strengthen the long-term career success of workers segueing into green industries by providing a way to assess on-the-job training for college credit. A real estate inspector who has picked up knowledge of green building and retrofits through a patchwork of training, reading, and on-the-job experience now can get a credential that validates his abilities. Credentials pave the way for gaining more and better work.

Latticed for a Change in Weather

Weatherization isn't a very sexy niche of general contracting, but it has been good to Mac Rattan so far.[38]

Since founding M and M Weatherization in 2002, Rattan and his partner have built a company with 110 employees solely on the basis of projects supported by government programs. In early 2013, however, many of those programs will expire. As Rattan reorients the company's revenue sources, partly by getting involved in San Antonio's Mission Verde Alliance, he is also ramping up programs to infuse new business skills and a new mindset into his admittedly old-school foremen and project managers.

Through the Mission Verde Alliance, M and M is exploring how it can install and maintain a rainbow of green products, from

Figure 1-4

Mission Verde Alliance Economic Development Model

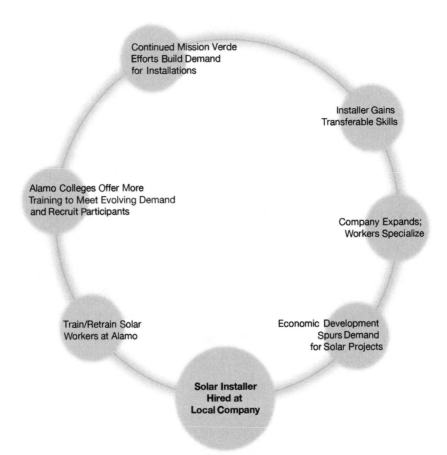

solar-powered ventilation fans to whole-building geothermal heating and cooling systems. With those new technologies comes a new expectation of what customer service means: more collaboration in advance on more complex projects, more collaboration as the work unfolds, and plenty of follow-through to make sure the moving parts are still moving the way they should. All in all, weatherization is quite a bit more complicated today.

"There's a green awareness out there that has not been there before," says Rattan. "For that career lattice, we'll take our veterans and management, determine the feasibility of it, and then teach staff. It will be a long time before we are functionally obsolete, but we have to continually reinvent ourselves. With the fast changes in technology, we'd like to be on the leading edge of the change that's coming."

Lessons of the Lattice

► Latticing will be the most essential career skill for the foreseeable future.
► Latticing makes sure that the right skills are in the right place at the right time, benefiting individuals, organizations, industries, and regional economies.
► Chronic skills gaps can be filled through targeted training and strategic lateral development.
► Successful latticing requires that three categories of skills develop in sync: technical, business, and relational/creative problem solving.
► Career lattices were pioneered in the 1970s and 1980s by educators and fully developed in the 2000s by the Council for Adult and Experiential Learning.
► The lattice is about continual career growth and development; it is not defined by aimless sideways changes, work-life solutions, or disguising subpar performance.

CHAPTER 2

CONSTRUCTING YOUR LATTICE

"It's a lattice, not a labyrinth," says Sabrina McCoy, diversity manager for Chubb & Son Insurance Inc. As a quantitative-minded auditor and compliance officer—the person who checks other people's work to make sure it conforms with regulations—McCoy never expected to be leading Chubb's diversity efforts. It took her a few cycles through lateral moves and subsequent promotions to figure out how to navigate the career lattice that Chubb was building a few steps ahead of her. Now she's in a position to shape the company's career paths going forward—and she is developing next-generation lattices for Chubb's four generations of employees.

Like many well-established companies, Chubb has for a long time used structured lateral moves to groom fast-track up-and-comers for the executive suite. "It's hard to get to the C-suite without having several lateral moves," says McCoy. "To get to that next level of officer title or role, in terms of being a branch manager or higher, they need to have certain experiences where they are a lot closer to the customer. They need to take on a corporate staff role. They need to round out those leadership competencies, financial acumen, strategic thinking."

But as Chubb streamlined its operations to become more competitive, some incremental layers of management evaporated, and with them went opportunities for minor promotions. Meanwhile, the company's employee resource groups (ERGs), launched in the 1980s to neutralize barriers to the advancement of women and minorities, were rising as an alternative channel for identifying and cultivating talent. As the enmeshed ladder-lattice model became more unwieldy, the peer-driven ERGs grew to offer more opportunities, more consistently, to more people. The ERGs offered democratic lattices that grew from the bottom up and have come to replace much of the top-down model of development.

"There are fewer positions at the top, and quite a few people competing for those positions. How do you continue to provide enriching, fulfilling experiences for these senior leaders and everyone down the pipeline? How do you engage them? The idea of lateral moves as a forethought emerged organically," continues McCoy.

Chubb leaders had to change the culture and the language of advancement as they realigned their definition of career development from ladder to lattice. Human resources and talent development staff started rotating all types of employees among staff jobs in parallel business units. They emphasized the importance of employees owning their own career paths instead of waiting for the infamous "shoulder tap."

Gradually, longtime employees began to realize that the ladder had quietly been dismantled. A new job-posting system that outlined specific skills required for positions made it easier to find developmental lateral jobs and to apply for them. Peer mentoring and coaching was organized through the ERGs, shifting accountability for career development from corporate managers to individuals and peers. Now, building, navigating, and strengthening career lattices is the explicit agenda of the ERGs, from their annual conference to monthly activities.

Where was McCoy while all this was going on? Happily running compliance audits. "I can't say I noticed it at the very beginning," she confesses. She benefited from the old top-down system when she rotated into a position that required her to gather information from senior managers across the company and present those results to top executives. It was career-making exposure . . . but McCoy says that the most important lesson she learned was how to wield influence. She had few direct reports but a great deal of direct responsibility.

McCoy could have been poised for a big step up the old ladder. But in 2005, a position in the company's diversity office opened up, and she started hearing from advocates around the company that she was the ideal candidate. Why?

Because she was such a skilled influencer. Affecting business results by fostering diversity was a big side step from the consequences-driven auditing work at which she excelled.

She did not realize what she had gotten into until she was well into it. Longtime colleagues responded to the announcement of her new position with congratulations on her "promotion," when in fact the job was precisely a lateral move. That showed McCoy just how much work she had ahead of her. As it turned out, her compliance experience was aligned with the original intent of Chubb's diversity programs: staying a step ahead of evolving regulations. At Chubb, as at many progressive companies, diversity and inclusion are seen as strategic business drivers. ERGs introduce ideas for new markets and vet products and marketing campaigns intended for specific consumer segments.

McCoy's office oversees Chubb's 23 ERGs and collaborates with the company's talent development staff. And McCoy herself is closer to achieving one of her own career goals: she is only a couple steps away from reporting to the CEO.[1]

Replacing a ladder with a lattice involves more than switching metaphors. It's a whole new way of thinking about how you combine your interests, skills, abilities, experiences, and contacts so that you are consistently evolving. Instead of assuming that a promotion is the only way to advance, you'll start to see how others have used lateral moves to go from stagnant departments to fast-growing divisions. You'll start to catch the vision for how you can think holistically about what you do, how you do it, and whom you collaborate with so that you develop a sixth sense for tomorrow's careers—today.

This chapter will help you understand the lattice from an individual's point of view. If you are using this book as a career guide, this chapter will help you define and collect the building materials for your own lattice. Chapter 4 and subsequent chapters will show you how to use these elements to construct a lattice that fits your age, career experience, and stage of life.

If you are a manager, talent manager, or HR staffer, this chapter will help you understand how lattices look from an individual's point of view. This is the mirror image of the organizational view of the lattice, which is explained in detail in Chapter 3. Together, these two chapters will help you diagnose your organization's cultural barriers and opportunities regarding lattices so that you can figure out the most effective strategies for establishing lattices. This chapter will also show you how to communicate the benefits of career lattices to employees, some of whom will be skeptical.

The Reinvention Misconception

Trial lawyer to yoga instructor.

Investment banker to organic farmer.

Advertising executive to vintner.

These are not career reinventions for the rest of us. That means those of us who do not have richly stocked investment accounts to tide us over until we reach profitability—or indefinitely, if profitability is not even a goal. Reinvention is a popular theme these days, understandable given the number of underemployed, unemployed, and stuck-employed. But the dirty little secret of reinvention is that it represents a serious failure of career management.

Reinvention need not—and should not—mean that you have to abandon all the skills, abilities, connections, and confidence that you have built up over the years. The great delusion of reinvention is that it rationalizes a failure to steer your career as a "fresh start." If you have to reinvent yourself with a completely new professional identity, chances are good that you have driven your career into a ditch by limiting your vision of yourself, your abilities, and the array of meaningful opportunities that are within reach of your current position.

Reinvention isn't a triumph. It's not a course correction. Reinvention, as it is now defined, is backing out of one dead end and heading down an unmarked path without knowing whether it is yet another dead end. The entire point of the career lattice is to help you avoid dead ends in the first place. This chapter will help you reorient your frame of reference from the ladder to the lattice.

As a latticer, you will gain career intuition that will enable you to pave your way a few steps at a time, while aiming for a destination job or level. Whether the organizations you inhabit are lattice-progressive or lattice-agnostic, or even clinging to linear career paths, you will be able to chart new ways to advance. Your career skills will include:

► A sixth sense for emerging trends and the implications of those trends for your career
► That much-coveted adaptability, with plenty of examples, starring yourself, that you can use when interviewing for new jobs
► A 360-degree network that includes peers who are looking out for you, and you for them
► The awareness of "unofficial" skills and interests that can quickly be put to use to achieve organizational goals
► A toolbox of resources and contacts to get just-in-time training, mentoring, coaching, and practice so that you can put those skills to use as you tackle lateral assignments
► The ability to pull together a business case for making lateral moves

The Lattice Is Not the Career Path of Least Resistance

Remember the fuzzy-focus career advice you probably got when you were just starting out: "Follow your bliss, and the money will follow"? The harsh truth is that you can follow your bliss all you want, but even when you find it, it is unlikely to be sprouting from a pot of gold. In the slow-growth economy that is predicted for the next decade, employers don't expect you to do more with less. They expect you to do more with *more*. If you don't have a certain skill that is essential for your new position, well, that's why online classes were invented. Meanwhile, training budgets are likely to be thin. You will build your lattice as you go, and invest in your own success.

To make the most of lateral moves, especially with minimal formal organizational support, you will have to find new ways to master skills, including skills that you might have hoped to avoid. "You will have to learn some things that come hard—math for journalists, communication for scientists. Some of the things you have to study, you study them *because* they're hard," says lattice proponent Henry DeVries, coauthor of *Closing America's Job Gap.* "The goal is to be strategic about it. Concentrate your scarce patience and aptitude on the hard things that you have to have."[2]

When in doubt, go quant. Analytical skills are becoming essential to nearly every type of operation and business. A report from the McKinsey Global Institute estimates that the United States needs at least 1.5 million more "data-literate" managers who can apply galaxies of data to specific business plans.[3] Certainly, nearly every manager must be at least conversant with technology and able to collaborate effectively with tech teams.

Meanwhile, career lattices are no substitute for work-life and workplace flexibility programs. Work-life programs traditionally address the needs of working parents and others with dependents, such as children of aging parents. The clash of daily caretaking and daily work may or may not be eased by taking on a lateral role. Chapter 8 addresses the ways in which lattices can be used as *one* avenue for reconciling pressing personal responsibilities with ongoing career advancement opportunities.

But make no mistake: managers and human resources executives in latticed organizations emphasize that diagonal career moves should not be confused with work-life programs. Often, a lateral move involves more work, not less, and that can exacerbate work-life demands. For example, a staffer who expands her role to learn a new function may well be working longer hours and at the same time taking an online class to quickly master a new technical skill. While she is on that learning curve, her work-life pressures are rising, not easing.

Besides, it is time that lateral moves started getting the respect they have long deserved. After all, lateral moves and developmental assignments have long been standard for the chosen few, hand-picked by talent scouts at big corporations. And, those lucky few have the advantage of being coached and mentored every step of the way.

Back in 1998, when the author was managing the "Top 25 Companies for Executive Women" cover feature for *Working Woman* magazine (now defunct), she interviewed a rising manager at Xerox. Ursula

Burns was processing the implications of several recent lateral moves. It appeared that Xerox was investing in her through these structured developmental rotations. It paid off: Burns is now CEO of Xerox and the first African American woman to be CEO of a Fortune 500 company.

Here is what Burns thought of her lateral experience while she was in the midst of it.

She started as a mechanical engineering intern in 1980. For her first three years as a full-time employee, she worked on product groups "just like any other engineer," she said. But then she met Wayland Hicks, who managed engineering development. He encouraged her to rotate onto teams outside the engineering silo. "I knew I wouldn't do engineering forever, but I didn't know what else I would do," Burns said.[4] She figured it out, pitching in on low-volume projects that allowed her the elbow room to figure out the financial and strategic planning aspects of new product introduction.

As an African American woman engineer, Burns was destined to stand out in nearly any setting. Corporate life got easier for her as she got involved in projects on which she was not the only woman or the only African American engineer. The 1980s were a good time to be questioning the status quo at Xerox: "Gradually, and with significant nudges from women's groups within the company, Xerox was broadening its career path to include experiences way beyond engineering," she said.

Burns caught a big break when her mentor (Hicks) also became her sponsor. He had advanced to lead marketing and research, and he asked Burns to become his executive assistant. "No, I won't be a secretary," she thought. But Hicks persuaded her that the position was "actually being chief of staff, helping him process decisions about people and projects." It was the ultimate lateral move; once Burns realized what was being offered her, she took it.

And she did a good enough job that the then-chairman hired her away from Hicks. Burns attended task force meetings on his behalf; she fielded consumer complaints; she researched options for reorganizations and helped enact the changes. After 18 months, Burns took over a small business unit to put into practice what she'd just absorbed. She turned around the unprofitable fax unit and moved on to run bigger lines of business. "It was clear by then that I was entrepreneurial, so they sent me to England to see how I was with an ongoing business," Burns said. In 1997, she was back in the United States and rocketing up the traditional corporate ladder. In 2009, Burns was named chief executive officer, taking over from Anne Mulcahy, in the first woman-to-woman CEO transfer in the Fortune 500. The official Xerox statement quoted Mulcahy saluting Burns as having landed the top spot "the old-fashioned way. She has earned it."

And she first earned it through strategic lateral rotations designed to, in Burns's own words, let Xerox leaders "see if I was as much hotshot high potential as people said I was."

On the lattice, every employee is as "high potential" as he wants to be. The career lattice is a framework that can adapt to nearly every employee and every organization. Lattices for all democratize opportunity. By latticing, you win in two ways: you gain new skills and experiences that position you for emerging positions, and the process of latticing (gaining the "muscle memory" of using lateral networking and learning adjacent skills to solve problems and get results) is an emerging career skill on its own.

Even in a very traditional organization, you will make a difference as you craft your lattice. As you explain to your peers what you are doing, you will soon have a group of like-minded latticers. Because your first focus will be on doing your current job better by gaining adjacent skills, the benefits to your boss and to your team will be self-evident. Your foray into latticing will become a living case study. And don't underestimate the influence you can have on your organization, your department, and your team. It takes only 10 percent of a population to change the mind of the whole group.[5] You will find that others have struggled with both the idea and the execution of career ladders and of "reinvention." They are groping for a fresh way to orient their career growth, and they will immediately recognize that the lattice is the solution they have been looking for. It only takes 10 percent of a population to spark change for the whole group. You and a few coworkers can be those change agents.

You are more than the sum of your résumé. Your constellation of skills, your experience, and your aptitudes equip you to lattice to new positions that show others that you can do more than they might have assumed. As you gain confidence and see results in your new position, you will develop additional skills and abilities as you solve fresh problems and do your bit to help your organization achieve its goals. You will learn to recognize skills and abilities in coworkers that you were not aware of before. It's all part of learning the culture and the language of the career lattice.

Plant Your Lattice Firmly

No industry can afford to dismiss the lattice, as this cultural change in Silicon Valley illustrates. ManpowerGroup, the international staffing company, conducts an annual survey of about 40,000 employers worldwide. The 2011 Annual Talent Shortage Survey (no hidden agenda there) found that 89 percent of the respondents cited "lack of experience, technical skills deficiencies, or poor soft skills" as reasons why they did not hire candidates.[6] Manpower's analysts concluded that employers' chronic frustration with the lack of candidates that match their long wish lists can be solved by internal programs that help current employees segue into those hard-to-fill jobs.

The skills required for key jobs are evolving faster than workforce training programs. Administrative assistants now have to be adept with web conferencing technology across global time zones. Engineers have to troubleshoot problems directly with clients, meaning that they require client management and negotiation skills, which are traditionally not engineers' strong suits. Sales reps can't just represent a product; they have to be brand ambassadors, able to articulate the company's stance on fair trade. Manpower's recommendation: figure out who can be trained to segue into these hard-to-fill jobs . . . and keep training people to meet anticipated needs, not just to backfill current gaps.[7]

Silicon Valley is a perfect case in point. The culture in Silicon Valley is legendary: mercurial managers, egotistical engineers, impudent interns, all of whom think that working 24-hour stretches, sleeping under their workstations, and unlimited free breakfast cereal are hallmarks of an excellent workplace culture. But when local employers commissioned a study to find out what skills they will need in a completely connected world, the results verified the importance of having everyone acting like adults.[8] With high-tech entering another growth cycle, company leaders are not replicating the hiring patterns of the past. They want employees with both experience and entrepreneurial abilities—and if these employers have to choose, they would rather have a candidate who is adaptable and is ready and willing to take on new tasks than one who offers superior technical skills. Silicon Valley engineers are now expected to have business, creative, and relational skills, too.

If engineers want to spend their careers inventing new technologies, they will get there by cultivating old-fashioned networks. As difficult as this is to accept, computer engineers must demonstrate that they play well with others; to land a plum job, they must prove to recruiters that they have dissected and solved complex technical problems, with corresponding business results. From entry level to the executive suite, employers in Silicon Valley prize candidates who are more than the sum of their technical skills. The top skills they seek are working well in a team setting and the ability to adapt to shifting business and technical objectives. In other words, the emerging criteria for success are about peer relationships and the ability to forge new solutions with the skill sets within reach—quickly acquired lateral skills.

Employers in different industries are coming to the same conclusions: they can either create career lattices or starve themselves of the talent they need if they are to grow. Employees who help lead this trend will advance their own careers.

Lattice Strategies for Employees in Fast-Growth Industries

▶ Look beyond superficial amenities to sniff out organizations that cultivate and promote a culture of opportunity for all.

▶ Make the most of cultures that are likely to be more team-centric and less hierarchical.

- ▶ Look for divisions within your current organization that are fast-moving or relaunching, possibly those driven by global sales and/or technology.
- ▶ Think fast and move fast to detect and get in on new teams for product launches.
- ▶ Bridge to new positions on the basis of your technical skills or core business skills (such as project management), and then rise on the basis of business and relational problem-solving skills.
- ▶ Build a network of peers to help you sense emerging opportunities.
- ▶ Realize that lateral moves may not be labeled as such.
- ▶ Find developmental opportunities in new product launches and in leadership of employee resource groups.
- ▶ Look for opportunities to shape the culture to be lattice-centric.

Lattice Strategies for Employees in Slow-Growth Industries

- ▶ Understand that organizations probably have few and shrinking opportunities for traditional promotions.
- ▶ Recognize that baby boomers lingering in the leadership pipeline are likely to be blocking promotions.
- ▶ Be aware that the company culture may have outdated notions of lateral moves as "dead ends."
- ▶ Expect to encounter lattice skeptics who are slow to grasp the new definition of developmental lateral moves.
- ▶ Realize that even lateral moves may be predicated on acquiring official certifications or other validations of technical skills.
- ▶ Look for ready-made latticing opportunities that are likely to be available through well-established industry associations, employee resource groups, leadership training programs, and networking groups.
- ▶ See if the industry has reinvention or innovation projects that link suppliers, vendors, and producers together. Get involved in these

to learn about adjacent positions in other organizations that might be an achievable side step from your current position.

▶ Seek lateral opportunities that are likely in fast-growing divisions, even those slated for spin-offs. Look for small departments or projects that need contributors who bring several skill sets.

▶ Consider joining a fast-growing division or spin-off where having several skill sets is an advantage—and where you can try out several roles to decide on a destination job.

Muscle Memory

The relevant technical skills are required to land a job (hopefully). But team-centric organizations count on individuals to anticipate, diagnose, and solve problems and to find and pursue opportunities— and accomplishing all that requires business, creative, analytical, problem-solving, and relational skills. To some degree, we all need some of these skills to get our jobs done. But the beauty of the lattice is that it gives you a framework for developing and showcasing these skills. A résumé is designed to show your business or technical skills in a linear progression. A résumé mirrors the ladder. But on the lattice, not only do you get to cultivate your creative, analytical, problem-solving, and relational skills, but you can't make lateral moves work without them.

The more you exercise these skills, the stronger they will become. Learning to climb the lattice is like, yes, riding a bike. With some practice, you will gain the "muscle memory" you need for latticing to become second nature. Before long, you will be accumulating examples that show how you put this constellation of skills into action. These case studies of your skills are invaluable in gaining your next lateral position or when interviewing for your destination job. Essential skills for success with the lattice are:

Influence. Learning how to persuade your peers to make contributing to *your* project one of *their* priorities is a core lattice skill. In global and multigenerational organizations, influence is swiftly replacing top-down power. Considerable academic and real-world research indicates that women, in general, excel at the skills that make for success on the lattice. For example, work done by David Gaddis Ross, an assistant professor of management at Columbia Business School, has found that women are especially effective at leading teams that need a "democratic and participatory approach" if they are to be successful at tasks such as innovating solutions.[9] Not incidentally, Ross's research found that companies with higher proportions of women senior executives deliver better economic results specifically because women's leadership styles are more inclusive.

Collaboration. Command and control is the militaristic term for the traditional corporate structure. Command and control doesn't go over very well these days. Collaboration—the ability to reach a genuine consensus that achieves business goals—is cited by numerous studies as the most desired (and most admired) leadership skill. Like influence, collaboration tends to be a strength of women.

Peer coaching and learning. Bosses are not the fount of all wisdom. They expect teams to collaborate to come up with effective solutions. Learning from peers is a skill that is best developed at the team level, because you will be using it at each plateau on the lattice. Your peers will change. The dynamic will not.

Personal perspective. It's not enough to be a self-starter. You have to know where to go once you start. The wisdom to set your own goals and measure your contribution to business goals gives you the insight you need if you are to see opportunities around you on the lattice. Personal perspective also enables you to scale your ambitions to accessible opportunities. The lattice is all about making achievable steps. Shoot for the stars, but practice first on some balloons.

Your Lattice Crew

By definition, it's impossible to lattice alone. You can accumulate degrees and certifications until you're in a rocking chair, but they won't do you any good if you can't enlist others to help you move from where you are to where you want to be. Just as your lattice involves a range of skills, experiences, and certifications, so your crew needs to include at least three types of members:

Spotters. When you are wading into new territory, you need someone to help you keep your balance. Just as a gymnastics spotter watches within reach as an athlete performs a new or tricky move, your spotter is nearby to help you over rough spots in your transition. The spotter is proficient at the skill you hope to gain, and has the patience and time to help you as needed. For example, if you are working on social media marketing skills so that you can lattice from technical development to marketing, your spotter might be a search engine marketing (SEM) whiz who can help you quickly concoct a strategy for boosting traffic to your brand's social media campaign.

Wingpeople. The wingperson is your partner and companion as you navigate your lattice. Whether your wingperson is working on a lattice plan similar to yours or is simply a fellow traveler who is at the same stage as you in learning the lattice, she is someone who shares the journey. She's your cheerleader, your sounding board, your talk-it-out comrade, and the person who fires you practice interview questions the day before an important interview. To continue our example of mastering the essentials of search engine marketing, your wingperson tests variations of your search engine marketing keywords to make sure your marketing plan plays out from different angles. Then, she gives you a supportive critique. She's also the person who forwards you news about trends in search engine marketing and careers and helps you figure out what that might mean for your goals.

Lookout. On the lattice, you are always on the lookout for your next opportunity. Unlike the ladder, which presents a narrow range of opportunities from a single viewpoint, opportunities to lattice will pop up in many directions—some of them unexpected. That's why you need several lookouts to tip you off to emerging opportunities. Your lookouts are advance scouts who are in meetings you're not, have networks beyond yours, and understand what opportunities would put your lattice into action. A lookout is different from a *sponsor*. A sponsor is a highly placed executive or influencer who advocates with other higher-ups for you to be given a choice assignment. A lookout is someone who is at your level, but is in a position to tip you off about opportunities that will help you accomplish your latticing goals. In the last step in our example of pulling together an SEM strategy for social media, your lookout would flag for you an upcoming marketing meeting that will require input about the social media project from someone in your department. By volunteering to represent your department in the meeting, you will have a chance to give a short presentation about your search engine marketing tactics to a group that you would like to join. You will have a chance to show that you have gained traction with search engine marketing—a skill you have identified as being key to your ultimate goal of moving into marketing.

Grow Your Lattice Where You Are Planted

If they are an especially collegial group, the members of your team may have already organized themselves into crews. Ideally, of course, the crews interlock, with each latticer also being in others' crews.

How can you help your team members identify their spotters, wingpeople, and lookouts?

Is someone alone?

Is this a good opportunity for an introduction to peer mentoring?

As valuable as they are, the members of your crew probably will not have the pull to get you into your destination job. The lattice is diagonal; your peers help you make the most of lateral moves, but you still must have organizational mentors and sponsors if you are to move up—especially to your destination job.

Mentors are usually a few steps ahead of you, whether on the lattice or on the ladder. Your mentor can help you sort out what next steps might be logical, given your ambitions and the direction of the organization. While mentors can be useful sounding boards, don't just use your mentor to process your thoughts. Ask your mentor to challenge your assumptions and tentative decisions—and challenge those of your mentor.

Sponsors are well-placed advocates who are in closed-door strategy meetings that you are not in—yet. Your sponsor is familiar with your work, either directly or through the recommendation of your direct supervisor. When you believe you are ready to go for your destination job, cultivate a sponsor and make your case for being given the job. A good sponsor will spare you humiliation and frustration by letting you know if you are not yet ready—or if the spot has been "reserved" for another candidate. Your sponsor needs to have enough clout and authority in the organization to be a force in meetings with other high-level peers. And, of course, when your sponsor comes through for you, say thank you directly and follow through with a stellar performance that makes your sponsor want to go to bat for you again.

A Star Lattice

Career ladders are firmly rooted at public accounting firms. The climb to partner is as cut-and-dried as an income tax form; built on the sturdy platform of the CPA designation, accountants start as staff accountants, then move up to senior associate, manager, senior manager, director, and then partner or principal (see Figure 2-1). It's a comfortingly familiar route for those who enter the profession because they love orderliness, logic, and consistency. Change in accounting is hard-won, even when the business case for adopting lattices is proven by a few progressive firms to retain and advance women—a goal that the profession says is a top priority.[10]

Some firms are finding that strategic lateral moves enable them to keep promising performers engaged—especially as they wait for baby boomer partners to retire. Star Fischer, a senior manager with Seattle-based Moss Adams, made the most of the firm's evolving culture. From a most unlikely entry point, she latticed to senior manager, and in the process, created a new career path.

On her own at 19, Fischer quickly realized that a paraprofessional cre-dential could serve as a foundation for any of several moves. She became a

Figure 2-1

Typical Career Ladder at an Accounting Firm

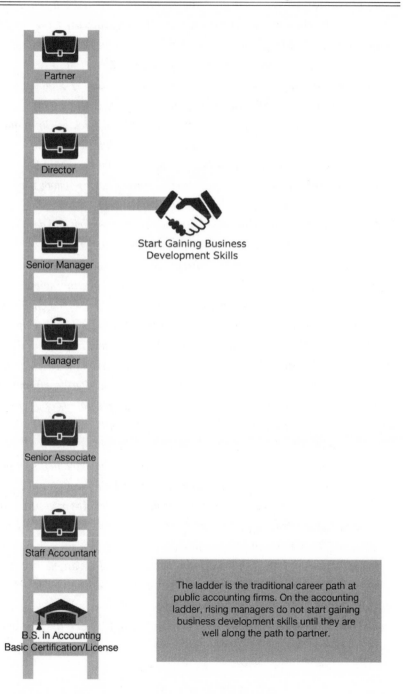

Partner

Director

Start Gaining Business
Development Skills

Senior Manager

Manager

Senior Associate

Staff Accountant

B.S. in Accounting
Basic Certification/License

The ladder is the traditional career path at public accounting firms. On the accounting ladder, rising managers do not start gaining business development skills until they are well along the path to partner.

paralegal and simultaneously started working for a small legal practice and began pursuing a bachelor's degree in accounting. An informal conversation between a sponsor (one of her attorney employers) and a partner at Moss Adams resulted in an offer for Fischer to step into a temporary administrative assistant job. "Even though I wasn't in an accountant's role, I saw how the practice worked," says Fischer. One thing was immediately obvious: the up-or-out ladder was the standard career path. (See Figure 2-1)

Fischer stayed on full-time while finishing school, picking up hands-on experience preparing tax returns, and became a staff accountant without missing a beat. A year later, she asked her manager what it would take for her to become a senior associate. The partners counted her in-school years, and Fischer became one of the firm's youngest senior associates.

Then Moss Adams launched a specialty practice in research and development tax credits, and Fischer was faced with a stark choice: stick with the well-worn, well-marked ladder or lattice to the entrepreneurial, team-centric unit.

She polled her peer network and her informal "board" of senior managers and partners—her lattice crew. She found that the new venture would enable her to gain practice development skills much earlier than her peers, but that the unit's structure meant that she would be short on learning how to adapt to different types of management styles. "My peer network has helped me baseline myself against others to see if I am ready for promotion based on what I see from them," she says. "You have to pick people you trust, who aren't jealous of your opportunities." She started expanding her network of lookouts and spotters.

Fischer questioned her mentors, including her then boss and women partners she had met through Forum_W, the Moss Adams women's employee resource group. "Some of them recommended that I stay with tax work, that it [the new venture] was too risky," she recalls. But the lure of gaining direct responsibility for attracting clients and managing client results pulled her in. She made a lateral move to the new division.

Fischer could backtrack to traditional tax work if she wanted, but it's her client management skills that will keep her on track to partner. "Part of my career path was being at the right place at the right time," she says. "But you have to take those opportunities. You can't say, 'Oh, I'll catch the next one.'"[11]

Figure 2-2

Star Fischer's Lattice

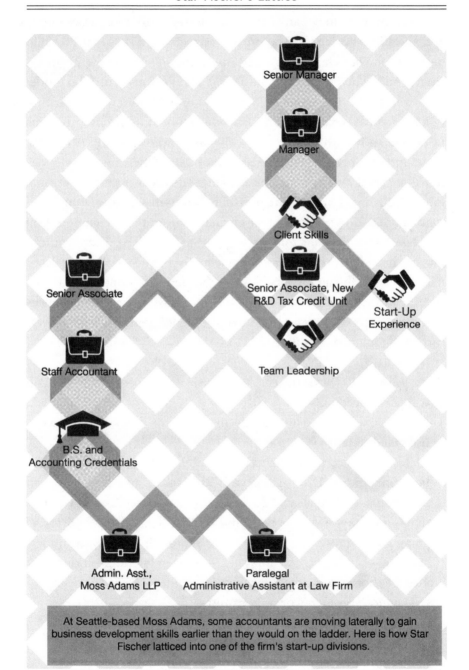

At Seattle-based Moss Adams, some accountants are moving laterally to gain business development skills earlier than they would on the ladder. Here is how Star Fischer latticed into one of the firm's start-up divisions.

The Why and How of the Personal Portfolio

It can be difficult to separate transferable skills from job descriptions and specific experiences. The process of creating a Personal Portfolio helps employees clarify *skills that can be transferred* to new positions from *activities that were situation-specific*. The Personal Portfolio model was created by the Council for Adult and Experiential Learning (CAEL), which develops workforce education and training programs in partnership with community colleges, employers, and economic development programs.[12] CAEL's method of helping employees navigate career lattices is grounded in the self-discovery of the Personal Portfolio. As you build your portfolio, you will see how your experiences break down into smaller elements. From those elements, you can detect specific skills that are relevant to other jobs. Then, you can line up those skills with the jobs you want to pursue—both your destination job and the lateral jobs that are the stepping-stones to that destination job. By building on skills you have mastered and experiences that show you how you have gained confidence, you will see how you can bridge into new positions.

Before doing a job. This is the challenge, task, or business result that you wanted to accomplish.

Transferable skills. These are the specific skills you gained that you can use in a different job.

Discussions, stories, and case studies. Start by shaping your experience into case studies. Discussions with supervisors and coworkers can help you see more clearly the skills you have used and how effectively you have used those skills. Talking through the process of gaining and improving your skills helps you fine-tune your understanding of how you can apply these skills to lateral positions.

Stories are short case studies that show how you used specific skills to:

- ▶ Diagnose problems or opportunities.
- ▶ Assemble the resources, people, and time to solve the problem or achieve the opportunity.
- ▶ Measure the results.

These short narratives prepare you to show your skills in action when interviewing for lateral positions or promotions. Table 2-1 shows you how to build a case study from your experience.

Table 2-1

Convert Skills to Case Studies

Job Function	Transferable Skill	Discussions, Stories, and Case Studies
Example: Technical Skill		
Review parts and equipment.	Assess for errors and defects.	How do you know what to look for?
	Set quality standards.	When did you decide you needed to do something about the defects?
Example: Business Skill		
Negotiate with suppliers.	Analyze pricing structure.	How did you assess the value of this supplier compared to the price paid for goods or services?
	Maintain good business relationships with supplier.	How did you understand the overall relationship this supplier has with the company?
Example: Relational Skill		
Coach others.	Facilitate learning.	Did you ever help new workers learn or do a job? How did you do that?
	Set performance standards.	How did you demonstrate good performance?
	Performance review.	What did you do if the new worker did something wrong?
		How did you know that the new worker was ready to do the job independently?
Example: Creative Skills		
Increase traffic to website.	Create team model for creating SEO content	How did you decide which coworkers would be trained?
	Design training modules for coworkers	How did you win buy-in from other managers?
		How did you measure results to validate the training and team model?

Assembling the Career Lattice Portfolio

On the ladder, you wait for validation of your accomplishments from higher-ups. A promotion is the ultimate validation. On the lattice, you are self-directed. It is up to you to identify adjacent opportunities, to figure out what skills you need to get to your destination jobs, and to assemble those skills. You validate your skills when you achieve personal productivity goals and track your direct contributions to team goals.

Staff members at CAEL find that gathering the various skills into a portfolio is extremely helpful. The primary purpose of this portfolio is to document college-level knowledge and skills from work experience. Not only does this help you inventory skills and accomplishments of all sorts, but the portfolio also helps you identify gaps that you must address if you are to bridge into new positions or obtain college credit for your learning. The portfolio is a refreshing change from the ladder-dictated résumé. The chronological construct of a résumé almost forces a ladderlike organization. But, just like the ladder, the value of the formal résumé is crumbling. Employers and recruiters are increasingly relying on software to filter résumés for specific skills and keywords. Portfolios enable you to see the full spectrum of your abilities and accomplishments so that you can confidently pursue your next positions.

For more information on building a portfolio, including how to gain college credit for your knowledge, please visit CAEL's Learning Counts website: www.learningcounts.org.

The Career Lattice Portfolio includes the following material.

Prior Learning That May Count Toward College Credit If gaining an associate's or bachelor's degree is part of your professional aspiration:

▶ Have you blended classwork with on-the-job training to such a degree that you could pass a formal test to prove your level of mastery?

Passing the test will validate your knowledge and give you credit for what you already know. (The College Board's College Level Examination Program is the largest program: CLEP.collegeboard.org.)

► Military, workplace, government agency, and professional association training may count for college credit under the American Council on Education College Credit Recommendation service (ACE CREDIT). Check with its ACE CREDIT program (www.acenet.edu) to see if you can get credit for training you have finished.

► Check www.learningcounts.org to see which colleges are collaborating with CAEL to grant credit for learning gained outside of college.

Degrees, Credentials, and Certifications

► Completed college degrees
► Completed postgraduate degrees
► Professional certifications
► Technical certifications

Skills and Knowledge Acquired on the Job

Business Skills

► Formal learning, such as certifications, licenses, and finished coursework and training
► Ability to translate business goals into a project plan
► Mastery of technical processes and tools
► Negotiation
► Participation in collaborative problem solving
► Quality control
► Business development
► Sales
► Customer retention and service
► Other

Creative and Relational Skills

► Flexibility
► Willingness to change and adapt

▶ Willingness to learn
▶ Ability to share knowledge with others
▶ Strong work ethic
▶ Peer coaching
▶ Mentoring/coaching
▶ Informal training
▶ Other

Life Experiences That Resulted in Work-Related Skills and Abilities
Relational, creative, and problem-solving skills often are honed outside the workplace.

Use this self-assessment checklist to isolate skills gained through volunteer responsibilities at all levels; group leadership; advocacy; and navigating complex situations.

Technical Skills

☐ Mechanical
☐ Cooking
☐ Construction/building
☐ Digital/web
☐ E-commerce
☐ Other

Business Skills

☐ Leadership—board
☐ Leadership—executive
☐ Leadership—committee
☐ Marketing
☐ Mentoring
☐ Project management
☐ Event planning and management
☐ Business management
☐ Financial management
☐ Creative problem solving
☐ Negotiating

☐ Communications

☐ Business development/sales

☐ Gaining sponsorships

☐ Client management

☐ Mission/message development

☐ Time management

☐ Other

Creative and Relational Skills

☐ Coaching

☐ Mentoring

☐ Crisis management

☐ Flexibility

☐ Analysis

☐ Recruiting volunteers

☐ Developing volunteers

☐ Retaining volunteers

☐ Resource acquisition

☐ Stick-to-it-iveness

☐ Time management

☐ Focus

☐ Self-direction

☐ Other

Using Stories or Case Studies to Showcase Your Skills

Stories or case studies show all these skills in action. Stories and case studies are essential for showing managers, coworkers, and potential employers how you have developed the skills you have and how you will grow in the new position you hope to get. They are invaluable for interviews (see Appendix A for more interview tips). The most compelling story format is to *present a problem* and *show how you solved it*. Aim to summarize your stories or case studies in no more than three paragraphs: one paragraph to present the problem and two more paragraphs to show how you solved it.

Use the categories shown in Table 2-1 to format your experience into specific skills that you have mastered. Use these questions to develop stories or case studies from these experiences:

► How did you grow professionally as you acquired these skills?
► How have you used one or a combination of these skills to achieve results?
► How did you realize that you needed to acquire some of these skills, and what did you do to get them?
► How did your problem-solving approach evolve to achieve results?
► How did you prioritize resources and time?
► What objections from individuals or groups did you have to overcome?
► How did you persuade others to adopt your point of view?
► How did you shape the mission to reflect the underlying goals of the group?
► What was the response of participants to the final result?
► What was the response of recipients, your audience, or the market to the final result?
► How did you measure your results?
► What would you do differently if you were to attempt the same project again?
► How would you coach someone else through the same or a similar project?
► How does your pursuit and use of your skills so far make you a good candidate for a lateral career move?

From Portfolio to Career Path

Once you know what skills you have, you can see what skills you need to get or improve in order to pursue your destination job. If there are many gaps between the skills you have now and the skills required for that job, lateral steps will bring you closer.

Identify the skills required for your destination job:

▶ How many of those skills do you need to gain?
▶ What jobs can you take that will help you gain one or two of those new skills at a time?
▶ How do those lateral positions align to bring you closer to your destination job?
▶ What other jobs might open up for you if you took one or two lateral positions?

Some industries have plotted out career lattices so that employees can see where they can go from where they are. CAEL has worked with organizations in several industries to develop online career maps that show industry employees a fuller range of job opportunities, and what specific education and training qualifications they would need in order to land their target jobs. See Figure 1-3 for a solar energy example, and Figure 3-1 for a telecommunications example. Career maps are also used as recruitment tools for industry employers to help job seekers clarify their career aspirations by providing information on the skills and certifications that employees would need to advance to a particular job.

The following case studies give some examples of latticing.

For an up-to-date list of the career lattices for different industries, visit our career lattice website, www.thecareerlattice.com.

Spiraling Success

About 15 years into his career with Chubb Insurance, David B. Williams realized that something was changing. The company was combining roles. Efficiencies were rearranging job responsibilities. Some jobs were evaporating, and more people were competing for fewer promotions. Titles were less important than what you could actually do.

Williams had started on an organizational ladder. Now, that ladder was morphing into a lattice. He had to adjust his career management skills and expectations even as the organization rearranged itself.

Williams, now a vice president, worldwide manager for Chubb specialty insurance—multinational solutions, coined a term for the new realities of lateral moves: PPS (personal professional satisfaction). He coaches other Chubb employees on how to reorient their career aspirations so that they go for the greatest PPS rather than defining their success in one-dimensional terms of promotion. "Chances are your next step will be lateral. The more you expand and broaden your foundation, the more prepared you will be when the step up appears," says Williams. "It doesn't have to be a promotion to be a rewarding move. You have to say to yourself, 'This is good; I'm making progress, and I'm doing well.'"

Fewer opportunities for actual promotions mean that there is greater competition for them. To increase your chances of getting a promotion, you have to have multiple points of strength that qualify you and multiple sponsors advocating for you.

Williams's own career at Chubb has been a ramp—a series of incrementally rising diagonal moves. He started as an underwriter and bumped up to assistant manager, then took a big sideways step to assist two chief underwriting officers. Connections made through that role set him up for a six-year spiral through the company's international division, running divisions in Asia, landing briefly back in the United States, then serving as an SVP in Canada, running a business unit. One thing he learned along the way was that in the new talent economy of latticing, success is not always defined by managing more and more people and bigger and bigger budgets. In Canada, Williams managed a business unit with $150 million in sales and oversaw all operations. Today, he has few direct reports, but he oversees a strategic initiative that supports customers all over the globe, and he accomplishes his business goals through influencing decisions in other business units. "One of the challenges of lattice management is that you are likely to have the same title for a long time," says Williams. "But you are making the job you do and your skill set expand."

When that occurs, it is up to you to make sure that your expanded, deepened, and proven skills show up in the organization's talent management system and are recognized by your managers and sponsors. "Generally there will be a disconnect between your perception of your skill set and the corporation's perception of your skill set," says Williams. "Inevitably you have a grander perception of your skills than the organization has. How do you close the gap so that the company also recognizes that you have those skills? Whether it's business acumen or strategic problem solving, you have to bring that to the surface. And you have to understand where you stand compared to your peers."

That's where aiming for the next developmental lateral move becomes critical, because filling small gaps in your experience and creating your own stretch assignments can make all the difference in being identified as the right candidate for a coveted promotion . . . or not. Not only do you have to shine in your self-designed stretch assignments, but you also have to make sure that your managers recognize that you created and mastered your own growth assignments.

Framing conversations about your goals and how you accomplished them is an essential skill for navigating the lattice, both up and over. Williams advises others to prepare and present evidence of this in scheduled reviews and career direction discussions. "That's the key difference between getting a promotion on the lattice and on the ladder," says Williams. "On the ladder, people were shooting for a particular promotion. It was predictable and obvious. Your timing was about pushing your case and determining when to advocate for being a candidate. On the lattice, you are keeping your brand and skill set top of mind so that when something comes along that you might not even know about, or that your sponsor might not have been aware of, you are brought up as a candidate on the basis of your skills, for any of several spots. They [the people offering the promotion] will define the skills, not the title, and they will start looking for people who have those competencies. You need to be on several people's radars and have several influential sponsors weigh in on your behalf."[13]

Rising as the Ladder Morphs

When she was partway up the ladder at Chubb, Nicole Brouillard found that the ladder was morphing into a lattice.

In 2005, she was the chief information officer for the insurance company's Canadian operation. She was asked—through the proverbial "tap on the shoulder"—to conduct a strategy review of the company's Latin American operation. It was an adjacent assignment, but it was consistent with Chubb's tradition of using lateral moves to develop talented middle managers who *appeared to have the potential to be senior executives. At the time, Chubb promoted people on the basis of their linear progression through clearly marked rungs on the ladder. Getting promoted was all about the list of titles that you'd held, including a few lateral moves required by talent managers, who used these assignments to plug skills gaps in promising candidates.*

But as Brouillard was delving into the details of the Latin American division's information technology situation, a sea change was taking place within the corporate culture. Human resources managers started talking about employees taking responsibility for their own career paths. The company began using the term career *lattice to describe planned lateral moves initiated by employees themselves, not dictated by corporate talent planners. Brouillard had taken on the task to gain expertise in an additional non-U.S. market, with the expectation that she would then be positioned for a clearly marked promotion.*

Instead, she asked to take on the CIO role for the Latin American division in addition to her ongoing identical role for Canada. By expanding her current role, she realized, she would solidify her platform for any of several international management jobs. "I thought, with only Canada, I don't have a good chance to get an international job. But with two geographies, and one being an emerging market, my knowledge of Latin America from a business and IT perspective would be critical."

Staying put with more responsibility also gave Brouillard a chance to catch her breath and integrate several new skills that she had developed on the fly—literally. She was either in Canada or at one of the five Latin American locations, but she could not be in all of them at the same time. That meant that she had to quickly learn how to manage virtual teams in several locations. Realizing that she had gained an important operating and communications skill opened Brouillard's eyes to the emerging reality of Chubb's new criteria for promotions: on the basis of competencies—what the candidate had proven to do well—instead of simply on the basis of tenure and titles.

While Brouillard was shifting her perspective, Chubb was accelerating its transition from ladder to lattice. Blending external research with HR's corporate initiative, the longstanding Women's Development Council started championing career lattice discussions in 2007. The 16 women executives on the council made robust development plans for their direct reports a priority, including lateral assignments and promotions. Latticing is now a core topic at Chubb's annual women's conference, addressed through panel discussions and year-round webcasts. Ongoing communications and manager training by the human resources group provided critical mass for shifting the entire company's culture to foster nonlinear, untraditional career paths.

In 2010, Brouillard's lateral strategy paid off. She was promoted to CIO of the personal insurance division. "My experience with the emerging markets, which are a big personal insurance market for us, was key to getting this role," she says. "It gave me visibility in an area that is highly important, and I got exposure to corporate executives who had personal insurance responsibilities. I do not think I would have gotten this role without expanding my prior role."

As her profile has risen, Brouillard has ramped up her advocacy for strategic lateral roles and career lattices. "A lot of people I mentor are going after lateral moves. One of my mentees needed people management experience and just took a lateral move to get it," she says. Chubb's corporate human resources department has continued to build out tools that equip managers to weave latticing and personal responsibility for career paths into planning discussions with employees. Hiring criteria have shifted to recognize the strengths added by lateral moves at all levels. "It's about not just creating a world in which lattices exist, but also creating recognition and success stories for managers who hire and promote through nontraditional career progressions," says Brouillard. "It's a recognition that lateral moves are key to your career."[14]

Build a Personal Business Case for a Lateral Move

Career lattices are great for organizations, as particularly outlined in Chapters 1 and 3. But even in a highly latticed organization, you still need to build a personal business case for pursuing a strategic lateral move. In other words, you have to show your supervisor that this lateral move works for his goals just as much as it works for yours.

First, get a reality check from your lookout, your spotter, your wing-person, and possibly your mentor:

▶ Do they all perceive the same opportunity for growth that you see?
▶ Do they agree that taking this lateral position will reposition you for your destination job in one or two more steps?

▶ Do they agree with you that you are qualified for the position, or do they advise you to gain or sharpen certain skills to increase your chances of getting the position?

If you are making the case for expanded responsibilities with your current supervisor, you must show him that this move will help your team and your business unit better achieve their goals.

If you need skills training, how much will it cost, where will that money come from, and how will your gaining these skills help your team contribute to the unit's goals?

Will you gain business skills that increase your team or unit's ability to:

▶ Gain clients or customers?
▶ Retain clients or customers?
▶ Increase the amount of work and revenue from current clients?
▶ Increase efficiency?
▶ Increase productivity?
▶ Help the team become more responsive to internal or external clients?
▶ Cover for anticipated or emergency situations that could disrupt business goals?
▶ Directly save money?
▶ Achieve a highly desired "soft" goal, such as cultivating environmentally responsible business practices?
▶ Position the team or unit for a desired project or goal?

A good format for outlining the business case is:

▶ Summarize the team or unit goal that the lateral move will assist.
▶ Summarize the problems or barriers that are preventing the team from achieving the goal and that the lateral move will alleviate.
▶ Show how you would solve or overcome the problems or barriers if you were in the lateral position.
▶ Explain how any new skills training would "pay for itself" by helping the team achieve its goals.

▶ Show how you will measure your effectiveness in the position.

▶ Propose a specific date to review your performance in the new position.

Don't forget: the very process of creating this business case helps you sharpen your business, communication, and persuasive skills.

Social Media and the Lattice

Who knows you better than your coworkers?

Nobody. That's why social networking sites are poised to displace traditional recruiters and job boards as the best channel for your next best-fit job. In the new world of peer recruiting, everybody's an agent and everybody's a client. In lattice terminology, everyone's a spotter—on the lookout for great opportunities for coworkers whose accomplishments they admire. And you hope everyone else will be on the lookout for you.

"Why should recruiters, who don't know much about candidates, be paid for hires when it's your friend who knows what you are good at and what you are passionate about?" asks Rotem Perelmuter, CEO of Top Prospect, which splits the traditional recruiting fee among peer recommenders. Off-job-description skills, interests, and aptitude are precisely the kind of things that friends know make you a good fit for a position, but that recruiters don't see—because such things aren't on résumés.

For example, your dedication to organizing and competing in triathlons gives a point to your interest in working for a company that makes high-performance sports shoes. You're the company's best customer. But triathlon experience is rarely included on a résumé. "People read your résumé, but they don't know that you're a great connector within an organization, or a great planner. But once you work with someone, you know what that person is great at. You are better at assessing what the fit should be," says Perelmuter.[15]

Serial entrepreneur Rick Marini formed BranchOut, which wraps around an individual's Facebook account, in 2010. "There are three reasons why employees become recruiters for you: they want a referral bonus, they are altruistic, or they want to work with their friends," he says.

With more than ten million monthly users, BranchOut goes beyond the traditional white-collar world of LinkedIn by creating a halo of connections for those in creative, healthcare, blue-collar, military, contract, and other categories. "BranchOut lets them unlock the professional power of their Facebook network," says Marini. BranchOut's professional profiles are a sanitized, streamlined version of a Facebook account, ensuring that comments from crazy brothers won't intrude on your professional image.[16]

LinkedIn doesn't take its status as the granddaddy of career networking sites for granted. Be sure to continually upgrade your profile and take advantage of new functions like the "skills tool," which can help you compare your skills point for point with the ones required at your job.

Social Recruiting Invokes a New Set of Career Management Skills

To be an agent:

- ► Work small talk. Even a small insight into a coworker's off-hours interests and activities can lead to a realization that she is attuned to dynamics that might make her perfect for a newly available position.
- ► Practice crystallizing someone's best-fit characteristics in a sentence or two. That's all you get in a social recruiting recommendation, so make those words count.
- ► Get to know what hiring managers and recruiters at your organization are looking for. Ask them what types of social recruiting they find most useful, and adapt your recommendation strategies accordingly.
- ► Consider how your professional reputation will be strengthened if you can develop a track record of recommending people who

are subsequently hired—and who thrive. What aspects of your recommendation process can you apply to hiring and managing staff or managing peer relationships? For example, BranchOut offers "connector" and "superconnector" status, which show you how well you are leveraging your real-world relationships for career networking.

To be recommended:

► Help your coworkers become aware of the skills, interests, and aptitudes that you cultivate in your personal life that might help them recommend you. For example, if you are a software developer who is the treasurer for the regional PTA, your basic accounting skills might open the door to work on a business development project with a defined profit-and-loss requirement. Say so.

► Consider a social recruiting exercise for your peer mentoring or peer coaching group. What hidden skills would you highlight in one another? What terms succinctly describe those skills? How do those skills line up with terms used in the job descriptions for positions you would like to pursue? BranchOut allows 140 characters for its recommendations. Can you recommend each of your peers in 140 characters?

► Comment—intelligently—on industry trends across relevant social networks.

Are You Ready to Lattice? Take This Quiz and Find Out

1. I have a very firm idea of what destination job I want.
2. I'd rather pursue a well-worn path in my organization or industry; why reinvent the wheel?
3. Breaking new ground is work, but it's worth it to forge a career path that is right for me.

4. I tend to advance, anticipate, or lead change.
5. I tend to reflect, respond to, or react to change.
6. My work will speak for itself.
7. I expect to get new positions on the basis of my performance.
8. I expect to get new positions on the basis of my potential.
9. Presenting, positioning, and selling my work is nearly as important as the work itself.
10. I expect to help invent my next position.
11. I expect to be chosen for my next position.
12. I define career success in terms of titles, regular salary increases, perks . . . and a corner office, of course!
13. I define career success in terms of continual growth, the ability to adapt to continually changing business conditions, and lifelong economic self-sufficiency.
14. I have a good idea as to what my destination job might be, but I am open to changing directions if a new and better opportunity pops up along the way.

If you answered yes to questions 3, 4, 8, 9, 10, 13, and 14, you are lattice-minded.

If you answered yes to questions 1, 2, 5, 6, 7, 11, and 12, you tend to be ladder-minded.

Lessons of the Lattice

▶ Latticing is continually bridging into new skills and qualifications to position you for your next job. Reinvention usually involves a full stop and restart, wasting prior knowledge, experience, and networks.
▶ You can lattice in any industry or organizational culture, using the appropriate strategies.
▶ Your performance grounded in your technical skills serves as the foundation for early career latticing. As

(continued)

you rise on the lattice, you will layer in business and relational/creative problem-solving skills, which will become preeminent at the top of the lattice.

▶ Peer relationships are essential to success on the lattice. Your lattice crew consists of a spotter, who provides peer coaching as you get a grip on new skills; your wingperson, who helps you practice those skills; and your lookout, who flags emerging opportunities.

▶ A Personal Portfolio combines traditional résumé elements with case studies that illustrate your performance and provide evidence of preexisting skill mastery. The portfolio is a way to organize your skills so that you can spot your qualifications for target jobs or obtain college credit for your learning.

CHAPTER 3

THE CAREER LATTICE TOOLKIT

For years, Danielle Schaeffer was content to be the activities director at the small nursing home in Scotland, South Dakota, run by the Evangelical Lutheran Good Samaritan Society, a multistate healthcare provider. The idea of gaining a nursing degree was appealing to her—but it was seemingly a logistical impossibility for a mother of young children, since the nearest facility offering classes and clinical rotations was nearly an hour away.

In 2002, Good Samaritan's Growing Our Own program broke Schaeffer's career stalemate. Part of a major effort by the Council for Adult and Experiential Learning (CAEL) and the U.S. Department of Labor to address the chronic shortage of registered nurses and to pave the way to professional careers as registered nurses for entry-level healthcare workers, the program put existing training programs in a new context: the lattice. With some of the cost of the program covered by Good Samaritan and its education partners, Schaeffer took long-distance classes and tests and commuted for the clinical rotations. "When I heard that there was an option that would let me arrange my work schedule to do distance learning right there at the facility, and that there was scholarship money available, I thought, 'How much better can you have it?'" says Schaeffer. Promising to stay in the Good Samaritan system as recompense for the scholarship seemed like a more than fair trade-off.

After graduating in 2003 with her nursing degree, Schaeffer rotated through several positions at Good Samaritan facilities. She was a floor nurse, promoted to charge nurse, then became a director of nursing; she then returned to directing activities, and now is a charge nurse in Scotland, back where she started. Her next aspiration is a specialty position as a case manager for residents, operating at the intersection of patient and family needs and policies and procedures.

The core lesson of Growing Our Own for other employers, Schaeffer believes, is to tap the talent they've got by recognizing and rewarding reliable employees who have bought into the organization's mission and culture. Skills can be taught, but attitude must be caught. "Select employees for character, and teach the skills," she says. "You want people to say, 'This is where I want to stay and work.'"[1]

CAREER LATTICES ARE not uncharted territory. This chapter lays out the pioneering work done by CAEL and the DOL (U.S. Department of Labor) in introducing lattices for healthcare workers, especially nurses. The proven processes of CAEL's nursing lattice program have been readily adapted to other industries, as illustrated in Chapter 1's case study of San Antonio's Mission Verde project and in this chapter's profile of the VIVID Future lattice for the telecommunications industry.

Managers, senior leaders, human resources staffers, and talent development staffers can use the templates and tools in Chapter 3 to adapt the CAEL's lattice expertise for their own organizations. Line managers will find this chapter helpful for designing lattices for their own teams and departments, although at some point they will want to coordinate their efforts with the human resources and talent management staff at their organizations. Individuals can use this chapter to understand how their own lattices fit with organizational growth goals and with industry trends.

During the most recent recession, lateral assignments were key to many employers' efforts to hold on to top talent.[2] Widespread layoffs and reorganizations meant that for many rising managers, the next step on the ladder simply evaporated. Many people accepted offers for jobs that were lateral moves because actual steps up simply did not exist; others took lateral moves because the alternative was unemployment; and untold millions had lateral growth thrust upon them as they took over tasks abandoned by laid-off former coworkers.[3]

The 2008 recession coincided with the final crumbling of the ladder. Deliberately diagonal career paths proved to be more flexible, sturdy, and sustainable—especially during a terrible recession. At progressive organizations, the recession cemented the confidence that lattices are the best model for developing employees at all levels. Employees' experiences proved that today's lattices are profoundly different from the holding pattern that characterized some types of lateral moves in laddered environments.

The CAEL Model

The beauty of the lattice model is that it can be adapted for nearly any industry or profession. Lattices can be individual, as illustrated in Chapter 2. Lattices can also be for teams, departments, or business units. Systems of lattices can form career maps for organizations and entire industries. Lattices can start with entry-level positions or with midcareer positions.

CAEL brought the career lattice into the mainstream. Previously, lattices had been largely confined to early childhood education (as outlined in Chapter 1). CAEL's mission is to enable lifelong learning and economic self-sufficiency for all workers. To accomplish that, CAEL designs education and training services in collaboration with colleges, employers, and industry groups.

Healthcare employers are chronically short of nurses. CAEL consultants realized that the concept of the career lattice could be adapted to develop nurses from among employees who were already employed in healthcare: assistants and aides. Assistants and aides do the backbreaking routine work of hospitals and care centers. They mop. They deliver. They ferry patients to and fro. Few of them can afford to take time off to immerse themselves in school, even with the aim of gaining a certification, such as LPN (licensed practical nurse), that would boost them to the next rung in both prestige and earnings. At the same time, healthcare employers were overlooking the potential ambition and abilities of assistants and aides, who, if trained, could fill needed spots as technologists and nurses.

CAEL connected the dots by creating a healthcare career lattice that consisted of short training modules that workers could easily master while working full time, coupled with career coaching so that they could position themselves for a variety of more highly skilled, better-paying jobs.[4] "People need a road map," says Pamela Tate, CAEL president.[5] "To have a lattice, you have to know all the jobs you could branch out to." CAEL identified seven healthcare systems to pilot the program, including the Evangelical Lutheran Good Samaritan Society.

Now CAEL is developing similar career-path blueprints for other industries. American employers are struggling with the skills gap, and American policy makers are scratching their heads over educational reform, economic stimulus, and job creation. Meanwhile, CAEL has already shown how to bridge the skills gap: grow your own talent, starting with employees you already have who have aptitude, experience, and potential that has been overlooked. Keep them productive in their current positions while they apprentice and cross-train for others. The talent is there. Programs like the Growing Our Own lattice propel that talent to fill critical employer needs.

From its work designing career lattices for entire industries, such as nursing, CAEL realized that lattices also needed to be scaled for workplaces. "We kept hearing from employers that they needed career maps within their organizations because they weren't doing a good job of telling people how they could transfer from inside," says Shawn Hulsizer, a CAEL senior program manager and one of its career-mapping experts.[6] These lattices can be scaled down for departments and business units and scaled up for your industry—something that is especially valuable for companies that are growing fast.

CAEL's staff also realized that employees needed more responsibility and power to know where they might aim so that they could plan their lateral moves accordingly. They developed these questions to shape large-scale career lattices and career maps:

- ▶ What type of growth is shaping your business or industry? What skills are you likely to need in five years? Where are the skills gaps?
- ▶ How can you grow your own employees to fill those gaps?
- ▶ How will employees find those opportunities?
- ▶ How will skills acquisition be supported by programs such as tuition assistance, formal training, on-the-job training, and leadership development?
- ▶ How will managers support skills development? How will managers support lateral moves? How will lateral career moves and related skills development be integrated into performance assessments?

"Well-articulated career maps allow employees to plan ahead. They give people time to earn credentials, and to develop the skills and competencies required for new roles and responsibilities. However, companies must engage a varied group of stakeholders from the outset," says Hulsizer. "If you don't, your strategic objectives may not align."

The CAEL Template for Designing Industry or Regional Career Lattices[7]

Outline your tactical goals. What measurable results are you trying to accomplish by having a career lattice? Goals might include:
- ▶ Developing employees to meet current demands and fill skills gaps
- ▶ Developing employees to meet anticipated needs and skills
- ▶ Retention
- ▶ Engagement and productivity
- ▶ Supporting workforce development initiatives
- ▶ Making the most of internal training efforts
- ▶ Recruiting

Then, put the plan into action. Here are the broad steps.

First Steps

Task 1: Focus on Communication

1. Scan the industry landscape in your area. Look for allies and potential partners in local employers, educational institutions, and other stakeholders.
2. Educate others about how career lattices can help address skills gaps, both current and anticipated.
3. Develop marketing materials for distribution and schedule meetings with key stakeholders.
4. Engage community partners in the project. Recruit an advisory committee to guide the planning. Work to clarify the direction the project will take.
5. Identify a site coordinator. The sooner a site coordinator is identified, the shorter the time frame for engaging partners and implementing projects.
6. Keep people informed about your progress. Find ways to keep stakeholders updated during all phases of the project.

Task 2: Identify and Begin Work with Industry Partners

1. Identify employers in the industry that show need or promise. Look for employers that are dedicated to addressing challenges and open to innovative approaches.
2. Learn about employers' unique workforce needs. Identify the needs, their scope, and existing programs. Use this information to construct the business case for implementation.
3. Lay the groundwork for the career lattice approach. Explain the concepts behind the model, talk through concerns, and share information on how other industry employers have used the concept.
4. Reach an agreement with the employer on how to proceed. Formalize the agreement with a written document or memorandum of understanding that includes all project partners.

Put the Plan into Action

1. Establish an advisory committee to guide the project. Include key players from participating employers as well as representatives from community organizations and other important stakeholders. Members of the committee formed during the planning phase of the project may also take on this new advisory role.
2. Design a program to meet the employer's needs. Identify the focus of the program, determine employee interest, assess barriers and resources, and identify appropriate training providers.
3. Inform employees of the projected training and engage them. Publicize the program widely and explain it clearly in information sessions, using materials that are specifically geared to the various target populations. Be sure to involve current staff members and supervisors in the planning and execution of these activities.
4. Screen and register participants. The enrollment process should be streamlined and easily understood by all candidates. It should include attention to both skills assessments and the individuals' eligibility for available financial resources. You may need to refer participants to remedial training where appropriate, and you may need to help them find funding. When available, tuition assistance from employers will cover some expenses, but employees may also be eligible for a variety of other funding sources, including Workforce Investment Act funds.
5. Implement the training. During training, the site coordinator and the advisory committee continue to play key roles by providing feedback and monitoring progress.

Keep It Going

1. Track outcomes against the initial goals. Follow and record the progress of all participants. Monitor costs, turnover, and retention as well.

2. Determine how expansion can be customized to support each employer. Revisit program design and customize the program to meet the employers' remaining workforce challenges.
3. Ensure continued financial commitment. Continue to make the business case to partners, and identify new sources of funding.
4. Share your experiences. Reach out to others in the industry within your community and your state to recruit new partners, funders, and champions. This outreach can also help to generate positive publicity for existing partners.

The CAEL Template for Designing Workplace Career Lattices[8]

When you create career paths within your organization, your current and potential employees can see where they want to go. When the path is clear, they are more likely to get there—and less likely to leave. Career maps support workforce development and internal training. Career pathing results in more effective use of tuition dollars, and can even augment your recruiting strategy.

Know where you're headed. What are you trying to accomplish by having a career map? Where is your organization headed, and where are the gaps? Include all of these stakeholder groups:
   ▶ Executive management
   ▶ Workforce development
   ▶ Training organization
   ▶ Staffing and recruiting
   ▶ Incumbent employees
   ▶ Skilled facilitators

Identify and rank in order the positions you need to fill. Gather, review, and assess job families, job briefs, and requirements. Make sure that you look far enough into the future to ensure that you'll have the talent you need—when you need it.

Create a "backward map." Speak with your current workforce to identify transitions and progressions. How can you replicate successful, existing skills development methods and career paths?

Validate. Draft your map and validate it with your stakeholder groups.

Develop an "asset map." What tools and resources are already available to you? Are there national, regional, or sector resources? Local or national grant funding? Your training organization? Tuition assistance? Local colleges?

Create education partnerships. If industry-specific education doesn't exist, your local colleges are likely to be able to help you customize content aimed at your needs.

Bring it all together. Consider a physical or electronic format.

Socialize your map. Make sure your map is known throughout your organization (leadership, management, and frontline workforce); embed it in your performance management; share it with local colleges, local high schools, and local economic development leaders.

Career Lattices Close Skills Gaps

Corporate leaders loudly lament the lack of critical and creative thinking in today's workforce. Yet, when they are faced with their own dead ends (such as evaporating market demand), their frequent reaction is to cut staff members who have been working in the now-nonessential operation, back up, go into another direction, and then start complaining anew about the difficulty of finding employees with the latest magic combination of technical skills plus creative and critical thinking.

Latticing helps organizations segue from this self-defeating cycle. A latticed organization:

► Is able to diagnose the soft and technical skills required by the new opportunities so that they can find the right people, looking internally first.

► Knows which individuals can be quickly redeployed to an emerging sector.
► Has a database of employees' skills and aptitudes that would qualify those employees for new types of jobs.
► Trains and coaches managers in the specifics of encouraging continual training, the value of lateral moves, and how to tap employees' "unofficial" skills.
► Unlocks the power of peer relationships.
► Shows employees through case studies, profiles, and personal stories how latticing has resulted in continued, satisfying employment.
► Continually supports the business case for latticing by tracking the results of having a nimble workforce that can rally to take advantage of new opportunities.

The telecommunications industry had all these goals in mind when it collaborated with CAEL to create an industrywide lattice to address current and anticipated workforce needs. Working with CAEL's Shawn Hulsizer, industry players threw their collective resources behind a career-mapping and employment site that integrates career lattices with immediate job openings. VIVID Future not only illustrates how current telecommunications employees can lattice their careers, but also provides an engaging glimpse of the possibilities for students and entry-level employees.

"If you do this with your business competitors, you stand to gain a lot more credibility than if you go it alone," says Jon Nelson, director— HR staffing for AT&T, one of the industry executives who has been intimately involved with VIVID Future.[9] The industry already had a group dedicated to training its workforce, the National Coalition for Telecommunications Education and Learning (NACTEL), which was a natural for leading the effort. "Framing the VIVID Future site as a 'one-stop shop' for learning about telecom initiatives, understanding job titles and projected career paths, and knowing general learning requirements and wage scales is unprecedented for this industry. You can then tie those benefits together with a job board, and the site visitors

start to see the big picture of how this industry comes together and how they can benefit from it," says Nelson. "It is also important to note that 'upward' movement is not always available and/or applicable. Career pathing means both vertical and horizontal opportunities. We wanted to show relational attributes between different fields and how they can align to benefit the individual and the company." A screen shot of the VIVID Future career map is shown in Figure 3-1.

To see the VIVID Future career map in action, visit VIVIDfuture.org.

Even the name of the site, VIVID Future, points workers to where the fresh opportunities can be found. The acronym VIVID includes each component of the evolving communications industry: Voice, Information, Video, Infrastructure, and Data. Furthermore, as workers within the industry seek lateral moves, they can easily remember the acronym as a way of orienting their career direction as they learn more within any one sector.

"An individual with strong technical skills and customer service experience can be hard to come by in any industry," reminds Nelson. "Also, 'high technical skills' is no longer a requirement exclusively for 'field' positions. Many of our industry's call center positions require technical skills far greater than anything required by a technician driving around in a truck. We want to keep skills relevant so that individuals can maintain employment and companies can improve retention rates."

A big push for VIVID Future came from one of its biggest supporters, AT&T, says Richard Hake, an analyst with the technical training department of CenturyLink Communications and a member of the NACTEL board of directors.[10]

The industry wanted to do more than retain technically proficient employees. Its leaders wanted to illustrate how certain levels of technical proficiency qualified employees to make lateral transfers so that they could continue developing. In addition, the leaders realized

Figure 3-1

CAEL VIVID Future Career Map Screen Shot

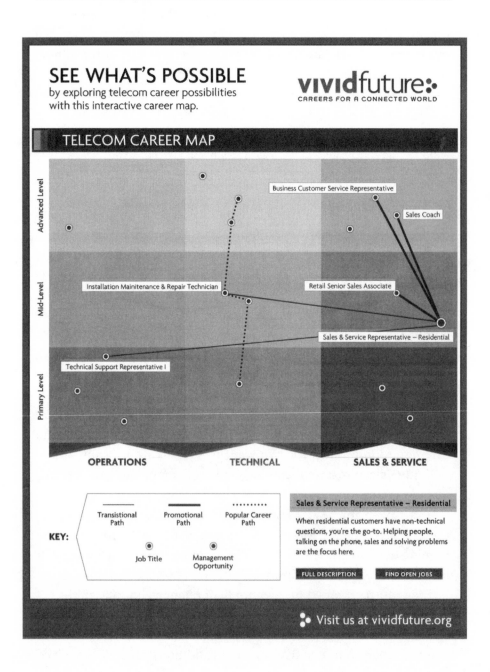

that continued consolidations and mergers had undermined many of the industry's historically solid employee development programs and cultures. VIVID Future's career-mapping tool provides an alternative approach for talent management initiatives. "We've been good at providing training to become competent. But where we dropped the ball was, we'd say, 'congratulations, you're competent; you're set for the rest of your career.' Now we have a website that gives managers a tool that lets them have meaningful discussions with their employees about their futures," says Hake. "VIVID Future gives people the chance to plot their own careers. Instead of just floating along, now they can see how they can position themselves as the leading candidate."

Tying the career paths to open jobs does more than give site audiences a sense of the lattices' immediate relevance. Visitors' travels through VIVID Future and their responses to open positions provide invaluable metrics that help NACTEL and CAEL continually evolve the site's content and design. "Statistics that come from our employers who post vacancies on the VIVID Future job board are extremely important," says Nelson. "At the end of the day, we want to provide a path to education that will lead you to a job. So, being able to numerically see an impact through job applications from this site is terribly important."

The next steps for VIVID Future include expanding its job board to link ever more specifically to the career, technical, and educational information on the site. And, NACTEL also aims to extend its efforts, partly through VIVID Future, to reach high school guidance counselors and students.

Realigning Organizational Culture from Ladder to Lattice

"A lot of companies are doing something [about career pathing], but are not pulling it together. Pulling it together is where we get the retention," says Lori K. Long, an associate professor in the business division of Baldwin-Wallace College.[11] "By moving up, down, and sideways, you can build more committed employees." When retention is redefined during a recession, it doesn't have to mean a dead end. On the lattice, it means new growth in new directions.

But organizational cultures can block lattices, both in spirit and in action. The more ladder-centric the culture, the harder it may be for it to make the transition to the lattice. When top executives achieved their position via the ladder, stories of their climbing prowess and their triumphs become hard-wired into the culture. Lattice career paths need to be clearly communicated. As sincerely as they might champion the lattice, it can look as though senior executives are pulling the ladder up behind them once they have scaled the heights, when they introduce lateral moves out of context.

Meanwhile, rank-and-file employees may not be aware of how many lateral moves have often been woven into the career paths of high-profile leaders. Breaking down the steps taken by top leaders and highlighting the strategic and tactical value of their lateral moves are the keys to successfully segueing from the ladder to the lattice. Especially when they can see lattice success in the careers of their peers, employees will intuitively grasp the greater significance of lateral moves. They may even help discover new career-pathing ideas for other employees.

"Lateral is different. It's expanding; it's learning. It's not that up is good and lateral is bad. You have to reward people who take those moves," says Jill Smart, chief human resources officer for Accenture.[12] She uses her own lateral-laced career path as a case in point for Accenture employees and managers. Employees need to see how they can link lateral moves to aim for a destination job, while managers need to have a "pay it forward" point of view so that they are willing to support developmental moves for team members.

Individual stories, believes Smart, are essential for reinforcing the value of lateral moves. "We show examples of people who are strong performers who take jobs that might seem smaller, but that really are challenging assignments," she says. "We give them a special performance management approach, and we give them different objectives. That helped us so that people would not avoid those kinds of assignments. If someone thinks he has to have $100 million in sales, he's not going to take the start-up assignment if he knows he can't make $100 million in sales." A situation like that recently unfolded at Accenture: a manager who was in charge of a major European operation was asked to start up a division in South Korea. The new job offered a rare opportunity to start a new operation from scratch, but in the traditional way of measuring corporate power, it involved managing fewer people, which could look like a demotion. The manager took the position, confident that the opportunity to build a country operation from scratch would outweigh the smaller staff size. After all, it's more impressive to build revenues from no dollars to any dollars than it is to accelerate an already-cruising sales operation.

Smart herself zigzagged to the C-suite. After two decades in technology consulting to the government and financial services sectors, she was asked to apply her technology, training, and client management skills to her own company, Accenture. "I was not quite sure where it would take me," she recalls. "But I thought, I'll learn something new; I'll get to know some new leaders in Accenture. Still, it was taking a chance." Her instinct that getting to know a new set of colleagues could prove valuable was on target. Not only did she expand her relationship base, but one of those new connections was on the fast track to COO. "He turned out to be a mentor and advocate. You get things out of these changes [lateral moves] that you might not expect," says Smart.

Because she had championed training, Smart was asked by the CEO to analyze and then reorganize training companywide. Abandoning client-facing responsibilities was contrary to everything Smart then thought she knew about how to manage her career. But one of her peers in financial services persuaded her otherwise by pointing out that she would gain a new set of business skills and get to know the entire organization. Most important, she would design and execute a major strategic plan, from start to finish. The unexpected benefit to this role: Smart became conversant in the cultures of many of the countries in which Accenture operates.

Informed by her own experiences, Smart has added structure and pathing around lateral moves. "We purposefully pluck people to move, and they volunteer. We move them to different clients and into and out of leadership roles," she says. Career counselors are a key component of her plan. Every employee has a career counselor, a professional who is a level or two ahead and who can both help with career navigation and serve as a sounding board. (See the section "Career Coaches for Everyone!" for another take on career counselors.) Every executive must be a career counselor, and each is equipped for the role through training, annual refresher courses, and an online career mapping and resource tool.

Shared responsibility for employee success has helped neutralize the fear that some managers understandably have that investing in key personnel with crucial skills will cause those people to disappear. Counseling employees who do not report to them helps managers stay focused on retaining talent for the organization. And, it forces them to continually develop succession plans for their own departments.

Research conducted by Dr. Long at Baldwin-Wallace College and other academics reinforces the importance of fueling motivation with a sense of personal and professional purpose.[13] The immediate effect of the lattice is to increase engagement, productivity, and retention, says Long. Continual growth and direction on the lattice provide a structure for engagement.

"The lattice reframes the whole discussion. For culture change, it supports from the top the view that this is a valued initiative that is focused on individual development and retaining valued employees. Then, if you take a lateral move, we see it as a sign that you are committed to our company," says Long.[14]

The Lattice Works, for Both Individuals and Corporations

Nancy Chagares has run grocery and food operations from store bakeries to regional operations. Some of her best career experiences were lateral moves that gave her the breathing room to integrate what she'd just learned in a new setting—in other words, the plateaus that grounded her.

Now an industry veteran, she advises ambitious up-and-comers to abandon the ladders that they lugged with them into the workplace and to craft their lattices. "I like to say that it's not good enough anymore to be smart, and book smart does not compensate for lack of experience. That justifies telling someone who is younger, 'You need to take this lateral move because it's good for your development. It will give you depth. If you do this right, you will have people who will be in your corner when you need someone, and that is invaluable.'"[15]

As the buyer for the bake shop of one of the largest grocery chains in Chicago, Chagares was told by her boss that she needed to take a side step into operations. As the new mother of a baby, this was the last thing she wanted to do. "When you're out in operations, you work holidays. You work weekends. Your hours are unpredictable. It's not being in the office from eight to five. But it was one of the best things I ever did for my career. You understand the fundamentals of the business when you see it through a different operating position," she says.

A roll-up-your-sleeves recommendation is not universally greeted with enthusiasm, but rising leaders need to understand that their response to the offer of a lateral move is likely to be closely evaluated. It's not just about the nuts and bolts of the new assignment; it's more about how a rising leader learns to adapt to a new situation, size it up quickly, and start delivering results. "We had a produce employee whom we moved to floral buying," recalls Chagares. "He didn't know anything about floral. That's not the point. You can train anybody the tactics and how-tos. What people bring to lateral moves is the ability to be innovative, to see things with fresh eyes, and to make things work."

Constructing a Healthcare Lattice

When CAEL and the DOL partnered to address the nursing shortage, CAEL adopted the lattice terminology to recognize that careers do not always follow a linear progression. Workers often make lateral moves in their careers, and these moves can be just as important for their career development. For example, a career ladder would focus only on the progression of certified nurse assistants to licensed practical nurses to registered nurses, while a lattice would recognize that LPN candidates can also be drawn from other branches of the healthcare field, such as lab technicians, and even from outside the profession.

CAEL also reinvented the concept of apprenticeship to rotate employees who were new to healthcare through several types of departments, such as pediatrics and geriatrics, so that they could see early on if they had an affinity for a particular specialty. And, CAEL designed online educational components to enable employees to continue working full time while taking classes. Community and state colleges joined CAEL in adapting their programs to incorporate online learning.

The nursing lattice was a perfect fit for the Evangelical Lutheran Good Samaritan Society, which runs a far-flung network of care centers employing 22,000 people (see Figure 3-2). Its most pressing need continues to be for registered nurses, and the Growing Our Own component of the lattice program has been the most successful, reports Dr. Neal Eddy, executive strategic administrator for Good Samaritan.[16]

Figure 3-2
Good Samaritan Nursing Lattice

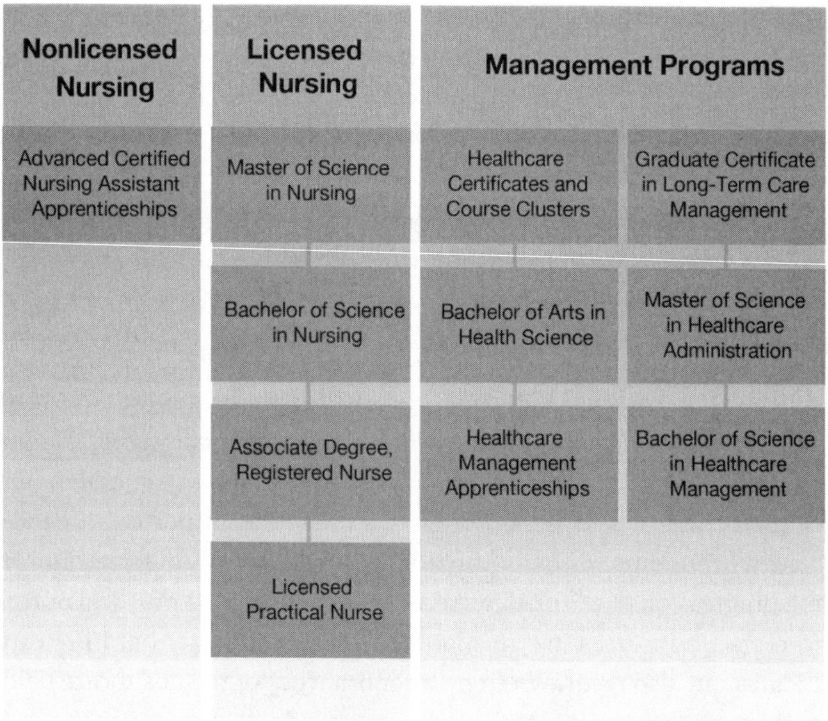

Nonlicensed Nursing	Licensed Nursing	Management Programs	
Advanced Certified Nursing Assistant Apprenticeships	Master of Science in Nursing	Healthcare Certificates and Course Clusters	Graduate Certificate in Long-Term Care Management
	Bachelor of Science in Nursing	Bachelor of Arts in Health Science	Master of Science in Healthcare Administration
	Associate Degree, Registered Nurse	Healthcare Management Apprenticeships	Bachelor of Science in Healthcare Management
	Licensed Practical Nurse		

But, as Danielle Schaeffer's story illustrates, the program's overlapping branches and intersections have kept candidates in its pipeline for administrators and specialty professions, as well. (Figure 3-3)

Program coordinators at each Good Samaritan facility are key to the evolution and ongoing success of the lattice programs. Every employee can meet with a coordinator to see what lateral experiences, training, and formal education link to a new job. Supervisors are expected to encourage employees to pursue training and certifications through the lattice program and to support that through flexible scheduling.

Figure 3-3
Danielle Schaeffer's Lattice

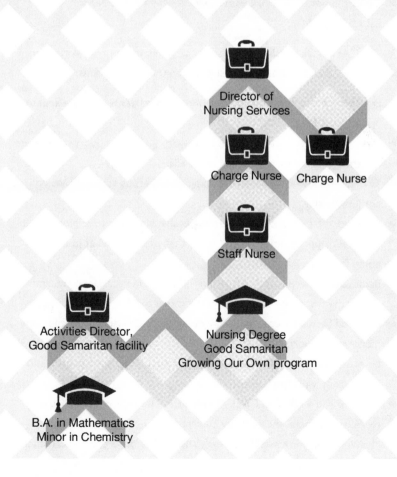

Director of
Nursing Services

Charge Nurse   Charge Nurse

Staff Nurse

Activities Director,
Good Samaritan facility

Nursing Degree
Good Samaritan
Growing Our Own program

B.A. in Mathematics
Minor in Chemistry

Danielle Schaeffer made the most of Good Samaritan's Growing Our Own program to become a nurse. Then, she rotated among several lateral positions to gain operating experience.

Elements of the Good Samaritan Nursing Lattice

► A clear direction through an individualized education and skills plan
► Mentors and coaches
► Affordable classes, some of them subsidized, but many low-cost because they involve distance learning
► Accessible classes, apprenticeships, and training through management support for flexible schedules and logistical support
► Opportunities to network with other members of the Nursing Career Lattice Program

The CAEL/DOL nursing lattice addressed a number of real-world dynamics that have undermined other well-intended training programs:[17]

► Employers customized the industry model to reflect their acute staffing needs.
► Latticing employees could continue to work—and to support themselves and their families—while gaining new skills.
► The lattice allowed employees to explore numerous advancement options, not just nursing.
► Apprenticeships and distance learning enabled latticers to explore potential career opportunities beyond those that were offered at just their home facilities.
► Because skills were linked to lateral or upward career development, employees for the first time could see how the career building blocks fit together.
► Logistical barriers were removed by offering flexible schedules and commonsense supports.
► Local advisory councils drew in related organizations, such as professional associations, workforce investment boards, and colleges.
► Each site had a full-time CAEL coordinator who promoted the lattice, recruited partners, and oversaw implementation at all stages.
► Measurements were established early and used to make course corrections.

Good Samaritan has learned that career lattices don't go on automatic pilot. Some educational components proved to be so effective that they became stand-alone programs, says Sonia Bury, manager of workforce programs.[18] Others, like the apprenticeship outreach, started strong but were overtaken by proliferating training requirements dictated by licensing regulators. Despite its ups and downs, the lattice program was validated by the retention and productivity of the employees who participated, says Bury.

"Growing Our Own is the starship of the program," adds Eddy. The program now has satellite locations to enable more nurse candidates to get their clinical experience and has just added a management component. "There are 120 nurses in seven states who would not have had the opportunity to become a nurse if it were not for this program," he says. Kelly Vig, another Growing Our Own alum, rose from certified nurse assistant to administrator of a nursing home in her North Dakota town. "The program makes any job not a dead end," said Vig. "Anyone can do it. It becomes a team goal to help that person achieve her goal." One resident was so impressed by Vig's achievement that he bequeathed money for Growing Our Own scholarships.[19]

Pennsylvania Early Learning Keys to Quality Career Lattice

Virginia, Pennsylvania, and other states have also adapted the career lattice for early childhood educators. The Pennsylvania Early Learning Keys to Quality Career Lattice program maps its lattice for workers, starting with aides and progressing to PhDs. At each level, this map shows the range of possibilities that open up with different combinations of experience, education, and credentials. This model can be adapted for other professions.

For more information on the Pennsylvania Keys to Quality Early Learning career lattice, visit their website www.pakeys.org and click on the Career Development tab.

Figure 3-4

Nine-Box Model

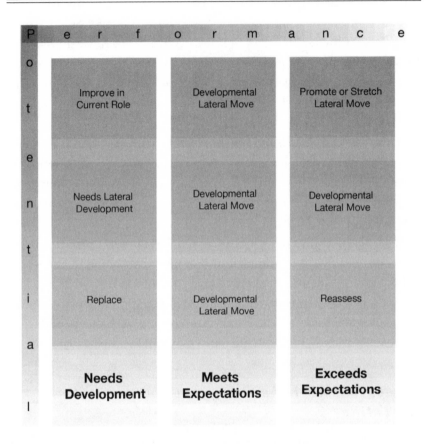

The classic nine-box model helps managers see which employees are the most promising candidates for leadership development and promotion. (See Figure 3-4.) The top right box represents the intersection of top performance and top potential, while the bottom left box represents the intersection of poor performance and minimal potential. Nancy Chagares and other latticing leaders recommend adapting the nine-box model to identify which employees are the best candidates for lateral developmental moves.

Blend the Lattice with Traditional Talent Development Techniques

Setting Up the Lateral Transfer

▶ Use the classic nine-box evaluation system to identify the best candidates for lateral moves.

▶ Share with each employee where he falls in the nine-box system—and why. High-performing employees need context for a lateral move so that they gain a broader understanding of what constitutes career development—and why it doesn't always involve a traditional promotion.

▶ Name the characteristics and work values that make this person worth the investment of a developmental lateral move. "We chose people who were flexible, motivated, and not afraid of hard work," says veteran retail executive Nancy Chagares.[20] "And they knew it."

▶ Not every lateral move is developmental, however. Some employees—hard workers who are not likely to become leaders—may permanently plateau. They also need to see where they fall in the nine-box schematic so that they can adjust their expectations accordingly. "Cycling through lateral moves keeps people engaged and motivated. It keeps people creative, solving different problems," says Chagares. If an employee is likely to continue at the same level, look for other ways in which she can develop professionally, such as becoming a coach or a mentor.

Setting Employees Up for Lateral Success

▶ Neutralize the assumption that a lateral move is moving aside. Employees may have heard that from baby boomers, for whom it might have been true—a decade ago. The more context the employee has about how this move will position him for a promotion, the better equipped he will be to make the most of his new assignment.

► Show the employee exactly where this position is situated in the company's organization chart. She may not realize that there are numerous positions at the same level, each with the potential to develop her career and her qualifications.

► Engineer the transition by enabling the new employee to work side by side with the departing employee for several weeks.

► Connect the employee with people who have made similar moves in the past year for peer mentoring. "When employees see others ahead of them make moves like that and be successful, they'll be enthusiastic about it," says Chagares.

► Identify one business skill and one relational/creative skill that the employee will need if he is to be successful in the new role, and arrange for that training. Not only will the employee gain the skills he needs, but he will feel validated by the formal investment in training.

► Emphasize the value of networking with a fresh universe of coworkers, suppliers, vendors, employees, and customers. The skill of introducing yourself to all those people and becoming oriented—with their help—is a professional skill in itself.

► Make several appointments for weeks and months into the lateral assignment so that the employee knows that she can count on "status check" discussions with a mentor or coach.

► When the time comes for a promotion or another lateral move, coach the employee through a graceful exit. Key to cementing these relationships is the employee's recognizing and thanking those whom he has worked with so that these connections will strengthen his network—and be valuable to him at a different point on the lattice.

Career Coaches for Everyone!

At first, Tricia Duncan's career path was traditional. She joined Jones & Roth CPAs and Business Advisors in the mid-1990s as a staff accountant, then rotated into its Business Advisory Group, blending consulting with a flexible schedule. That was when she had her epiphany: if her coaching delivered results for her clients, what would happen if she applied the same skills to Jones & Roth's talent pipeline?

Her solution, universal coaching, illustrates how a small workplace can transform its culture and drive business results by continually coaching its employees through structured lateral assignments. "Mentoring and assigned advisor programs were not conveying the consistency of the message," says Duncan.[21] "We needed a dedicated person for in-depth career coaching, and that melded with what I do best."

In 2007, Duncan became the firm's full-time career coach. Working with the firm's managing partner and its training and development director, she tracks the success of each of the firm's 85 employees, from receptionist to partner. The effort has decreased turnover and improved productivity. "It has really forced us to look at our competencies at each level. We're more confident that we are advancing the right people," says Duncan.

One early win was formulating consistent communications and top-line measurement standards, and gaining buy-ins from all partners. Every professional has a development plan, and the plans of up-and-coming younger employees are reviewed monthly. With the employee's supervisor and, when warranted, with the partners in charge of the line of business, Duncan reviews each employee's advancement in the areas of soft and technical skills, current and next assignments, and peer relationships. Short- and medium-term performance goals are adjusted accordingly.

The ongoing reviews are complemented by an ever-expanding array of training and business development programs that are open to all employees. Topics range from basic networking and client skills to joining the board of directors of a local nonprofit.

Jones & Roth had struggled to gain what it needed from mentoring programs, explains partner Doug Griesel. "Straight mentoring has not worked consistently, because people have responsibilities to their clients to get their work done. What ends up at the bottom of the heap is that mentoring relationship. If it doesn't get done for three months, well, that's the way it goes," he says. The coaching model solved that problem because it "ensures that everyone gets tools and training, and that they are held accountable for their goals," he says.[22]

In early 2010, the firm relaunched its mentoring program as a complement to the ongoing coaching. The coaching structure also has equipped staff, managers, and partners with a common language and common expectations for career advancement.

For example, when a woman manager found herself uncomfortable in her first forays into business development, it was easy for her and her partner to redirect her career plan to complex audits, and to reorient her business development aspirations accordingly, Duncan says. Popular work-life concepts, like flexible schedules, are tools that employees use to achieve their next career steps, not goals in and of themselves.

"We're teaching them the skill of assessing their flex situation so that they can identify ongoing solutions," Duncan says. "We coach self-awareness and self-accountability, and how to look at the deeper drivers."

In 2011, Jones & Roth integrated its compensation and performance review process into the "coaches for everyone" model. "Shareholders and managers had expressed concern that team members were not advancing," says Duncan. "By including mentors in the process, we have a new set of people accountable for and focused on developing our team. Mentors know that the results of the review process will have a financial effect on their mentees and will help the process by setting clear goals, gathering timely feedback, and working with the mentee to move forward."[23]

By blending structured career paths with structured coaching, Jones & Roth has created a lattice model that ensures that the firm is developing the right mix of skills to meet current and anticipated business demands. "The committee process has helped the entire firm clarify expectations at each level," says Duncan. "The meetings enable us to talk about general areas of concern, qualifications for advancement, and succession planning. Everyone has benefited from being on the same page: the firm, the employee, and the supervisors."

Is Your Organization Lattice-Ready?

Is your organization poised to take advantage of the lattice? This quiz will help you detect where your organization falls on the ladder-to-lattice spectrum.

1. Departments and divisions are in strict "silos."
2. Senior leaders spend at least 30 percent of their time on talent development.
3. Employee resource groups (ERGs) are a primary channel for identifying and developing talent.
4. Your HR systems inventory employees' skills and aptitudes— both those acquired on the job and those gained outside of work.
5. Employees have a self-directed training allowance.
6. Your recruiters stay in touch with valued former employees via an alumni network.
7. Suppliers, especially minority- and women-owned firms, deal only with buyers.
8. Virtual training enables employees to access courses at any time or place.
9. Midlevel managers are formally evaluated on their ability to cultivate talent.
10. Internal business plan competitions are open only to high-potential employees and/or employees in certain divisions.

Score your organization! Give your organization one point for a yes answer to questions 2, 3, 4, 5, 6, 8, and 9, and one point for a no answer to questions 1, 7, and 10.

7–10 points: Your organization is already latticing, whether you call it that or not. Your challenge is to tie together the various lattice programs into a coordinated whole that will exponentially increase results.

4–6 points: Latticing is probably happening organically in some divisions or regions. Exploring and analyzing these programs and cultural lattices will help you see how to cross-pollinate their success to the entire organization.

0–3 points: The lattice is probably a new concept at your organization. You'll need to build the business case for a pilot, possibly using the few examples that you can find.

How to Recruit Lattice Participants

Employees who are unfamiliar with career lattices will need to see what's in it for them. Here is an employee communication template developed by CAEL that can be used to recruit participants.[24]

Join the >> specific career<< Lattice Program

What's in it for me? Why enroll?

▶ The lattice provides a support structure for your own personal and professional growth.

▶ A mentor assists you in applying new skills and knowledge on the job—you earn and learn!

▶ It allows you to develop your own skills at your own pace during your current work schedule.

▶ You develop creative problem-solving skills that you can apply to any job, such as time management and improved communication.

▶ Professional growth is the first step of a career lattice that could result in bridging to lateral roles that help you develop key skills for future advancement.

▶ Increased pay and recognition for your advanced knowledge and skill.

▶ Build your own confidence by validating your competence and experience.

▶ Convenient and varied learning options! With a combination of distance learning, self-study, and on-the-job training components, you have the convenience of learning according to your schedule and with minimal travel.

Here's How to Get Started

1. >>Summarize here who is eligible, based on technical skill level, certification, or job title. <<
2. Complete an enrollment application. >> contact information here<<

Lessons of the Lattice

► Lattices can scale for any size organization, industry, or region.
► Creating a regional or industry lattice enables employers with interlocking interests to share resources, best practices, and expenses for programs that can help fill shared needs. Regional or industry lattices can develop and direct talent to address specific skills gaps, retaining valued employees within the region or industry.
► Integrate existing resources and talent management techniques into your organization's career lattices. Certification courses, distance learning, apprenticeships, as-needed learning, and other traditional modes of workforce training are more relevant when they are set in the context of an appealing career path.
► Use latticed career paths to accelerate the growth of employees with proven track records and to address weaknesses and gaps in other employees' skills and experience.
► Career counselors or coaches are key for facilitating essential employee conversations about career paths. Since they are unfamiliar with the value of lateral moves, employees need stories of successful latticing by employees and leaders at all levels.

THE LATTICE IN ACTION

In the daily crush of producing CNN's never-ending cable television news programs, editors Alison Hashimoto and Ben Kaiser had rushed by each other in the hall, but they had never met, let alone worked together. Editors who managed segments of CNN's torrent of news, Hashimoto and Kaiser each assumed that the only way to move up at the network was to wait for one of the positions above them to open up, then compete for that position. Neither of them gave much thought to applying his or her technical or management skills to jobs producing cartoons or drama at other channels within the Turner Broadcasting System subsidiary. They had plenty of ideas for news shows, but neither of them knew a thing about how to convert those ideas to new services that would bring more money to Turner. And neither of them knew anyone on the business side of Turner—the advertising, sales, and business development staff members who brought in new revenue and converted it to profits.

In short, before they took advantage of an innovative program at Turner designed to equip employees with career lattice and related skills, they had no idea how to apply their ambitions and energy to anything but the ladder.

Then Hashimoto and Kaiser met Leslie Kleine and Cathy Kononetz, both producers with Turner's Cartoon Network, and Marsha Maldonado, an MBA, a former PricewaterhouseCoopers consultant, and a staffer in Turner's finance department. These five made up a team in the KEYS (Knowledge Energizing Your Success) program, an internal business plan competition intended to deepen participants' knowledge of Turner's operations while they sharpened their business acumen and collaborated with high-performing peers. Their assignment: to come up with a new product that would bring in fresh revenue. They had their combined abilities, they had access to an array of business skills crash courses, and they had a deadline: eight weeks.[1]

THE WHOLE POINT of the career lattice is to use what an individual has, or can easily acquire, to daisy-chain to a new position. This chapter shows how individuals in several types of situations have done just that. Some have made the most of organizational programs, such as Turner's KEYS program. Conceived and run by Turner's senior women's network, Turner Women Today, KEYS accelerates lateral career development for the women who lead it and for the hundreds of employees who participate. Other profiles in Chapter 4 show how self-directed individuals have crafted their own lattices.

By illustrating several lattice models in action, Chapter 4 shows individuals, human resources staffers, and senior leaders how to combine the elements outlined in Chapters 2 and 3 into career paths for all, one at a time.

Assemble Your Portfolio

Before you can apply your abilities to your first move, you need to know what you are working with. CAEL researchers found that adult college students who consciously build on the skills and abilities they had gained before enrolling (or reenrolling) in college were more than twice as likely to complete their degrees.[2] What you already know gives you a huge head start toward achieving your career goals. You already know a lot; build on it.

This chapter puts the skills portfolio model outlined in Chapter 2 into action. Your skills portfolio is the foundation for your lattice. It inventories the skills that you already possess so that you can identify what skills and lateral opportunities you need to pursue to qualify for your destination job.[3]

Current skills + bridging experiences and/or skills acquisition = lateral move = one step closer to your destination job

Chapter 2 shows how to build the individual elements of your portfolio. You need to apply that technique to build case studies for these categories of expertise:

Technical skills. How do you do what you do? Technical skills deliver measurable results. Doctors diagnose and treat people; mechanics diagnose and treat cars. Degrees and certifications are a good start, but you might have significant on-the-job training, too.

Transferable skills. Transferable skills are business, creative problem-solving, and relational skills that you have acquired on the job and that can apply to a new job or challenge.

Experience. Gained at work, through volunteer work, and through personal pursuits, experience is the insight and maturity you have gained in the process of using your technical skills and picking up transferable skills.

Performance. Performance is what you've accomplished so far with your aptitude and skills. What are your measurable results? How have your results contributed to your organization's results?

Aptitude. What are you naturally good at? What comes easily to you? These are clues to what destination jobs might be good fits. You will want to make the most of your aptitudes to get there.

Ambition. This translates to everyday perseverance. Think of ambition as the determination to overcome obstacles to accomplish your goals.

Intuition. This is your ability to read trends, which will enable you to trellis to the right place at the right time. The more you test your intuition, the better you will understand how to trust it.

Personality. This shapes your attitude about all of the previous categories. Are you a "glass half-empty" or a "glass half-full" sort of person?

Network. Know who can give you a hand as you move from one point
on your lattice to the next. Revisit the crew section of Chapter 2 for
more on the three types of crew members you need in your lattice:
spotters, wingpeople, and lookouts.

Values. Is all of this worth the effort? What is the bigger mission of
your career? Knowing what makes it all worthwhile arms you with
personal guiding principles when you must make judgment calls.

Home School to High School

Deb Davis set herself a very specific and very challenging stretch
goal. At age 45, she had a dusty degree in elementary education, two
decades of experience home-schooling six children in everything from
arithmetic to Latin, a flair for languages, and a general desire to keep
teaching, this time at a school.[4]

Her first step up was a very big one. She was 45. She lived in a rural
area where opportunities quite literally were few and far between. Her
credentials were not just rusty, they were Iron Age. She still had two
teenagers to home-school and a husband to feed and water.

First, she identified how she could gain the technical credentials that
would validate her skills with eventual employers. Her first step was
to renew her elementary education certificate, which had expired while
she was teaching at the kitchen table. In order to do this, she had to
enroll in a Spanish class at the local community college. It wasn't long
before the language department instructor labeled Davis a prodigy
and asked her to teach part-time. (And this teacher is still her mentor,
whom Davis identifies as her wingperson to this day!)

To her surprise, the community college asked her to be a regular
adjunct. With some money rolling in, she decided to enroll in an
online program and earned a master's degree in teaching. Her very
first academic paper was chosen for publication by a scholarly journal.
(One of her professors was her lookout there. He knew the journal was
looking for an article from someone at a community college.)

Adjunct faculty positions can be the deadest of dead ends, but Davis
latticed it. She taught for several semesters, establishing her credibility

with college administrators by doing a great job and revising the adjunct handbook. She also created a hybrid version of the beginning Spanish class (partially online) and designed a tutorial version of the intermediate class. In the summer of 2009, she took a little stash of cash and went to a high-level language immersion course for international students. Before she went, she was relieved to have a colleague from Spain (one of her spotters) rate the program an A+.

Upon returning, she discovered that the local parochial high school was frantically looking for a part-time Spanish teacher for the about-to-start school year. Barely over her jet lag, with her suitcase still on the floor by her bed, Davis landed the job. After her first week, the principal asked her to design an independent study course for the most advanced French students. A year later, the school expanded the position to become the full-time head of the foreign language department, including the task of creating a new French program. By late 2011, Davis had gained a master's in Spanish from the University of Salamanca.

Here is what is in Davis's skills portfolio:

Technical Skills
Davis earned her master's in Spanish and her master's in education as she latticed back into the workforce. She had earned her bachelor's in education two decades before.

Transferable Skills
Acquired over the years, Davis's transferable skills included classroom management (six kids are a one-room school), curriculum design (she wrote unit studies for literature and history), lesson planning, a working knowledge of state testing requirements, and time management.

Experience
Gained as she wove together postgraduate degrees and eased back into the workforce, Davis's operating experience includes knowledge of educational bureaucracies; three summers living and studying in Spain, taking university courses in Spanish; and empathy for elementary, high school, and adult learners.

Ambition
Davis delivered results because she made her career goals a priority.

Intuition
Davis tracks trends in educational funding, testing, and other areas to ensure that she gets whatever additional training she needs to ensure that her skills are what schools need.

Aptitude
Davis has innate language talent, and she continues to seek out advanced language courses.

Performance
Standardized tests reveal that Davis's students perform well; she was asked to mentor younger teachers.

Personality
Davis is a high-energy person with an adventurous spirit. Travel and different cultures are exciting to her, not scary.

Network
Davis is now connected with Spanish teachers from around the world who can direct her to additional continuing education programs, especially those geared for teachers.

Values
Language and cross-cultural fluency are hallmarks of Davis and her family. She lives her values, which gives her credibility with her students.

The Lattice in Action: Technical Skills

Technical skills are the easiest qualifications to gain simply because there are so many people and programs available that are willing to teach you. Often it's in your employer's best interest to support you in your quest for greater skill. As mentioned in Chapter 3, employers are most likely to cover the cost of getting or expanding technical skills, often through tuition reimbursement programs, in-house training, and, increasingly, virtual training through online and self-directed classes.

Based on the skills portfolio that you assembled in Chapter 2, ask yourself:

► How do I use the technical skills that I learned?
► How are the technical skills that I have already learned of strategic value to me, given my ambition and aptitudes? Are there other skills that would be a better fit for me?
► If some of the skills I have earned seem like a waste of money or time, why do I feel that way? What other technical skills would be a good investment, and why?

What if you aren't sure what technical skills would help you move toward your destination job? Here are some ways to find out:

► Examine the career map for your organization or industry. The map should show what technical and transferable skills lattice from one job to another. See the VIVID Future career map in Chapter 3 for a sample of a career map. If you can't find a career map for your function or specialty, sketch one with your crew, your manager, or your career coach.
► Discuss your target job with your manager, mentor, or career coach and find out what incremental steps can help you bridge to that job.
► Talk with people who are doing what you want to do, virtually or in person. BranchOut, LinkedIn and other professional social media tools are terrific resources for this, as are industry networking groups and internal employee resource groups.

It takes time and energy to build your roster of skills. If you're feeling drawn to an entirely new career field, you may need a new skill set to qualify for your dream job. If so, now is the time to find out exactly what skills you need to master.

The Lattice in Action: Transferable Skills

You might not realize that running a meeting efficiently and getting everyone to agree—and like it—is a transferable skill. It is. Transferable skills are often integrated with the process of using the technical skills. Business skills—how your accomplishments contribute to your organization's achievements—become more relevant as you gain responsibilities for resources. Relational and creative problem-solving skills become increasingly imperative as you manage more people.

How do you:

► Apply your technical skills in collaboration with others?
► Coach others?
► Train others?
► Diagnose and solve problems?
► Realize when a project needs a course correction—and persuade others to make that correction?
► Manage up?
► Manage down?
► Measure the results of your effort?

The Lattice in Action: Experience

You can be a technical whiz. You can surround your technical skills with impressive business and strategic knowledge. You can infuse all of this with interpersonal finesse and be a genius at coming up with creative solutions for difficult dilemmas. But all of this is academic until you start using it. Street smarts, a sixth sense for organizational politics, and the ability to set realistic goals—all of this comes from experience.

Experience is the wisdom you have gained through navigating work situations and responsibilities. Whether they're good or bad, or just are, your experiences shape your expectations of your upcoming career moves.

On the ladder, you pretty much follow in the footsteps of the person who had the job before you, and presumably was promoted. If you aspire to the next rung, you have a good idea of how your current experiences will prepare you for that job and what you will experience when you get it. What will your life be like when your boss shuffles upward and you shuffle into his job? You already know: your day then will be just like his day now. You could argue that accelerating business cycles and rapidly evolving technological evolution mean that when you get your boss's job, you'll face a very different set of challenges from those that he faced when he got it. That's true, but you'll still be reacting to circumstances, not choosing them.

The lattice forces you to be proactive. You don't have to wait for experiences to happen to you. You pursue experiences that you believe will build your qualifications for your target job or jobs. Because you're choosing them strategically, you can seize on experiences that dovetail with your other responsibilities or your career aspirations.

The classic example is the international assignment. On the ladder, you get an international assignment after you've successfully handled a national assignment. The trouble is that by the time you climb that high on the ladder, you've generally picked up a spouse and kids. The international assignment often collides with your spouse's career aspirations and your children's schooling and friendships. Hey, everybody, we're being transferred to Beijing! Hooray! That's why some companies, like big accounting firms and Bloomberg News, are rethinking the timing of international assignments. It makes more sense for you to be part of an expansion into a new country when you're either in your twenties with small or no children, or an empty-nester in your fifties. If you aspire to be a senior executive of a big organization, international experience is likely to be in your future. By leveraging the lattice, you can angle for that experience when it's best for you, not just wait for a higher-up to remember you during annual succession-planning season.

Your experience is a huge advantage when you're navigating the lattice. The more people you know, and would like to work with, the more helping hands you can grasp as you seek your lateral moves. Diagonal moves are, by definition, gradual. That gives you plenty of time to develop alliances, advocates, and influence with an ever-expanding network of colleagues. One of the most valuable experiences you can have is to mentor others. Your protégé will (hopefully) advance, thanks to your help, and inevitably will be in a position to recommend you for a project or position that could turn into your next diagonal move.

- ▶ What experiences have proven to be most effective for your career, and why?
- ▶ How have you proven your leadership skills?
- ▶ How do your experiences match your career ambitions? What do you need to prove, and to whom?
- ▶ Have you gotten valuable experience outside the office, perhaps on the board of a nonprofit or an educational committee? How can this benefit your career?
- ▶ Have you managed people or resources successfully? How can you lattice to a situation that requires "bottom-line" results?
- ▶ What narratives can you construct from problems you have solved? The classic narrative structure is: problem, conflict, resolution or solution. What problems have you diagnosed and solved? What were the measurable results? (Are you still fuzzy on how to build a case study from your experiences? Revisit Chapter 2.)
- ▶ How have you quickly adapted to changing circumstances? Did you still achieve your original goal, or did you persuade your manager and your team to achieve a more appropriate goal?
- ▶ How have you advocated for improvements in a process or procedure?

If you have had an unpleasant leadership experience, bracket your feelings, and ask, "What did I learn?" This will help you zero in on the likely gain in any situation, especially if you are facing an interim lattice move that you'd otherwise avoid.

The Lattice in Action: Ambition

How badly do you want to move ahead? Ambition is how you focus your attention and energy to achieve your dream. Ambition requires bringing energy, self-discipline, and effort to bear on achieving a particular goal.

Ambition can motivate you. As reported in the *Journal of Experimental Social Psychology* by Garriy Shteynberg and Adam Galinsky, setting "specific stretch goals" makes it more likely that you will achieve, and even surpass, your ambitions.[5] Make your goals both challenging and specific, and set yourself up to measure the results. Merely telling yourself to "do your best" is more likely to result in excuses than in results.

True ambition focuses the mind. If you want to move ahead, your ambition is one of your secret weapons. Other people will confuse ambition with envy, dreaming, and scheming. Envy focuses on others, distracting you from doing what you can for yourself. Dreaming is untethered to reality, which makes it a fun escape, but doesn't result in concrete plans. Scheming is the dirty art of plotting to get ahead through the misfortunes of others. Not only is that not nice, but it's the opposite of the sincere goodwill you will need if you are going to work the lattice.

► Do you set specific challenges for yourself? If so, what are the results? If not, why not?

► Do you tend to give up easily? Why?

► When you settle for the status quo, is it strategic or apathetic?

► Does your ambition spark your creativity, or, when you are faced with obstacles, does it crumble in a pile of excuses?

► Sometimes, unfocused ambition is expressed as frustration. Do you have an identified career goal? What are the obstacles to your goal? Can you think of three ways you could achieve that goal in several smaller steps instead of one big step?

The Lattice in Action: Intuition

Actually, the ladder is a lazy way to plot your career path. It's one-dimensional. You don't even need a map. You just plod in the footsteps of the person in front of you. The lattice requires a strategy, and a strategy requires you to think several steps ahead. Some people call this "seeing around corners." Others are surprised when you accurately anticipate a turn of events, and just happen to be in the right place at the right time. "How did you do that?" they wonder. Are you eavesdropping in the executive washrooms?

Fortunately, no restroom lurking is required to cultivate your career intuition. You do need to pay attention to economic, industry, and societal trends. A good understanding of human nature in general, and the culture of your workplace in particular, is essential. As you become skilled at reading the subtle messages of your workplace and our economy, you'll get a sense of where you need to be positioned if you are to catch the next wave.

Nobody beats Barack Obama for career intuition. For years, he harbored the ambition to rise to the highest level of political office that he could. He didn't have the advantage of being born into a family with connections, so he created his own political family through asking others' advice at nearly every career turn. He apprenticed in Chicago, first as a community organizer. Frustrated by machine politics, he applied to Harvard Law School, intent on learning the skill of trading power. He returned to Chicago to work as a civil rights lawyer. He had a gift for oratory, and he honed that by teaching. He shrewdly outed himself through two autobiographies, so that when he burst onto the national political scene in 2007, there was no dirt for his enemies to find that he hadn't already dished himself. Regardless of your political leanings, you have to give Barack Obama credit for latticing his way from community organizer to commander in chief. Every step he took brought him a little closer to his ultimate goal, even if it looked to the uninformed observer like meandering.[6]

When was the last time you heard of a new product or service in your industry and exclaimed, "I thought of that six months ago!" You did? What happened to that great idea? Pay attention the next time you have that feeling of a dawning idea. Get in the habit of following through with initial feasibility research and finding out how you'd introduce the idea to the right folks. Soon you'll learn to trust your intuition, and that will point the way to a secure step on the lattice.

▶ How could you have explored that idea a bit more?

▶ Could you have researched one way in which the idea could have been used at your workplace?

▶ Whom would you have approached to brainstorm with about the great idea?

▶ Specifically how could the great idea have generated sales, revenue, and profits?

▶ Are others already doing something similar to your idea?

▶ What parts of your great idea would you want to do, and what parts require partnerships, delegation, or teamwork?

The Lattice in Action: Aptitude

What comes naturally to you? At work, what would you do even if they didn't pay you? (Lunch does not count.) Your aptitude is what you're wired to do. It's the flow you have to go with. Ambition is the motivation, intuition the where, and aptitude the how.

Sue, a human resources staffer at a major communications company, was competent at her job of managing relationships with the department's suppliers. She negotiated the best deals with benefits providers, and figured out which software would equip executives with the reports they needed in order to track who was getting promoted and why. She was so good at doing all this that, of course, she was moved a notch up the ladder to run a section of the human resources department. Managing people turned out to be completely different from managing suppliers and software. Sue was frustrated and impatient with staffers who seemed slow to grasp the bigger picture that she deciphered so easily. She would just as soon do the work herself, so she did. Thus a micromanager was born. Soon, she asked for a demotion back to her old job.

Fortunately, her boss recognized the difference between a bad fit and a bad person. Her boss was also catching on to the lattice. Instead of simply letting this staffer slide backward on the ladder, she assigned Sue to a couple of cross-departmental projects where her knowledge of human resources and her analytical abilities were invaluable in diagnosing problems and quickly finding affordable solutions. Soon, Sue developed a reputation as an internal consultant and the go-to person for on-the-spot problem solving. Several routes to advancement are now open to her. She's now the finance analyst for the human resources department and is pursuing finance courses to expand on her natural ability to analyze problems and see solutions. Had she not tried and failed at climbing the ladder in the traditional sense, she'd simply be stuck on the ladder, not far from the ground.

Your aptitude sets you up for success. However, it doesn't guarantee it. You probably know people whose aptitude appears to be for the slippery category of "people skills," which they seem to interpret as sucking up, schmoozing, and sliding by on charm. Someone with the aptitudes for easy conversation, genuine interest in others, and the ability to understand what people truly want (as opposed to what they say they want) still needs a solid grounding in business finance and operations to become, for example, a truly successful salesperson.

Recall a moment when you were "in the zone" and emerged with a huge piece of work done and done well. Chances are your aptitude was in full gear. Think through the types of assignments, challenges, and situations in which you have felt naturally confident.

- ▶ Who else shares your aptitudes, and what are his responsibilities?
- ▶ What parts of your current work do you relish? What parts do you recoil from?
- ▶ When you were in school or in training, what were your best subjects?
- ▶ Do you feel that your talents are overlooked in your current work? Why? How could you help others see your strengths?

Opportunities often lurk at the intersection of aptitude and ambition. Some lateral moves are more challenging than others. Is the challenge worth it? Based on CAEL's coaching models, the matrix in Figure 4-1 will help you figure out whether an opportunity is a good stretch assignment, or whether it is more likely to be a waste of time, effort, and motivation.

Figure 4-1

Lateral Opportunity Grid

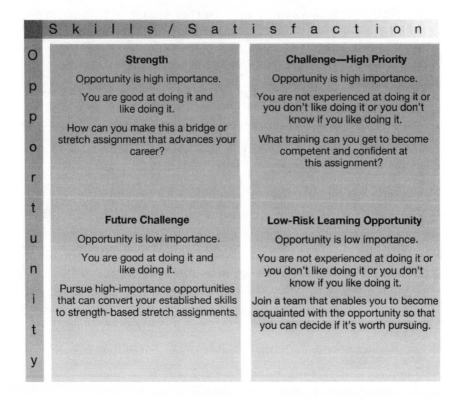

S k i l l s / S a t i s f a c t i o n	
Strength	**Challenge—High Priority**
Opportunity is high importance.	Opportunity is high importance.
You are good at doing it and like doing it.	You are not experienced at doing it or you don't like doing it or you don't know if you like doing it.
How can you make this a bridge or stretch assignment that advances your career?	What training can you get to become competent and confident at this assignment?
Future Challenge	**Low-Risk Learning Opportunity**
Opportunity is low importance.	Opportunity is low importance.
You are good at doing it and like doing it.	You are not experienced at doing it or you don't like doing it or you don't know if you like doing it.
Pursue high-importance opportunities that can convert your established skills to strength-based stretch assignments.	Join a team that enables you to become acquainted with the opportunity so that you can decide if it's worth pursuing.

(Opportunity — vertical label on left margin)

The Lattice in Action: Performance

Aptitude is something that God gave you. Skills are things that you acquired. What happens when you put your aptitude and your skills together? Your performance shows how your aptitude and your skills deliver results. The lattice is a structure. You must power your own moves. At each step—over, diagonal, or up—your performance will set the stage for your next move.

On the ladder, a lateral move is a move to the side, as in sidelines. If you're sidelined, you become obsessed with getting back onto the field and into the action—any action. On the lattice, a lateral move is a goal in and of itself. If you bring a ladder mindset to a lattice move, you'll assume that nobody will care what you do while you're on the supposed shoulder.

On the contrary, higher-ups are keenly interested in what you make of a lateral assignment. Executives say that a lateral move tests how the individual handles a new challenge when she hasn't gained any power on the organizational chart, how well she understands the strategic value of what she'll learn through this new position, and of course, how well she delivers.

- ▶ Be honest: based on your track record, would you choose yourself for a "stretch" assignment?
- ▶ What does your current boss say about your performance? If you are not sure, steel yourself and ask. If you're not sure you want to ask your boss, hash it over with a mentor. (If you don't have one at work, find one through a professional organization.)
- ▶ What have you done since your most recent performance evaluation? Address the problems, document your improvement, and prove to your boss that you're worth the investment of a lateral move.

Accidental Teacher, Purposeful Project Manager

Being "good with kids" landed Loren Rogers in education. It was true: he *was* good with kids—high school kids and even junior high school kids. But after seven years teaching reading, language arts, and social studies, he was ready to spend the day with adults. Which adults, in what capacity, he wasn't sure.

His aptitude for software was the first step on a new career path. During a summer testing software for a Fortune 500 pharmaceutical company, Rogers discovered a previously underestimated aptitude for technology.[7]

He moved from teaching to the corporate world and soon realized that he liked programming software more than he liked testing it, so he transferred to a developmental position on a software team. In this position, Rogers was surrounded by senior software engineers, and it became obvious to him that unless he retooled his technical skills, he was doomed to perpetual runner-up status. Therefore, he took a development position on an IT team that was part of a spin-off company. The hours were longer and the pay pretty much the same, but there was headroom to grow. And, he would have a shot at one of the step-up vacancies created by the spin-off.

Being in a smaller organization meant that he got to know managers at all levels, from team leaders to the president of sales. Rogers's communication skills, creative problem-solving track record, attention to details and results won him champions among the team's internal clients. When one of those clients took on a major project, he created a project manager position on his team and encouraged Rogers to apply. He landed the job—a major promotion. Rogers credits his performance with winning the trust of internal clients and building his reputation as a focused and results-oriented collaborator. He continually solicited his internal clients' feedback so that he could improve his understanding of their goals and how to anticipate how shifting business conditions would shape what they needed next. "Happy customers are the best form of advertising," says Rogers. "Performance matters, but advocacy closes the deal."

Sold on latticing, Rogers is sharpening his sixth sense for emerging opportunities and how he can better advocate for himself so that he can land in the roles he has targeted. He is networking with several like-minded managers in other departments to understand how he is perceived and what functional areas he needs to backfill to solidify his qualifications. One insight: according to an internal study of its culture, the company profiled several common management styles. One style dominates; Rogers has a different style. His crew is coming through for him as he adapts to the dominant culture without diluting his own strengths.

"One of my biggest challenges in preparing to take a management role has been to 'flex' to the dominant way of perceiving and operating," he says. "I have to go through a pretty rigorous mental checklist prior to having a business conversation with sponsors and stakeholders, and I have actually rehearsed these conversations with my mentors who share that style. In the same way, I am very careful to review my presentations thoroughly and run them by confidants and advocates prior to show time to make sure that the information is organized in a way that plays to, 'be brief, be bright, be gone.'"

This strategy is working. Stakeholders and sponsors who operate in the company's dominant style have given Rogers strong reviews. Because of his strong lateral network and stellar results, he is now taking management classes sponsored by his employer in anticipation of being promoted. He reached outside his day job to gain management responsibility for a nonprofit project that he can offer as proof of his management potential. At his company, interim assignments are often used as a trial run before an official promotion. He and his lookouts are scanning the landscape for the right interim assignment.

Loren Rogers's lattice is shown in Figure 4-2.

The Lattice in Action: Personality

Your personality is one of your greatest assets. You may develop your aptitudes masterfully with Ivy League skills, but if you camouflage your personality in the process, you'll come off as phony and insincere.

If you're funny, be amusing (without being sarcastic and cutting). If you're quiet, let people assume that you're infinitely wise because you say so little. Every personality has its advantages and drawbacks at every point in your career. On the lattice, you are free to pursue the situations and settings that best fit your personality.

▶ Are you a different person with family and friends from what you are with coworkers? Is that a bad thing or a good thing?

▶ Are you comfortable with the culture in your office? Why or why not?

▶ Are you comfortable with your personality today? Have challenges in your personal life pushed you to emphasize different parts of your personality? How does this affect how you see your current job situation?

▶ Do you feel stifled at work? Is it time for you to lattice to a situation where your personality is an asset? Or are there elements

Figure 4-2

Loren Rogers' Lattice

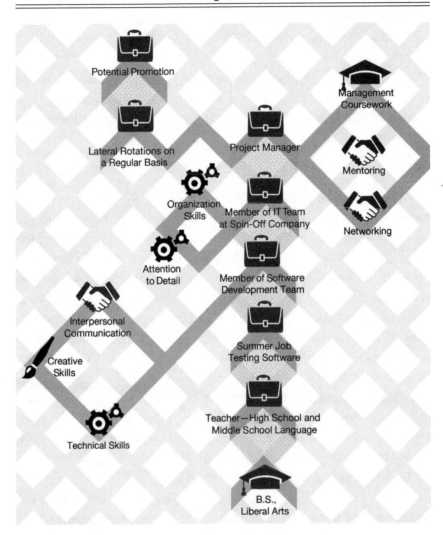

of your current situation that make "lying low" for a time
worthwhile?

▶ Women executives often feel that they have had to squelch part
of their personalities—usually the outgoing, fun-loving parts—to
fit in with sober-minded, usually male, colleagues. Often, these
women move up the ladder based on their skills and experiences.

They feel that they have to achieve a certain level or title before they can relax and truly be themselves. Then, when they do, they suddenly become so much more effective that they can only wonder what doors would have opened if they had been true to themselves all along.

▶ If you're having trouble diagnosing why your personality doesn't seem to be a good fit, take a work-oriented test that identifies personality characteristics and how to make the most of them at work. A good one is StrengthsFinder by Gallup Press (www. strengthsfinder.com).

Myrle Croasdale is a naturally neon redhead with a personality to match. She's quick, sharp, and funny, and she never hesitates to say what she thinks. All of these attributes worked well for her when she was covering commodities for a wire service. She thrived in the atmosphere of short deadlines and shorter tempers. Croasdale assumed that she was a lifelong fit for journalism . . . until the life went out of journalism's underlying business model and career options collapsed.[8]

So why is she so happy to be on the other side of the equation, managing daily public relations for a big-city hospital? Could sassy Myrle Croasdale make it as an official spokesperson?

Public relations staffers do need to be diplomatic, but even more important, they need to set priorities so that their organizations communicate clearly and authoritatively. For the hospital where Croasdale works, that means getting the word out about a medical miracle or the car that just crashed into the lobby (really).

After 20 years as a journalist, Croasdale was craving a new situation. She loves long-distance bicycling, and she wanted to be closer to her extended family. For her, working the lattice meant making a lateral move, from staff reporter to public relations staffer in a bike-friendly location only an hour from her beloved nieces. After three years in her new job, she is scoping out the potential for a diagonal move up, coordinating bigger projects and marketing campaigns.

How did Croasdale's no-nonsense personality mesh within a highly structured healthcare system? As it turned out, her aptitude for simplifying complex topics, combined with her fearlessness, has made her a favorite of doctors, marketing executives, and even the reporters she deals with. Her strong personality can stand up to doctors who think that every synapse deserves a headline. She tells camera crews where and when to shoot, and they do. Because she's known for concentrating only on what's most important, others, both inside and outside the hospital, take their cues from her. It's a match made in heaven. Who knew?

The Lattice in Action: Network

As we are reminded constantly by media that are all a-twitter, it's a networked world. As you plot your first latticed move, sweep the landscape for connections who can help you make that transition. It's a little more complicated than simply saying, "Hi, I'd like to join your team—but only for as long as it takes to pick up skills working with your manufacturing clients so that I can get a job with one of them!" Successful latticing requires a bit more finesse.

No doubt you've kept up with people you have worked with in the past. But have you reached through them to expand your network to help you unearth connections that might be just a transition away from your next job?

▶ Don't lunch with only your friends; ask them to bring along someone they currently work with—a coworker, client, supplier, or colleague—whom you might like to meet. Do the same with them.
▶ Always follow up with new connections by sending a brief e-mail that includes both your personal and professional contact information. Include a link to an article that the person might be interested in. Doing so signals interest in him and makes you memorable.
▶ Leverage online social media like BranchOut (which adds professional networking to your Facebook account) or LinkedIn (see Chapter 2 for more on professional social media). Sure, it

sometimes seems that the news feed from LinkedIn is a constant stream of requests to read other people's blogs. But here's what you may not know about LinkedIn: in its first burst of growth, it made most of its money by selling souped-up access to recruiters. Recruiters are masters of BranchOut and LinkedIn. Here are some of their strategies that you can use for yourself:

- ► Scan all the people listed for a particular employer to detect titles, responsibilities, recent hires, and recent departures.
- ► Parse descriptions of jobs you covet to pick up applicable keywords that you can embed in your résumé.
- ► Those keywords are vital clues to the skills and responsibilities you need to work your lattice. If the jobs you want are not described in terms that reflect your current responsibilities, figure out what training or experience will enable you to list those keywords honestly.

Hood & Strong, a San Francisco Bay Area accounting firm, has a long roster of nonprofit clients. New accountants have to advance their technical skills, including passing the CPA exam, but they also need to cultivate business development skills. Promotions go to those who develop the ability to become valuable advisors and bring in new clients. Local firms, like Hood & Strong, and regional firms are big enough to support technical specialization while also fostering hands-on business development early on. Savvy accountants pick up on this and start looking for ways to network that will result in new clients. How can they acquire business development skills?

At Hood & Strong, young associates accompany the firm's partners to nonprofit board meetings and events. Involvement in nonprofits, typically on boards, is golden for solidifying relationships with local business leaders. Joining a committee of a smaller nonprofit is a first step; chairing that committee comes after a couple of years of good work. Productive volunteers who lack both diva and martyr complexes are often invited to become board members. Once you are a board member, you are often asked to join meetings of other boards, and you might be invited to join other boards, too. That expands your profile in the nonprofit community, and with it, the reputation of your employer. Nonprofits always want financial services experts on their boards—something that is convenient for rising accountants.

Accountants especially, but all latticers as well, need to be cognizant of potential conflicts of interest. This is where checking with a mentor or career advisor can flag looming pitfalls. For example, if along the way you discover that you like nonprofit work better than you like your current job, you are then positioned to lattice to upcoming staff openings before those jobs are advertised. At the same time, you might also be among the first to hear about up-and-coming nonprofits that might need the kind of services that your organization provides. Either way, you and your organization can take a cue from the tactics that have been used successfully by others to lattice up and over it, through strategic volunteering.

The Lattice in Action: Values

Just as you are more than the sum of your work, so your work can be more than the sum of your accomplishments.

Is your work changing the world? Even a little? Grinding through a list of tasks is meaningless without a mission. Your organization may have a mission statement. (Warning: if it can't fit on a bumper sticker, it was concocted by a committee.) From your inside perspective, that statement may be hilariously ironic, given the decisions you witness every day.

No matter what it claims in its annual report, your organization displays its true values every day. Those values are manifested through the workplace culture. Have you ever encountered an organization that doesn't claim, on paper at least, that its greatest asset is its people? Too often, this pronouncement comes just days before a mass layoff or the news that the company has just been slapped with a discrimination lawsuit.

Are your values aligned with those of your workplace? Leaving aside the garden-variety bully, the clueless boss, and other evidence of management by bumbling around, do you generally believe in what your organization does? If not, consider finding a different department or team whose values are in sync with yours. You might even need to move to a different organization. The beauty of the lattice is that you can get there without starting over.

What does your workplace subsidize? Executive bonuses? On-site wellness clinics? Childcare subsidies for hourly workers? Base your assessment of your organization's values on metrics and third-party analysis, not just on cafeteria scuttlebutt. If you truly can't find its soul, act accordingly to save your own. Ask yourself:

▶ Are you comfortable with how your values compare with the values of your company?
▶ Have your personal values shifted over time? Does this make them a better match for your current job, or not as good a match?
▶ If you could change one thing about your workplace values, what would it be? What would have to happen to make the change?
▶ How does your workplace rank with outfits like the Calvert Group, which runs investment funds of companies that walk the walk?

The leaders of San Antonio's Mission Verde project, profiled in Chapter 1, are committed to growing an economy that's just as good for the earth as it is for the people living on it. Values add meaning and even passion to careers.

Plot Your First Lattice Move

Doing the same old thing in the same old department with the same old people is not progress on either the ladder or the lattice.

That leaves three options for plotting your first diagonal move:

▶ Apply your current abilities to a new challenge.
▶ Apply new abilities to a current challenge.
▶ Apply new abilities to a new challenge.

Now that you have a better understanding of the array of skills, aptitudes, and attitudes that you have to offer, you've no doubt thought of several diagonal directions for your first latticed move.

It's tempting to stretch, especially if you've been inching up the ladder. Resist that urge. The time for stretching will come. Make your first move a smooth one that blends your well-established skills with a challenge that's just slightly different from what might normally come your way. Your goal in this first lateral move is for it to feel natural, because you're adding just a bit of the unknown and unpredictable to your well-established repertoire.

Your first order of business is to locate the lattice. Does one exist at your workplace, or must you BYOL (build your own lattice)?

This chapter opened with a scene at CNN. Its parent company, Turner Broadcasting, has several intersecting lattices designed to give employees plenty of directions for growth. If you're at a company like Turner, you're probably already aware of programs designed to help you gain additional skills and experience while you stay at your current job. Employee resource groups (ERGs) are growing fast at many companies, such as Chubb, which was profiled in Chapter 2. Look into ERGs. Get involved. Nominate yourself. Coach your boss to nominate you. Get a friend to pull you in.

What if your workplace doesn't have a handy lattice ready to climb? In that case, you will have to BYOL. This isn't as hard as it sounds, because most bosses like problem solvers. Position your latticing as a solution to one of your boss's problems (simply put: make your boss look good to his boss) and you've just constructed the first diamond of your own lattice.

Here's how to start:

Apply your current abilities to a new challenge:

(Experience + skills + personality) + new challenge = success

Apply new abilities to a current challenge:

(Aptitude + new skills + networking + performance) +
familiar challenge = success

Apply new abilities to a new challenge:

(Aptitude + new skills + ambition + network) + opportunity = success

Sometimes, a diagonal move is also a leap of faith. When there's a chasm between where you are and where you want to be, you'll have to jump. That's risky on the ladder. If you miss or lose your grip, you'll slide down. You might even fall off.

On the lattice, you've got more places to land. In a workplace that is formally adopting the lattice, you'll get coaching and advice from a mentor, a human resources staffer, or someone else who realizes that letting go of one spot on the lattice and stepping over to another can be scary. It's worth it for organizations to support risk taking in diagonal moves. New market opportunities are opening up all the time. By definition, few people have the exact mix of skills needed to step in and tackle those new opportunities. If you've got many of the qualifications, plus a willingness to stretch, you can get in on those jobs. When a new challenge calls for new skills, your main qualification is your ability to learn on the job—fast. Leaders will look at your ability to rise to the challenge when prior diagonal moves forced you to quickly adapt to a brand-new situation and immediately apply new skills.

Here are two ways to lattice confidently into a new position, especially when companies are scrambling to keep up with quickly changing economic and business conditions. These examples are from workplaces that are openly using the lattice to develop employees. If your workplace isn't quite there yet, you can use these proven practices to build a lattice proposal.

Job swaps. At some companies, job swaps are starting to take root.[9] A swap requires two people who are evenly matched in experience, each of whom wants to take a spin in the other's shoes. Over several months, each of them gradually takes over more of the other's responsibilities, with the two training each other along the way. At the six-month mark, they've completely switched places. At the eleven-month mark, they start to reacclimate to their original positions—if they haven't trellised their way to other positions in the meantime.

Short-term rotations. Turner Communications needs more information technology managers who know how to develop new lines of business quickly. The proliferation of mobile media alone is spawning so many new types of markets that the company can hardly keep up. Turner developed Technology, Strategy & Operations (TS&O) specifically to rotate midlevel technology managers into stretch positions for a short, intense burst of development. The managers are moved into brand-new positions that force them to remix their technical and managerial abilities in completely new ways, while also applying what they are learning in business and finance classes designed to address their current challenges. Mentors provide weekly coaching so that the TS&O participants don't get overwhelmed. The hardest thing for the participants to deal with isn't technical mastery—they're already good at that, having risen through the geek ranks. What drives them crazy at first is that they don't know what results they are supposed to be delivering. TS&O is about solving problems that aren't clearly defined, while you are still grasping some of the skills you need for the situation. When you're trying to hit the moving target of an emerging market, you must be able to cope with ambiguous goals.[10]

First Steps on the Lattice for Managers and HR Staff

Especially in very traditional, laddered organizations, it can be difficult to figure out where to plant a pilot lattice. These factors will help managers, human resources executives, and talent management staff identify fertile ground for a hothouse lattice.

Paths. What skills gaps do you need to close immediately? What gaps do you need to close in the near future? Choose a need that is urgent enough to get attention, executive buy-in, and resources, but that also allows enough time for measurable results to unfold.

Pace. How quickly do you need to roll this out? The faster the rollout, the smaller the pilot.

Positions. What types of jobs do you want to link together in a pilot lattice? Where would lateral transfers naturally occur? If lattices spring up spontaneously, you might have quick success by building structures around those organic bridges.

Point of entry. What are the qualifications for entering the lattice? Is there a baseline of credentials or experience that is a prerequisite for success on the pilot lattice you envision? It's important to make the foundational criteria crystal clear so that you can measure results unambiguously. Also, muddied criteria will only confuse and disappoint potential participants. How will you recruit qualified participants?

Performance. What pressing problems will be solved by the pilot lattice? Managers are unlikely to greet a new program with enthusiasm unless they can see exactly how it will help them achieve their department's goals. What training, coaching, and support will you offer to managers to help them make the most of lattice opportunities for their teams? And what overall criteria will you use to measure the results of the pilot?

Returning to the KEYS Team and Its Assignment

The U.S. economy plunged into turmoil in the fall of 2008, while Alison Hashimoto and Ben Kaiser's team was researching and rejecting idea after idea for its KEYS project at Turner. "Our challenge was to create something for an international audience that could also be used domestically to draw in viewers," explains Hashimoto. "We were supposed to look at emerging markets, tech trends, and so on. And pick a product."[11]

With only two weeks remaining in their KEYS challenge, the team members realized that any winning idea would have to be low-cost (because of the increasing economic uncertainty) and have both immediate and long-term growth potential, because that was what would keep Turner financially viable if the recession worsened (as it did). Latin Americans, they discovered, were enthusiastic users of mobile telecommunications tools and, better yet, used their phones and video gear to stay in close contact with friends and family who had recently immigrated to the United States.

"We knew that the Latin American community likes to tell stories, and we knew that more iReports [cell phone pictures and anonymous news tips submitted by citizen journalists] were coming from international contributors," says Kaiser. *"We knew that Turner was interested in Latin America, because it had recently bought a company there, and that Internet usage in Latin America was up by a factor of 7 over the last decade."*[12]

Finally, the team had its brainstorm: create a version of iReport, the popular, user-generated CNN news site, for native Spanish speakers. Then the team started working its lattice crew. One of the team members knew the manager for the existing iReport service and persuaded her to be a spotter and provide technical and marketing input for the concept. The team members had to figure out how iReport en Español *would handle translations (via volunteer users), how to engineer a technical platform that would let viewers toggle between English and Spanish, and what technical equipment would be required in CNN's Latin American operations. They applied their brand-new skills, like financial analysis, to build their case.*

The team's presentation to top CNN executives went smoothly. The proposed budget of $100,000 to launch the service was $1 million less than the next-cheapest proposal. CNN brass immediately figured that the idea could bring in $3 million in new revenue over its first several years. Within two weeks, the leaders green-lighted the project, which went live in September 2009.

"One of our teammates said she thought she'd get a promotion from the project, but it was really about horizontal growth," says Kaiser. *"My understanding of the company is much broader and deeper."* For Hashimoto, the breakthrough was, *"How do I innovate within my brand? It opened my eyes to what Turner can do as a company, and to what I can do,"* she said. *"If I want to go in a totally different direction, and work for entertainment or go to corporate, I know how to take the steps to do that. It's an eye-opening experience for the potential of the company, and for my potential."*

Keys to Turner's KEYS Program

Turner isn't a company that rests on its laurels. KEYS is continually evolving. Employees now must have at least five years with Turner before they can apply to the expanded 10-week program, which now includes elements of emotional intelligence and management, complementing the "mini-MBA" business courses. The KEYS work groups now introduce their ideas in a format patterned after venture capital pitch sessions instead of informal executive presentations.

Turner Women Today has started a follow-up program for KEYS alumni: the Turner Journey MAP (My Action Plan). It loops the KEYS experience into an individualized career plan so that participants can see how to directly apply what they learned in KEYS to their ongoing jobs.

Core elements of the Turner Journey MAP include:

▶ Creating personal brand assessments

▶ Identifying personal strengths

▶ Framing those strengths into an individual development plan that aligns with Turner's talent management strategy

▶ Reinforcing and expanding the peer network established during KEYS

▶ Hearing the career stories of current Turner leaders

"In the last four or five years, there has been more limited opportunity for advancement upward throughout the organization. We are really shifting the focus to developing our skills, reaching and making contacts with people at all levels of the organization, growing visibility, and expanding business acumen," says Michele Golden, Turner's vice president of talent management. "KEYS does a nice job of aligning with that objective."[13]

Your Style, Lattice Substance

Latticing might come easily to you. Or, it might feel like an awkward transition.

Some of this might be due to your personality, your career experiences, your learning style, and the organizational culture you are navigating. However, you might not be aware of a dynamic called the *directional pattern model* of career advancement that describes four types of career path cultures. This model was developed by the career researchers and advisors Ken Brousseau and the late Michael Driver.[14] This Career Model can help you see whether your organization's culture supports or clashes with your own career development preferences. While the Career Model has been used for more than three decades, the demands of today's flattened, team-centric organizations are condensing and blending many of its previously separate categories. In other words, the venerable Career Model is most useful today for identifying areas of lateral growth and development (see Table 4-1).

TABLE 4-1

Directional Pattern Model Adapted to the Lattice

	Style			
	Linear	Expert	Spiral	Transitory
Path	Up	Stays put	Over, up, repeat	Over, maybe up
Personal drivers	Power, status	Skills mastery, recognition	Fresh applications of core skills	Completely new skill sets
Lattice strategies	Build business skills and network	Expand core mastery; adopt adjacent responsibilities	Fresh applications of core technical skills; new markets and creative growth	Completely new technical skills; build on business and creative/relational skills
Career outcome	Power, title, organizational results	Respected for knowledge, longevity	Personal satisfaction, serial accomplishments	Independence, variety, seized opportunities

Diagram Your Lattice

Figure 4-3 is a "fill in the blanks" model to help you think through a lateral move. This diagram shows two ways to arrive at your destination job. The left side illustrates a lateral move made on the strength of technical skills, with the goal of gaining the business skills and experience necessary for the destination job. The right side illustrates a lateral move made on the strength of business skills, with the goal of gaining a technical certification and the related experience necessary for the destination job. Experiment with different combinations of bridges using technical, business, and creative/relational skills to plot the first steps of your lattice.

Figure 4-3

Generic Lattice for Technical or Business Skills

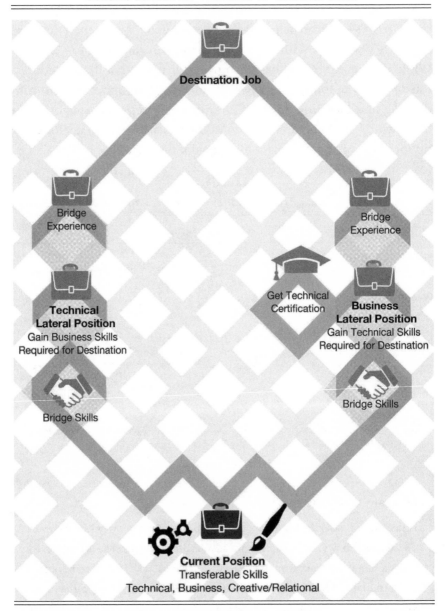

Destination Job

Bridge
Experience

Bridge
Experience

Get Technical
Certification

**Technical
Lateral Position**
Gain Business Skills
Required for Destination

**Business
Lateral Position**
Gain Technical Skills
Required for Destination

Bridge Skills

Bridge Skills

Current Position
Transferable Skills
Technical, Business, Creative/Relational

Lessons of the Lattice

▶ A lateral move = current skills + bridging experiences and/or skills acquisition.

▶ Using the case study technique outlined in Chapter 2, develop experience = results stories that quantify your skills: technical, transferable skills, experience, performance, aptitude, ambition, intuition, personality, networking, and values.

▶ The three typical modes of first lateral moves are:

  ▸ Applying your current abilities to a new challenge
  ▸ Applying new abilities to a current challenge
  ▸ Applying new abilities to a new challenge

▶ Short-term rotations and assignments are ideal first steps because they provide low-risk lateral experiences while filling immediate business needs.

CHAPTER 5

START DIAGONAL

Call centers come with revolving doors for a reason: turnover in these high-stress jobs is notoriously high.

However, in the depths of the Great Recession, a call center job was all that Jason Smith[1] could land. He had graduated in 2008 with a bachelor's degree in media marketing and had spent a year managing an entertainer whose up-and-coming career went down-and-gone as the economy crumbled, taking Smith's career down with him. By mid-2009, Smith had to cover his rent. He took a job taking calls from potential customers in the advertising department of a major media company. In his job interview, he asked about opportunities for moving on and moving up. The answer was a vague, "Of course." Does any recruiter ever confess that a job is a dead end?

But "within the first few months, it was clear that we were all seen as interchangeable cogs in the machine," says Smith. It dawned on him that, given the absence of a discernible career ladder—or even an obvious next rung—he would have to map a new route. "You have to look at it as a rock-climbing wall. You can't just go like this," he says, stretching his arm over his head. "You have to reach over here." He stretches his right arm out. "And you have to hold over here," he continues, reaching diagonally with his left arm, "to go there."

139

To carve a foothold for a move out of the call center, Smith took on the responsibilities of a vacancy in a different ad category. He quickly discovered that both ad categories suffered from identical inefficiencies in work flow. Reordering the way the ads were assigned to the staff and how the staff communicated with advertisers freed up $1.2 million in revenue—and landed Smith a "Who is this guy?" interview with his boss's boss.

He told her that he wanted to move up in the company, and a few interviews later, he joined the new leadership team of a smaller department that had just been reorganized. The call center had a different function, too: calling customers to pitch an array of consumer services. Since the marketing function was in flux, Smith offered to help out with social media. After all, customers asked many of the same questions through the company's Facebook and Twitter accounts that they asked over the phone in the call center. Conversely, he figured that callers' questions probably reflected the confusion of many consumers, and that answers to those questions could be useful social media fodder.

He was right. As the marketing team grew, its new director recognized that Smith had solved one of her problems—how to continually increase the brand's social media following. And he volunteered again, this time to design and implement specific strategies to build fans and followers. His willingness to take on lateral responsibility—and his ability to more than triple the brand's social media following—convinced the department manager to create the position of marketing coordinator for Jason. Now, he's back on track in the field he started pursuing before he was thrown off course by the recession— though, thanks to latticing, not for long.

Jason Smith's lattice is shown in Figure 5-1.

IF THERE EVER was a career escalator, it's even more broken than the career ladder. Latticing from the start channels millennials' hopes for their careers. Managers and human resources staff members can catalyze organization-wide culture change by building lattices for those who are just starting their careers, because the implications ripple up and out. It can be difficult to pry embedded ladders from the upper echelons of an organization, because those ladders are how many senior executives got where they are. But millennials know that

Figure 5-1

Jason Smith's Lattice

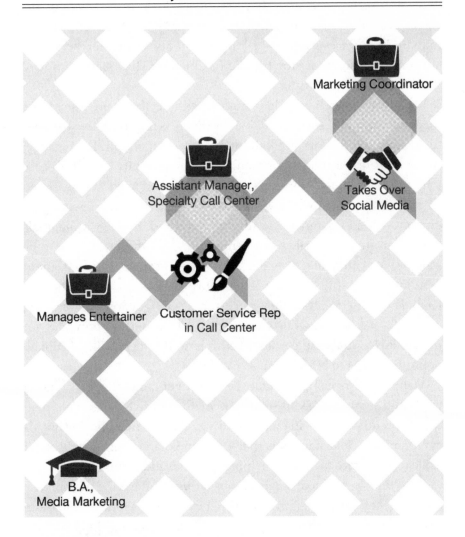

the old methods of advancement won't work any more. They expect to advance through collaboration and teamwork. Latticing their ambition is in sync with their generational outlook.

Millennials—those born since 1980—are entering the workforce in a slow-growth economy. This accident of timing sets back their earning power by as much as 10 percent compared with those in classes that graduated just prior to the recession. One researcher found that the earnings of those who graduated during prior recessions were still 2.5 percent lower 15 years after they graduated. Even worse, these grads' career prospects were curtailed, too, especially for those who earned humanities degrees from lesser-known schools. The researchers' conclusion: if these grads don't make up for their slow start within 10 years, they will never catch up.[2]

And that research was done after recessions that were less severe than the Great Recession of 2007–2009. Even as the economy struggles to recover, employers are caught in a perpetual spiral of restructuring and offshoring that obscures career visibility even for those who are entering the workforce confident of their skills and seasoned by internships. Meanwhile, opportunities to advance are few, as generation Xers and boomers seem to be cemented in place. Millennials know that they're starting out behind and that they will have to be innovative if they are to make up the lost ground. Worried about handling student debt in the face of shriveled career prospects, millennials need to see how they can structure a tight spiral of learning and skills acquisition while gaining career traction. The only way for millennials to make up earnings setbacks and to cope with shrunken opportunities is to branch out—to lattice.

Manufacturers complain that they can't get apprentices with good math and analytical skills—even as math-minded millennials read about continual layoffs in manufacturing. Understandably, this breeds cynicism: why invest in skills that will immediately become obsolete? College grads face the same dilemma, with the added burden of having to shoulder student loans. Numerous surveys reveal the millennials' mindset: they expect that their working lives will be longer than those of their parents and that they will have to keep gaining skills.[3] What's missing is how they can manage that continual evolution of skills and experience. The lattice provides the framework that millennials need if they are to plot their paths so that they can get back what they have put into education and training. As word spreads among millennials that the lattice is the way to stay relevant, employed, and growing, they will see why it's worthwhile to gain the technical skills that employers covet.

Starting their careers in an erratic economy, only 56 percent of those graduating early in the decade found jobs in their fields within 12 months after leaving school, according to a survey by jobs site Career-Builder.[4] Fast-forward 10 years, and 27 percent have never succeeded in finding a position rooted in their majors, while 36 percent wish they'd concentrated in a different field. Another study found that 57 percent of millennials expect to stay in their current jobs for only two or three years.[5] Arizona State University researcher Dale Kalika suggests that the millennials' expectation that they will have a dozen or more jobs is actually an advantage because they are always preparing for their next best opportunity and are less likely to settle into a career-stifling rut.[6] The career lattice helps them sort their skills, aptitudes, and experiences into a plan that can build on much of what they bring. Employers that equip them early on to build their lattices will be more likely to retain millennials.

Hard-Wired to Lattice

They don't know what to call it, but many millennials already have a lattice mindset. Opportunities for learning are their first career priority, with quality of life and relationships with colleagues tied for second, according to a Johnson Controls–sponsored study.[7] In a study by a different group, Corporate Voices for Working Families, employers cited millennials as already being excellent in the skills required for lat-ticing: critical thinking and problem solving, lifelong learning and self-direction, teamwork and collaboration, and creativity and innovation.[8]

Millennials and their employers need to count work-relevant skills they might have acquired while taking a recession-forced scenic route to full-time employment. Adapted from the Prior Learning Assessment tool developed by CAEL,[9] this list can help both millennials and employers to inventory work skills disguised as life experience:

► Military and related training
► A year or more living abroad

- ► AP credit earned
- ► Portfolio (a body of creative work that shows progressive skill advancement, such as new media skills—see Chapters 2 and 3 for more on portfolios)
- ► Student leadership
- ► Projects designed and accomplished during internships
- ► Part-time work
- ► Volunteer leadership, as validated by specific results
- ► An intuitive grasp of using mobile technology to get work done
- ► An intuitive grasp of solving communication, marketing, and other problems using social networking
- ► Mentoring
- ► Collaboration
- ► Cross-generational communication and collaboration

Entry-Level Programs in Lattices

Math and science are exacting disciplines. It is understandable that high school students want to know what they will reap in return for sticking out pre-calc. Through programs like CAEL's Light Up Your Future, high schoolers get a glimpse of how they can put math and science to practical use in the trades. For energy, steel, and other industries that need millennials with the aptitude and perseverance to master precise technical skills, CAEL has designed entry-level lattices that rotate math-minded high school students into job shadowing so that they can glimpse the careers that lie ahead. As the students progress in associate's or bachelor's programs, they spend summers in paid internships that put their nascent skills to work.

Lay Out the Lattice from Day One, Especially for Women

Yes, millennials want and expect additional technical training. But without the context of career pathing, employers will see their training investment walk out the door. To the degree that the lattice is only a partial solution to work-life issues (the topic of Chapter 8), millennial women need to see how their lattices can keep their careers on track. An Accenture study of the career expectations of millennial women found that a third of them believed that they would reach the top of their professions. At the same time, half of them put great faith in flexible hours as a key to career success, with only 37 percent citing ongoing training.[10] Both advancing over and advancing up require continued cultivation of technical, business, and creative/relational skills. An interruption of as little as six months that involves shorter hours—not even a full-fledged leave of absence—can lead to a detour in a woman's earnings and career trajectory, especially for women with MBA degrees.[11]

Millennial women who assume otherwise are in for a shock that could jar them off their career tracks. Internal communications that illustrate a variety of braided career paths, plus explicit career-path training, coaching, and mentoring, will reset the expectations of young women so that they are lattice-minded from the start. When the path ahead is obscure, many women lose sight of their career aspirations. They self-deselect.

Self-deselection undermines many of the best-intentioned, best-planned, and even best-resourced workplace women's initiatives. When women talk themselves out of their ambitions and quietly drop their commitment to career advancement, they have already made the decision to leave. When they do, talent management leaders are dismayed to see their high-potential investments take their skills and acumen to industry or to government.

The assumptions that frame self-deselection go both ways, so they cannot be unilaterally dismantled. Both men and women must be ruthless in recognizing cultural barriers and in stripping away assumptions. And, often, the locus of transformation is in the first level of management, for the youngest employees.

The power of the individual conversation cannot be overestimated. The author's research firm, Wilson-Taylor Associates, has found that confidential, one-on-one conversations are the single most powerful tool for calibrating career expectations and tailoring career paths accordingly.[12] Company leaders must not underestimate the power of responsive listening, which signals both that the conversation is worth having and that the woman is worth retaining. Ideally, such conversations start in the first year and occur consistently, especially when a major life event looms.

"Though it may be a decade into their future, the time to talk with millennial women about achieving partner is before they take themselves off that track," says Tammy Young, managing director of human resources at Moss Adams LLP.[13] She and key Moss Adams managers deliberately address a self-defeating behavior that they call "future tripping": women making premature decisions about their ability to advance to leadership roles based on conclusions about how their careers and their personal lives might unfold. "We tell them, 'Have all the right facts before you make big decisions about your career,'" says Young.

Forum_W is Moss Adams's approach to long-lasting culture change supporting women's careers. Through its annual report, both men and women are made aware of Forum_W's goals and results. Programs at each office are designed to foster thoughtful discussion about career steps, including messages and role modeling intended to spark dialogue rather than "future-tripping." And, each Moss Adams employee meets regularly with a career advisor to discuss her next career moves. In this way, millennial women can purposefully plan their career paths.

A few employers and women's professional groups have introduced career-pathing programs for millennial women. The Inforum Center for Leadership, the education arm of the Michigan-based women's networking group, has reinterpreted its long-established leadership development programs for midcareer women to focus on millennials. "NextUp" blends training, coaching, and networking to equip young women with business and relational skills so that they can better navigate the workplace. Employers of all sizes pool their resources so that women executives are not overwhelmed with requests for mentoring. Along the way, rising women gain exposure and contacts in a constellation of industries and functions.

Employers are starting to plant lattices early to keep millennials on track for the long term. These best practices are ripe for widespread adoption.

Cultivate Peer Networks by Schooling Millennials in Professional Social Networking

Online social networks are good fun until it's time to apply them to career goals. Big Four accounting firm PricewaterhouseCoopers (PwC) saw an opportunity to become a career advisor for college and graduate students by coaching them through the transition from social to professional online networking. PwC collaborated with LinkedIn to co-brand Career Explorer, which lets college students map career options in a range of industries based on their majors—any majors. Students enter their majors or areas of interest, then Career Explorer pulls up possible postgrad jobs and the next steps from there, and highlights those majors in real LinkedIn profiles. This skills-driven start lets students see where their current qualifications can take them. Career Explorer includes a menu of additional supports, such as live chat and links to hiring events at—you guessed it—PwC.[14]

Appoint Millennials to Mentor Interns and Apprentices

Paying it forward early and often gives millennials perspective on the investment that others are making in them through mentoring and networking. Entry-level "paying it forward" is a component of programs such as Year Up, a Boston-based program that helps inner-city youth make the transition into the workforce by combining career and technical training.[15]

Leading employers such as Aetna Insurance, cable operator Bright House Networks, and grocer H-E-B[16] have created lattices that start in college and technical schools and continue into the student's first years on the job. These trellises blend internships, apprenticeships, and mentoring to establish relationships between students and employees, then expand after the new grad joins the company full-time, with career-path training, first-level business skills, and peer networking. New hires who prove adept at integrating these experiences are candidates for management training.

Link Them Early with Advocates and Mentors

Millennials doubt that their older colleagues will advocate for them.[17] That's understandable: as upward mobility has congealed, there is more competition for each actual promotion. And millennials' presumption that they should have immediate access to organizational leaders is legendary. Instead of letting them stew (and it won't be in silence), organizations should address both dynamics by connecting millennials early with midlevel mentors and advocates.

Circle mentoring is a proven practice that both cultivates peer relationships and amplifies the influence of mentors (this is especially valuable at workplaces where women and minority mentors are both scarce and in high demand). Circles comprise four to six protégés and two mentors. The protégés are at a similar career level; ideally are drawn from several functions and departments; and share a similar focus for the mentoring, such as handling issues that are commonly faced by first-time managers. With coaching and support from an assigned human resources consultant, the mentors agree on topics for the mentoring sessions and how they will share leadership of the sessions. The mentoring cycle is designed to gradually shift the responsibility for leading group discussions and developing protégé action plans from the leaders to the protégés, usually over a period of six to eight months. Circle mentoring helps millennials build strong lateral relationships, modeled in part by the mentors. It also conveys in form and focus that protégés are responsible for building their own lattices.

Commission Millennials to Collaborate with Retirement-Track Employees

Numerous studies indicate that millennials get along famously with their grandparents—the so-called silent generation—and with older boomers who are segueing into retirement.[18] Eager to solve problems with technology and comfortable with "mentoring up," millennials are perfectly positioned to collaborate with retirement-track employees on telecommuting and making the transition to positions that bridge into retirement.

Unleash Millennials to Improve Productivity with Technology

If millennials hadn't been born with opposable thumbs, they would have invented them: how else could they text? The younger the millennial, the more intuitive his grasp of mobile and collaborative technology, according to Accenture.[19] Pull millennials into cross-functional teams that are applying technology to functions like collaboration, security, remote work, communication, and brand building. They will have a tailor-made showcase for taking the lead, and, in addition, managers will have a chance to glimpse latent tech abilities that might be cultivated to fill current and future jobs. The same "grow our own" tactic that enabled Good Samaritan (see Chapter 3) to lattice more nurses into its system also works for home-growing technology employees. One telecommunication provider screens all employees for technical aptitude and streams promising candidates into technology careers through latticed training and internal rotations.

Strengthen Lattices with Employee Resource Groups

Leave it to the generation that invented social networking to reinvent the employee resource group.

In 2008, when Vanessa Wilczewski landed at Aetna, she looked around for other twenty-somethings. She found them, but it took more work than it seemed to her that it should. Aetna already had more than a dozen employee resource groups (ERGs), some of them dating back to the late 1980s. It didn't take long for Wilczewski to latch on to the idea of creating an ERG for millennials, and with it, a lattice for her own career.

"A representative from HR informed us that we could use employee resource groups to build on our desire to interact with other younger employees. We realized we had to write a business plan," says Wilczewski, who was in a three-year rotation through multiple departments. She and four other millennials dug into it, persuading executives to be sponsors and researching the market potential for their generation.

Word spread fast, even to nonmillennials. "We started making connections with people who ran HR, the office of diversity, communications, marketing. I would get e-mails from executives saying, 'I need someone with an MBA to join my department; can you recommend someone?' or, 'We want to survey Gen Y within Aetna; can you help?'" she says. As soon as the group was announced, 100 people joined. It hit cruising altitude at 600.

Wilczewski included her work with this group, EnRGY, in her weekly reports, making sure that it was included in her professional development plan. To manage the flow of requests coming at it from all points in the company, the EnRGY steering committee started an internal mentoring website. The group produced a recruiting video designed to attract other millennials to Aetna. EnRGY programs focused on early-career topics, such as etiquette in the workplace and first steps in money management.

"Along the way, people would ask me, 'Well, Vanessa, what are you doing currently? What do you want to do next?' I was surprised at times that I was being approached about specific job opportunities that could have taken my career in a very different direction. My loyalty was to the rotational program, because it was very structured. I knew that there were rotations in front of me so that I would learn different things," she says.

As she finished up her rotations, Wilczewski was underwhelmed by some of the career options she had seen up until then, but the possibilities that kept popping up as she worked in EnRGY made her realize that she didn't have to wiggle into an uncomfortable fit in a traditionally defined position. Instead, a new international division offered her a role that combined her technical skills with the entrepreneurial and project management experience she had gained through starting EnRGY. She now works in international IT strategy as a project manager.[20]

Employee resource groups are built-in lattices. Originally designed to help women and diverse employees connect for mutual support and mentoring, some, like Aetna's, have evolved into internal consulting groups that help vet marketing and customer service ideas for the markets their populations represent. A few, like Turner's KEYS program (profiled in Chapter 4), run programs that help employees gain new skills and clarify their career paths. Chubb Insurance, profiled in Chapter 2, promotes its ERGs as a chance for employees to network beyond their departments with the aim of designing lateral moves and lattices.

Here is how leading ERGs are weaving lattices into their purpose and programs, drawn from Wilson-Taylor's research, dating from 1998, on analyzing the effectiveness of ERGs in advancing women and people of color.

Leadership Development

ERGs take a lot of work, which is why they are the perfect setting for developmental assignments. General Electric's Women's Network, for instance, invites women to join committees with the aim of taking on responsibilities that are complementary to their official job descriptions. Engineers figure out how to market the group's events to employees; women in IT plot meeting agendas and vet speakers; communications staffers manage projects. Not only does this enable members to develop and showcase new skills, aptitudes, and experience that might not otherwise be relevant to their jobs, but their responsibilities and performance are reported to their managers and are included in their evaluations and career planning.[21]

- ▶ Committees are the perfect forum for first attempts at project management, leadership, presentations, and meeting facilitation.
- ▶ Cross-functional teams and mixers help participants connect across organizational "silos" so that they can glimpse potential career moves and know whom to contact to learn more.
- ▶ Budgetary oversight can also be the occasion for gaining financial statement skills that will be needed in the future.
- ▶ Large ERGs offer the chance to grow in project management, communication, internal marketing, and presentation skills.
- ▶ The guarantee of meeting with C-level leaders at least annually motivates the ambitious to rise through the ERG.
- ▶ Managers take ERG responsibilities and results seriously, incorporating them into career planning and performance reviews.

▶ Such programs can be used as a platform for organization leaders to tell their own stories of latticing and career pathing.
▶ Consider the portfolio, crew, and skills identification modules in Chapters 2 and 3 as modules for small group discussions and exercises.

Tackle Real-World Business Projects

CNN's *iReport en Español* bubbled up from an internal business development project—KEYS—sponsored by Turner's senior women's network. ERGs are the perfect context for creating and testing business ideas. Entrepreneurially minded employees often feel that they have nowhere to turn with their great ideas. Programs like KEYS channel their ideas by replicating the venture capital pitch process that winnows start-ups with potential from those that are unlikely to succeed. At Aetna, ERGs serve as internal reality checks for marketing, communications, customer service, and other functions that need insight into diverse markets. Tackling real-world projects and problems lets employees discover for themselves what skills they need to acquire, what aptitudes and skills are most valued by others, and what adjacent positions they might pursue.

▶ Open competitions and consulting to all employees; this is a chance to detect quieter talent that might be overlooked by traditional fast-track processes.
▶ Clearly outline expectations for career development and networking; use the "lattice crew" concept outlined in Chapter 2.
▶ Require sign-off by managers in advance so that supervisors can help employees integrate career development goals into the exercise.
▶ Create teams that mix employees from different departments, functions, and levels.
▶ Start with self-diagnostics so that participants can quickly identify the skills they have and the skills they need to acquire. (Use the Personal Portfolio outlined in Chapter 2 and the "lattice in action" modules in Chapter 4.)

▶ Require participants to take at least one training course scaled to the intensity and duration of the project; for example, KEYS offers a "mini-MBA" so that participants can grab new skills and go with them.

▶ Set clear criteria for evaluating new business ideas, such as a minimum amount of projected revenue.

▶ Have a step-by-step guide to provide structure to the program. Each phase, from choosing a focus through polishing the final presentation, should have guidelines.

▶ Provide career coaching and debriefing so that participants can apply their experience to their career development and next steps.

Provide a Safe Place to Discuss Caregiver Issues

Millennials are outspoken about their desire to blend their work and their personal life in a more balanced way than they believe their parents did. It pays to provide a forum for this activity, but not in the ERG. Set up separate groups for employees who are immersed in parenting young children, caring for elderly relatives, and coping with disabilities. Focused groups provide a safe, supportive, and contained environment where employees can work out solutions without diluting the mission of the broader-purpose ERGs.

The Networking Nanny

Not even close to 30, Pamela O'Leary performed a Herculean feat of latticing to rise from grad school to executive director of the Public Leadership Education Network, a nonprofit in Washington, DC. How she did it is a crash course in squeezing the most from every opportunity. Considering that she even managed to network during a brief stint as a nanny, O'Leary's is a tale with takeaways for nearly every millennial.[22]

The University of California at Berkeley has radicalized more than a few students. O'Leary entered as a geology major and exited determined to pursue feminist activism. She pitched in to help organize women's events, and while she was in graduate school, she helped colonize a new chapter of her college sorority, interned with Human Rights Watch, helped plan a conference in international feminism, and organized annual fund-raising events and campus operations for the Feminist Majority Foundation. By the time she learned of a United Nations internship, she was able to talk about problems that women faced in the workplace, and show how her project management had delivered results in short order for a variety of groups.

O'Leary's unpaid U.N. internship introduced her to a boss who became a demanding mentor. "She showed me how to be an effective advocate, the value of lying low and choosing your battles," says O'Leary. "Focus on the cause daily. Go out to lunch with people who don't necessarily care about your issue because you may need them later. The more marginalized your issue, the more you must rely on intellect, grace, and professionalism. The power of advocacy is authenticity."

By the time she was 23, O'Leary had parlayed her U.N. internship into a congressional fellowship that had her researching issues important to a New York congresswoman and writing a resolution (which got passed) condemning rape in the Democratic Republic of the Congo. Washington offers an encyclopedic range of networking groups—so many that even O'Leary had to pick and choose. She zeroed in on the Women's Information Network (WIN) and attended every weekly meeting, introducing herself to speakers after their presentations.

But in the midst of her rounds of unpaid internships and relentless networking, O'Leary's funds ran out. In the fall of 2008, during the nadir of the economic meltdown, she resorted to "line standing," or being a paid placeholder for lobbyists, in the same building where just months before she had been a congressional staffer exulting that her resolution had been passed. Nannying pays more—and involves occasional sitting—so that's what O'Leary did next. When she wasn't at the playground, she also worked as a docent at the Sewall-Belmont House and Museum, helping out with special events. That was where she ran into the congresswoman whom she had worked for—who needed a fund-raising staffer.

"It was very hard, but I really saw how hard it is to run for office," says O'Leary. Having established herself in the community, she was elected to the board of the Women's Information Network. Impressed with her work—not to mention her work ethic—a Sewall-Belmont House and Museum board member recommended O'Leary for an open development position at the Sewall-Belmont House and Museum. "They were looking for someone with more experience, but I had existing relationships with people on their team, so that was really helpful," understates O'Leary. It also helped that O'Leary had worked side by side with other board members on menial tasks like event registration.

O'Leary wasn't shy about her aspirations. She wanted to be executive director of a nonprofit that advances women. It wasn't long before a WIN friend passed along word that the Public Leadership Education Network (PLEN) was looking for an executive director. PLEN prepares women for careers in public policy, a perfect fit with O'Leary's career goals. By then O'Leary had connected with strong supporters of PLEN from different directions. In January 2011, she was offered the job.

It took more than superhuman networking to land O'Leary in her dream job. "Volunteering builds your professional reputation—people say, 'Oh, she'll get it done,'" she says. "And networking is the ability not just to see how others can help you, but how you can help them." She sends handwritten thank-you notes to those who help her out and always tells them how they've helped her toward her destination job. "I looked for opportunities in every direction, to grow in different ways. I can always get better at something," says O'Leary. "Even though I haven't had 10 years of work experience, because I've done all these things, I have lots of experience."

Lessons of the Lattice

▶ Career lattices reflect the generational outlook of millennials, who expect their skills and positions to continually morph. Employers and industries that plant career lattices in high school and college can pace career development with millennials' emerging job and leadership skills.

▶ Career latticing, and the ongoing, incremental decisions that shape lateral moves, disarm the insidious deselection dynamic. Young women often silently discount their ambitions and "self-sideline," evaporating from the leadership pipeline. With its many checkpoints, the lattice creates a culture of open discussion that gives young women permission to stay the course.

▶ Link millennials early with mentoring, business development, peer coaching, and cross-generational mentoring to help them cultivate relationships across the organization.

▶ Mine millennials' aptitude for technology; consider "growing your own" tech staff by latticing tech-oriented millennials into tech careers.

▶ Employee resource groups are becoming a key framework for career pathing. Create and nurture ERGs for all employees; millennials especially crave immersion in career guidance, networking, and hands-on business challenges.

CHAPTER 6

TEAM LATTICE

"How much is that going to cost us?"

That is what Jill Kaplan is in charge of figuring out. As manager of product cost engineering for Navistar, Inc., which manufactures trucks and other heavy vehicles, her six-member team of engineers pencils out the expected expense of using new materials and processes.

This is a function that demands diplomacy and collaboration; the team influences decisions across the company, but it doesn't have the final say on the final outcome. Effective cost engineering involves strong listening, analysis, and communication skills—not the kind of things that engineers are usually known for.

Fortunately for the team, Kaplan is a natural at those skills. She realized that her team members could advance their careers by becoming experts at collaboration and communication, because the team's assignments gave them so many opportunities to showcase those skills.

One member came up with an "elevator pitch" version of the team's complex mission. His crystal-clear summary won him a dotted-line relationship with a corporate finance executive—a potential sponsor for a lateral or developmental move.

For a project examining why a key process kept breaking down, one team member developed a simple model for choosing the best materials for different purposes and the relative cost-benefits of each. His training sessions and materials for buyers and managers were so successful that he is now the team's lead for developing training materials. His reputation grew, and he was appointed to a high-profile remanufacturing project. "He'd been wanting to work on that kind of big capital project for quite a while," says Kaplan. "Being known for his expertise got him to the right place at the right time."

Another team member has a knack for launching projects. That's a skill that Navistar calls "dealing with ambiguity"—defining the amorphous resources and goals of a brand-new project. He's now the launch consultant for the team's projects, validating his aptitude and giving him a channel for applying his mastery of ambiguity to an ever-widening range of situations.

Kaplan drives her team's productivity by coaching its members to continually evolve their skills, aptitudes, and internal relationships. "You have to convey that you genuinely do want your staff members to be successful within the company," she says. Her approach is to mirror back to them the strengths she observes and encourage them to reinvest in their own success by building toward stretch assignments and expanding their internal networks. "If an employee wants to grow in a different direction, he might be hesitant to tell you, because he is afraid you will squelch his ambitions because you are protecting your own headcount," she says. "But it reflects well on you as a manager to 'hold lightly' to good talent."[1]

MORE THAN 40 percent of American workforces count on project teams to get work done.[2] Teams are the great democratizing dynamic of the American workforce, and teams are the organizational building blocks of the lattice. Skills are honed, vetted, and diagnosed while working in teams. Teams encourage peer networking, the energy source that keeps a lattice alive and expanding.

Chapter 6 outlines how team dynamics and leadership are the proving ground for individual and workplace lattices. If you are a team leader, use Chapter 6 to weave the lattice into your team's culture so that you can expand your team's capacity to achieve your goals. This chapter also illustrates how team leaders and middle managers can graft their own careers onto the lattice through reorienting their own career paths from ladder to lattice, in the context of managing teams and projects.

Diagonally Speaking

What replaced the corroded ladder? Without an army of middle managers to parcel out work and direct traffic, employees organized into self-directed teams. These teams tackle projects—solving problems or building new products—by drawing on the variety of skills contributed by their members. Instead of waiting for a work assignment to drop into their laps, team members define the goal, determine how to achieve it, and keep one another accountable for achieving results. In the process, they represent their own work; they are not as dependent on managers to recognize their work as employees in ladder-dominated workplaces.

The intrateam lattice model is shown in Figure 6-1.

Figure 6-1

Intrateam Lattice Model

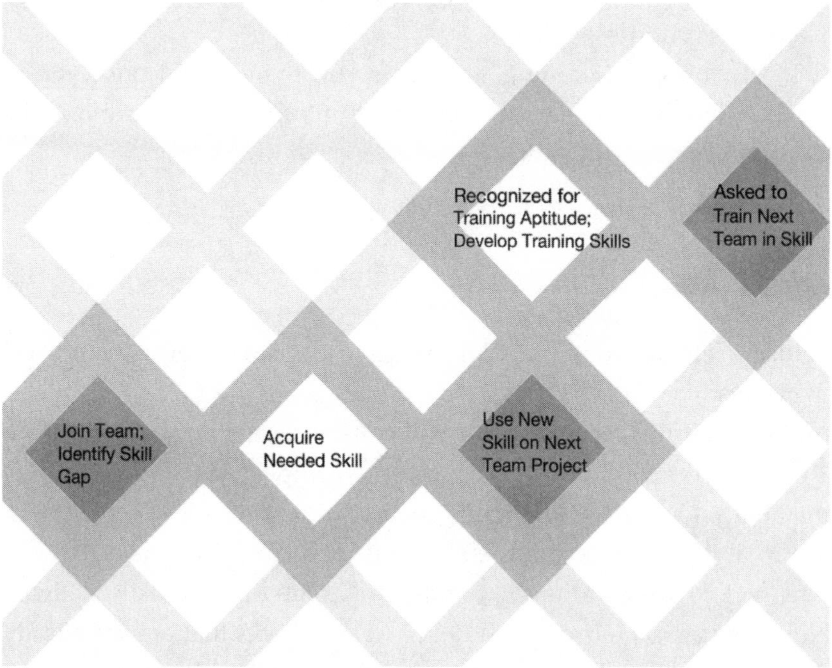

The contributions of each team member are clearly visible, which spurs its members on to gain new skills, to keep up with teammates, to share the workload, and to pursue intriguing new abilities. The team dynamic is especially powerful for women and minorities, who are often subtly blocked out of traditional power structures. As determined by the research of Alexandra Kalev at Tel Aviv University, "job-training programs" that focus only on equipping women and minorities with technical skills don't increase the presence of women and minorities in the long term.[3]

But teams that are focused on a bigger goal—solving a problem or achieving a goal—have the unintended, though welcome, side effect of retaining and advancing women and minorities. Why is that? Because the team itself is a mini-lattice. In functioning teams, members benefit from one another's complementary skills: the point of the team is that it takes what everyone brings to get the job done. Meanwhile, in a cohesive team, members learn from one another and detect what skills they need to improve. They hear news of problem solving and intriguing opportunities in other departments and maybe even at suppliers and vendors.

In other words, gaining skills gets you the job. But once you're on the team, it's the team dynamic that unfolds the lattice and all its possibilities.

Lead Latticer

Latticing requires you to coordinate with other team leaders and midlevel managers. You will work with them on designing specific tactical moves (more about those shortly). As you collaborate with them, you have a chance to expand one of the emerging competencies of this decade: the ability to manage ambiguity. A precarious economy, accelerating technical change, and rapidly shifting business conditions mean that you have to know how to tackle problems that are only partially defined. Not many employers offer training or assignments that are specifically designed to help managers manage ambiguity; the irony of acquiring the skill of figuring it out as you go along is that you figure it out as you go along. Latticing enables you to cultivate this skill in bite-sized bits, with minimal risk, in concert with like-minded peers. By the time you have become confident at managing ambiguity, you will be able to define it— and you will have good case studies for your Personal Portfolio.

Track and Measure Your Investment in Your Team Members' Lateral Moves

▶ How does your organization track, report, and analyze employee development? Be sure you understand what criteria human resources staff use to label, track, and forecast competencies so that you can accurately report advances by your team members.

▶ Many software systems have components for forecasting competency needs for changing business goals. Scale the system to track your team's development so that you can specifically report the return on lateral moves to employees, HR, and your own manager.

▶ Find out how the talent tracking system used by your organization counts "off-job-description" development, such as skills gained through prior learning and volunteer work. Employees naturally develop skills for the fun of it when they have the aptitude and opportunity to do so. A graphic designer who runs a side business as a wedding planner, for example, clearly has an aptitude for project management (and probably has formidable emotional intelligence skills, too). Ask for guidance from your talent management coach as to how to blend these skills into development.

▶ Understand how your organization views and tracks on-the-job learning. How are competencies gained through teamwork rolled into the overall assessment of the employee's abilities and potential?

▶ What percentage of your own performance is predicated on your developing talent and retaining top performers? At some leading employers, 40 percent of midlevel managers' performance scores are grounded in these competencies.

Ready to Lattice?

How do you know when members of your team are ready for lateral moves? The "Ready to Lattice?" grid in Figure 6-2 will help you figure out when the members of your team are positioned for a successful developmental lateral move, and when you need to keep them "in house" to strengthen their essential skills. Use this grid for each type of competency: technical skills, business skills, and creative/relational skills. The following questions will help you zero in on exactly what types of lateral moves will help you achieve your team's goals, both immediately and in the future.

Are your team's competencies aligned with the team's current business goals?

It is self-defeating to rotate out employees who have the skills you need if you are to achieve your team's current goals. However, if the "Ready to Lattice?" grid indicates that your team needs to borrow skills in order to achieve its goals, can you arrange to be on the receiving end of lateral rotations to fill those competency gaps quickly?

How are your organization's business goals likely to change in the near term? This will dictate your emerging need for team competencies.

Once the team has achieved certain milestones, what mix of competencies will you need for the next project, or to complete the current project? What rising priorities are likely to soon affect the competencies you will need to assemble to rise to those challenges? What lateral developmental strategies will ensure that you will have that mix?

What longer-term industry and economic trends will shape your organization's growth trajectory? These will dictate your future need for team competencies.

Industry, regional, investor, and company news can help you forecast the competencies your team is likely to need. You may not know what technical skills

Figure 6-2

Team Leader's Lattice Readiness Grid

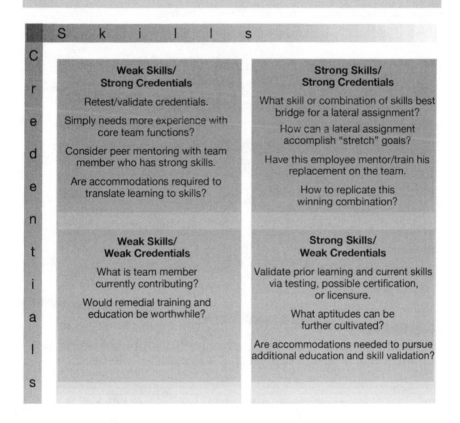

READY TO LATTICE?

Skills / Credentials

Weak Skills/ Strong Credentials

Retest/validate credentials.

Simply needs more experience with core team functions?

Consider peer mentoring with team member who has strong skills.

Are accommodations required to translate learning to skills?

Strong Skills/ Strong Credentials

What skill or combination of skills best bridge for a lateral assignment?

How can a lateral assignment accomplish "stretch" goals?

Have this employee mentor/train his replacement on the team.

How to replicate this winning combination?

Weak Skills/ Weak Credentials

What is team member currently contributing?

Would remedial training and education be worthwhile?

Strong Skills/ Weak Credentials

Validate prior learning and current skills via testing, possible certification, or licensure.

What aptitudes can be further cultivated?

Are accommodations needed to pursue additional education and skill validation?

your team will need in 18 months—in 2007, few people forecasted the need for full-time social media managers—so focus on aptitudes and creative problem-solving skills. You have plenty of lead time to give team members longer-term lateral rotations, chances to gain or validate technical and business skills, and opportunities to collaborate with talent development staff and other managers on structuring lateral moves that help everyone.

What resources are available to support your team members' lateral assignments?

Training budgets might or might not be available when you need them. This is where the prior learning assessment tools available from the Council for Adult and Experiential Learning (CAEL) are invaluable. Employees with strong competencies can develop a portfolio to document their learning for credentials, or even "test into" credentials, bolstering their platform for lateral moves.

▶ Low-cost training and peer training are often available through industry groups, economic development councils, community colleges, and local workforce training coalitions.

▶ Remove logistical barriers to training and test taking. Grant employees permission to study, take classes, and take tests on company time. Support flexible time and place arrangements that enable employees to get class and study time.

▶ Offer company resources, such as conference rooms, teleconferencing facilities, and administrative support, for groups of employees taking online courses and tests.

▶ The Lifelong Learning Account is a method of supporting ongoing employee education that was pioneered by CAEL. Modeled after individual retirement accounts, or 401(k)s, which involve an employer matching an individual employee's savings for retirement, Lifelong Learning Accounts let employees invest more of their own incomes in their own careers.

Tools for Framing Out Your Team's Lattice

These best practices from CAEL and from leading employers that participate in Wilson-Taylor research projects (managed by the author) will help you become an Olympic latticer. The key is to make latticing work in both directions—for members of your team and for members of other teams with which you collaborate.

Job sharing. Even organizations with traditional cultures can get behind job sharing. Job sharing pairs two employees with adjacent responsibilities, with each learning key functions of the other's job. By the end of the rotation, both employees can do both jobs. This is a perfect way to cross-train for planned leaves (such as maternity leave) and as part of disaster recovery plans. Meanwhile, employees get to try out a new skill set that is a close side step from their own, minimizing personal and professional risk. They get acquainted with employees in each other's departments and gain a new boss (or half a boss), exposing them to different leadership styles.

Peer mentoring. Using the "Ready to Lattice?" grid as a guide, pair employees who can learn from each other. The best combinations pair employees with complementary competencies and aptitudes so that each can draw on his own strengths to coach his partner. For example, a user experience web designer who has strong graphic design abilities but poor time management skills might be paired with a marketing manager who is adept at prioritizing and accomplishing tasks, but who struggles to manage freelance designers.

Lattice performance reviews. Weave lateral development into employee performance reviews. Reframe performance reviews as forward-looking, not just postmortems. Explain what new lines of business are emerging in the company, and what new positions are becoming in demand. That can help employees concentrate on training and cross-functional experiences that pave the way to those fast-growing categories.

Cast department and company decisions and performance in terms of the entire industry. That helps employees understand how suppliers and customers are interconnected, and the related career implications.

Cross-team brainstorming. A short, focused brainstorming session is a stage for employees to show creative and problem-solving skills that they might not use in their daily responsibilities. Joining with a team from another department creates an open forum that welcomes any idea from anybody and increases the chances for serendipitous breakthroughs from unlikely pairings of ideas and collaborators. You and your team members might come away with ideas for longer-term collaborations.

Cross-team task forces. Cross-departmental task forces let people exercise talents and skills that they might not use in their everyday jobs. One way to create such a task force is to first list the competencies, aptitudes, and creative and problem-solving skills that the task force will need and then have team leaders nominate members to fill those slots. Starting with a list of skills rather than individuals will place the focus on the group's function, so that the organizing group can concentrate on the dynamic of the group, not the personalities and preferences of potential participants.

Once you have identified the required competencies, aptitudes, and creative and problem-solving skills, you can then decide which skills are core for the task force and which slots can be developmental. One creative media company that used this approach invited an executive assistant who liked to write to join a new product development task force. She turned out to be an undiscovered star and rapidly latticed to a copywriter job.

When managers interview internal candidates, they ask them to explain the logic behind their lateral moves, and what they learned by making lateral moves. If the position they are applying for is also lateral, the interview also explores how the new position fits into the employee's career path.

Employees who transfer laterally are expected to pay it forward (or back) through their willingness to act as consultants to other teams, especially on high-profile projects where their expertise can backstop the current team. Organizing and running a cross-team task force is a developmental assignment in itself, especially for an ambitious team or middle manager who is itching for a higher-profile assignment.

Coach or Poach?

Latticing strengthens teams. However, managers understandably wonder whether lateral rotations might boomerang on them, especially if a number of productive employees lattice out and few lattice in. The short answer is: latticing enables you to maximize the talent available to you because you create a halo of talent and relationships that your team can draw on.

But wait—there's more! Latticing builds your reputation as a manager who is generous with good talent. Teams interlock, and members talk. Fostering lattices for your team members not only makes you the boss that everyone else wishes she worked for (and thus, a latticing magnet), but also builds your own brand.

At some companies, top managers strive to model the value of lateral moves—and with that, how to build their personal brands by becoming "talent developers." At one technology company, the one woman at the C level took the lead to ensure that midlevel women were rotated through lateral developmental assignments. The organization had traditionally promoted people through vertical "silos" on a narrow ladder. The executive was concerned that high-performing women, in particular, were becoming tired of treading water while waiting their turn for a small step up. Rival employers circled, eager to poach female talent to meet their talent and diversity goals.

Structured lateral rotations broke the cycle of being stuck. The company recast its definition of midlevel women. Its prior model had been to define jobs and titles based only on credentials. That was replaced with a multidimensional model of technical, business, and creative/relational competencies and aptitudes.

That is how a midlevel corporate lawyer became a vice president for technology policy and industry affairs. She had joined the company as a lawyer specializing in negotiating operating contracts. When she started managing ongoing relationships with a key sector of industry partners, she realized that she was adept at framing agreements that were not just technically correct, but also anticipated the changing needs of her employer. This business competency was noticed by the lawyer's manager and reported to a senior executive, who moved her into a lateral slot running a slice of the business. Two years later, with operating experience locked down, the lawyer was promoted to a strategic role that blends her mastery of law, her aptitude for forging agreements, and her ability to see around corners and anticipate future business needs.

Operating experience, via the lateral move, was essential, says the lawyer. "If you don't understand how the technology links to the market, you won't have credibility," she says. "The more engaged I am with what the engineers can deliver, the more I know what I'm talking about when I am negotiating with policy makers."

And the senior executive? Having replicated the lawyer's lateral success with several other women, she was asked to speak at an industry women's event about her talent development philosophy. That led to an article in an industry magazine spotlighting the company's success in retaining and advancing women, which fueled more requests for interviews. Both the company and the executive now are marked as proactive, thoughtful advocates for talent development.[4]

Lattice New Tech Talent

The chronic shortage of high-tech workers is a classic case of skills mismatch. But not every tech job requires a black belt in computer engineering. Teams are the perfect lab to allow tech-oriented employees to segue into tech positions that your company needs to fill now and in the future.

Deborah Westfall earned a bachelor's degree in marketing, so she assumed that marketing was where she should be.[5] And, she did like her first postgraduate job as a sales rep for a small broadcasting company. To her surprise, what she liked most was cultivating tech projects that she had tackled in school. She earned a master's in marketing communications to sharpen her research capabilities. In graduate school, she realized that she had a more intuitive grasp of interactive marketing than many of her classmates did. They had more business experience, but she was usually the one who figured out how to solve a business problem with an Internet tool.

Still, as Westfall reentered the workforce, she continued in marketing, first as a part-time business consultant on marketing for a small company and then joining the American Society of Plastic Surgeons as a marketing associate. That was where she hit her stride—in no small part because of the feedback of her coworkers. As the society circled the major project of redesigning its e-commerce functions (it sells manuals, software, and other practice management–related materials to members), Westfall represented her department and coordinated its contributions. After the project was completed, the IT director continued to pull her into meetings without prompting. It turned out that Westfall was adept at translating big-picture goals into specific phases of a project. She also had the innate ability to steer the design of the website so that it was user-friendly. She was able get the technical staff on board. "I don't have the technical background to actually build a website, but I can work with talented individuals and get my vision realized," she says. In 2008, "interactive product manager" was just beginning to emerge as a discrete career. Westfall was doing a job she'd never heard of. It wasn't until she moved to a major media company to manage the redesign and relaunch of one of its stand-alone e-commerce sites that she gained the title of product manager.

Now senior online product manager for a division of the American Hospital Association, Westfall credits her good working relationships with her colleagues—her lattice crew—with helping her identify the career path that blends her interest in marketing with her aptitude for solving business problems and envisioning technical solutions. "You start to see a job that's emerging under your feet when you're on a project that taps into something that's not your core strength, but that you're better at than others on the team," she says. Getting in on new projects afforded her the headroom to solve problems from different angles with different subgroups of coworkers. That process alone showed her that the skill of navigating through ambiguity is essential in an ever-accelerating technical realm. "You have to be comfortable with being 'in process' on it," says Westfall. "Goals will shift as you go along, rather than having everything all planned out in advance. . . . When you can trust your team members, you can really learn a lot about yourself. Listening to incremental, ongoing feedback can help you recognize in yourself strengths that can help you latch on to an emerging career."

Deborah Westfall's lattice is shown in Figure 6-3.

Figure 6-3

Deborah Westfall's Lattice

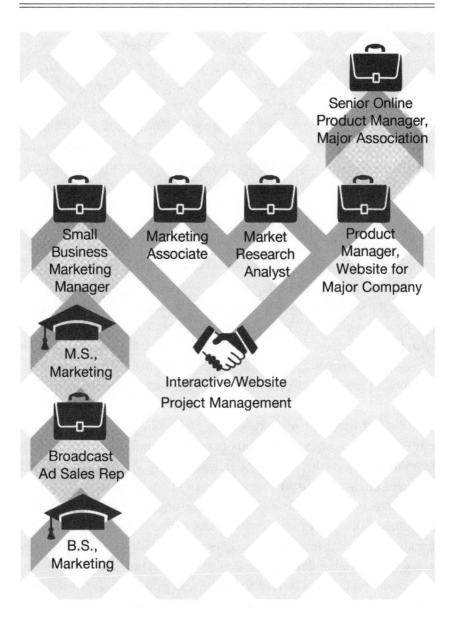

How Thrivent Grafted the Lattice

Being satisfied is not the same thing as not being stuck. In 2006, Barb Foote realized that Thrivent Financial had a lot of satisfied employees. However, many of them were also stuck on the career ladder—unable to move up, but unwilling to move over. Meanwhile, the not-for-profit, membership-model financial services firm was starting to need skills that were alarmingly absent in the talent pipeline. Foote decided to ditch the ladder and build a team-centric lattice that would democratize talent development and advancement. Employees would figure out where they wanted to go and how they wanted to get there. Managers would run interference and coach. Foote called her lattice "the Career GPS."[6]

Thrivent, says Foote, is a bit different from most employers. Its 5,000 employees serve members, mainly Lutherans. The organization's values mirror those of its Christian members, and its culture openly celebrates those values. And while fiduciary responsibility is part of Thrivent's mission, it also considers itself a steward of members' assets.

That filter shaped Foote's thoughts as she heard about latticing at a work-life conference. She had already been thinking about how to reorient Thrivent's career ladder. "In the old model, a silo model, you started as a junior analyst and ended up as the head of whatever. It called for incremental growth within a specific area of expertise, but what it didn't really build was people who knew about more than one area," she says. "In 2006, at Thrivent, it was not considered a good thing to take a lateral move: 'What's wrong with you that they wouldn't give you a promotion?' People would stay in place until they could move up. We had strong workforce engagement, but we knew we needed to address the career piece. And when the economy went south, there were not that many moves to be made. You could really only go sideways or even backward to get some expertise to grow."

By then, Foote had built out the platform for the Thrivent lattice. Drawing on the experience of the mass career customization concept developed by the accounting and consulting firm Deloitte LLP, which Thrivent already worked with, and based on her own decades at the organization, Foote created a four-phase model anchored in the employee-manager relationship.

Employees were commissioned to:

▶ *Assess.* Review your skills and abilities, and research opportunities.
▶ *Discuss.* Gather input from others about your goals.
▶ *Plan.* Write your career development plan.
▶ *Implement.* Carry out your plan and measure your progress.

Each phase is broken down into specific steps for both the employee and the manager.

Individuals' responsibilities are to:

▶ Set goals.
▶ Review their plan and goals with their manager.
▶ Gain peer support.
▶ Execute the plan.

Managers' responsibilities are to:

▶ Hold development discussions.
▶ Understand employees' career goals.
▶ Coach employees.
▶ Help the employee get the contacts and information he needs across the organization.
▶ Participate in building the entire organization's talent pool, and not hoard talent.

The goal is to find the "career sweet spot": the intersection of the employee's talents and passions with the organization's needs.

Piloting the Career GPS with a few managers helped her to fine-tune the plan. Foote believes that every lattice should be custom-built to reflect the culture and growth priorities of each organization. "Where can you make a contribution? That's the centerpiece of the career conversations," she says. "Then you create a map to get there." Personally, she says, she is passionate about leadership and helping people grow, though she has spent 30 years in marketing and sales at Thrivent. "I've only applied for one job my whole career, the first job I got. The rest, I approached with this sweet spot approach. I believed Thrivent needed to do talent management, and so I made a proposal, and really, in effect, I was advocating for that passion and how you can contribute. To me, it's not about always applying for a job or waiting for someone to come up with a job, but for you to use the sweet spot to think of where you can contribute."

Managers to whom coaching came naturally quickly got on board. Others needed training; a few needed prodding. But grounding each employee's lattice with his manager ensured that growth expectations started with what more the employee could contribute to the team right away. That not only addressed managers' concerns that lateral moves would become a merry-go-round of employee transitions, but also reinforced the message that employees were to look for feedback first from those who knew them best—their teammates.

The Career GPS immediately affected the development cycle. Employees pursuing their sweet spot submit ideas. If one of an employee's ideas is chosen, or if she hears of an intriguing project, she can petition to join that team as an adjacent, sometimes layered, assignment to develop goals that she has already identified through her GPS plan. Some employees have permanently transferred to new lines of business that they helped incubate.

"In human resources, we felt we should eat our own cooking. Change begins at home, right?" says Foote. "We were not necessarily the best at having people take lateral moves, and we needed to do a better job. In March 2011, 25 percent of the HR staff made some bold moves to move people around and take on new assignments."

The new talent economy at Thrivent requires an investment by all team leaders and supervisors; talent development is included in their performance reviews. "Let's be honest," says Foote. "Talent goes where it is valued and grows. It's no secret that there are people who are good at growing talent, and that others want to be mentored by them and talk with them. In the past, there was a fear that you developed all this talent and the people moved on. Now, it's expected that you develop talent for the organization."

The Thrivent Career GPS Toolkit

- ▶ Lets employees take ownership of their careers.
- ▶ Defines the "sweet spot"—essentially, what does Thrivent need that you can do and like to do?
- ▶ Lists values, career interests, and long-term goals; strengths and talents; what the company needs; and your passions.
- ▶ Gives a template for spelling out the steps to getting at the sweet spot:
    - ▶ Development goals
    - ▶ Financial leadership competencies linked to competency assessment at iThrive
    - ▶ Project roles that you can take on in your current position
    - ▶ Mentoring: who on your team can help you mentor, and who can you mentor?
    - ▶ Feedback from managers

Reaching Out for Lateral Skills

Industry groups can provide just-in-time opportunities to close skills gaps, as Dianne Blackwood learned.[7] Today, she serves as the area vice president of operations for the Carolinas region (which includes some parts of Alabama and Virginia) of Time Warner Cable. Blackwood began her career in the call center. Her "defining moment" occurred when she applied for a general manager slot at a small unit with 13,000 subscribers. Given her rise up the ladder, she felt that she was the perfect candidate. The hiring manager felt otherwise. "I was courageous, and I went to the divisional vice president and said, 'What do I need to do to show you I'm ready for this job?' What he said floored me: 'I haven't had enough opportunities to see you in motion in front of groups, negotiating with public officials, and handling complex situations.' He saw me as the manager of a 100-head call center. The general manager had let me do much of his job, but the hiring manager hadn't seen that. I had to figure out, how can I get that kind of exposure when the job I'm in doesn't give me that kind of exposure?"

She left that meeting with a developmental lateral position—business manager of a much larger unit where she could officially gain experience and visibility. But more important, the divisional vice president suggested that Blackwood start a regional chapter of the cable industry's women's association, Women in Cable and Telecommunications (WICT).

"Until then, I had not questioned the career ladder, but then I started to see value in lateral career moves," says Blackwood. "This particular division vice president was very open about my need to gain experience. That's the essence of general operations leadership. It's knowing the components of the business and how they fit together. I see that clearly now as I look at Time Warner Cable. [Rising leaders] have done a stint in marketing and in public relations and in finance on their way to the operations role."

Eighteen months after Blackwood took the lateral move, the same general manager job opened up again. This time, Blackwood got it. She rose to vice president of operations, with multiple general managers reporting to her and more than 400,000 subscribers. Not only did her star rise at Time Warner Cable, but she also found her voice at Women in Cable and Telecommunications. "It gave me wonderful opportunities to run an organization, do multifunctional roles, public speaking, and negotiation," says Blackwood, who rose to national president of WICT. "I didn't realize when I started down that path that it would be an opportunity to fill in my skill gaps."

Frame and Expand Your Own Lattice

Remember the lattice crew from Chapter 2? As a manager, you are perfectly positioned to lattice in all directions. As you support latticing team members, you can build your own lattice.

Your lattice is distinct from your personal "board of directors." Your board of directors should include mentors and well-placed advocates and sponsors who can speak for you in executive strategy meetings. Your lattice is a network made up of peers (other team leaders and managers at the same level), colleagues (professionals and former coworkers at levels at or below yours), and industry connections at all levels.

► Ask your boss to introduce you to a few other managers at her level with whom your business unit collaborates. A quick cup of coffee is long enough to find out what business trends these managers see on the horizon and how they might affect your respective teams.

► Take the time to get to know the leader and members of teams that your team is newly assigned to work with. A mixer will help team members get to know one another, and you will be able to pick up on potential opportunities for your team members—and vice versa.

► Ask a trusted peer for a short series of coaching sessions in a business or creative/relational skill that you are cultivating. For example, one New York media company paired each department head with an executive in the finance department for coaching and fill-in-the-gap financial skills education.[8] While the department heads sometimes struggled with aspects of managing budgets and finances, the difficulties were disparate enough that having all heads go through the same class wouldn't have been efficient. In this case, talent management staffers assigned six departments to each of the company's five finance executives. Each finance executive met with the department heads monthly, reviewing their budgets, tracing the impact of individual financial decisions through to the P&L, and helping them see how their department's financial performance affected the company's overall performance. The net result: departmental budgets are now accurate, as is forecasting. As department heads are promoted, they take with them their knowledge of P&L.

▶ Cox Communications took this concept one step further with its "Finance Matters" program.[9] The one-day course is customized for each department's metrics and business drivers. Participants work in teams to address financial decisions that reflect real-life priorities. The facilitators are leaders from the Cox finance department, not local academics or accountants. Not only does using finance department staff make the finance simulations more credible and relevant, but it is a lateral developmental opportunity for the finance team to build presentation and meeting facilitation skills.

Supervisor Circles

New managers need extra help in mastering the functional and relational elements of supervising others. CAEL's "supervisor circle" model and consulting work show how to lattice the process of helping new managers with this critical transition.[10]

The Supervisor Toolkit approach teams supervisors and managers in an experiential learning environment, guided by a trained facilitator who introduces the customized Supervisor Toolkit "Tools," each of which focuses on a critical supervisory or leadership skill. Participants practice these skills using the tools on the job, and at follow-up training sessions, experiences and learning are shared and debriefed. Tools that have been found effective and relevant in other settings and are frequently included in the toolkit include:

▶ Dialogue: When You Need Everyone to Be Part of the Solution
▶ Appreciative Interviewing: The Power of Positive Questions
▶ Leveraging Learning Through Meetings
▶ Maximizing the Impact of Formal Learning
▶ The Water Cooler: An Aid for Learning on the Job
▶ Work-Based Learning: Being Intentional About Informal Learning
▶ Huddle: The "Just-in-Time" Meeting

Experienced supervisors trained by CAEL lead the sessions, helping new managers make sense of workplace situations as they unfold. "It's a way of making a case study of what's happening right now, in front of you," says Phyllis Snyder, a vice president based in CAEL's Philadelphia office. "It applies theoretical learning." The program, now being used at a hospital system and a utility company, concentrates on the most vexing issues that typically trip up new supervisors:

► Making the transition from being a coworker to being a manager
► Leading meetings effectively
► Communicating
► Dealing with problems in the moment (and avoiding "blame cycles")
► Managing up
► Reading the business implications of changes in the economy, the industry, and the organization

Wide-scale layoffs have pruned the number of managers available for traditional transition structures, such as job shadowing. And, the remaining managers rarely have the time or the patience to work through beginners' dilemmas one-on-one. Supervisor circles complement the technical and human resource policy and procedure training that is required for most new supervisors.

Supervisor circles each include several new managers and a professional coach, either external or from human resources. Participants bring their issues and analyze the underlying dynamics; inevitably, they discover that among all of them, they can come up with the solutions. In the process, they learn new ways of approaching these common difficulties and practice patterning their responses so that they are thoughtful and responsive, not defensive and reactive. "Because everyone is at the same stage and going through the same challenges, you know that the others in the group are credible and will not be judgmental," says Snyder.

Because the group is made up of people at the same career stage, not the same age or tenure, its members become the nucleus of lattices for one another. Supervisor circles are most effective when they are led by seasoned coaches; CAEL has found that participants' gains are reinforced when they are paired with "field coaches" who mentor them for a specified period. Retirement-track employees often want to share their knowledge before they leave, and they have the life and career wisdom to serve as field coaches.

Supervisor circles "connect the classroom learning to the real issues in the company, and use the resources of that workplace to solve the issues. It's a way of thinking differently about the solutions," says Snyder.

The sessions are based on case studies and open with a story about a situation that has gone awry. In the prototype case study, the new supervisor is called on the carpet, and his first impulse is to assign blame. Inevitably, the new supervisor gets a call from his own manager. Participants work through solutions that can keep the situation from spinning out of control, and also learn how to diagnose where the interaction went off track, how to correct it, and how to respond to their managers with a proactive plan. "The facilitator we have trained helps them recognize the better way, through stories, and helps them own and integrate a new way of dealing with it," explains Snyder. "It's not lecturing. It's telling a story, and through that story, you start to think about how you can develop a new story."

Lessons of the Lattice

- ▶ Lateral rotations within a team are a proven technique for making the most of all the talent embodied by team members.
- ▶ How you lattice shows your team members how to lattice. Consciously expand your own career options, knowing that you are modeling latticing to your team members and your peers.
- ▶ Becoming known for finding and cultivating talent can build your reputation as a manager.

(continued)

▶ Use available corporate talent management tools to mine talent so that you can find and encourage lateral moves for your team members.

▶ Align lateral moves with your team's emerging skills needs. Use intrateam cross-training and lateral assignments to help achieve business results.

CHAPTER 7

LATTICE TO LEADERSHIP

"If you move someone straight up, he becomes deep but narrow, and it will be hard for him to become a general manager," says Shellye Archambeau, who has been CEO of MetricStream, Inc., a Palo Alto company that produces software for governance, risk, and compliance, since 2002. She spiraled to the top by plotting a series of lateral moves that not only qualified her to run a company, but increased her chances of long-term success.[1]

In the midst of the 1990s Internet boom, Archambeau was one of hundreds of IBM vice presidents. After years of ping-ponging between staff and line positions—IBM's standard use of lateral moves to develop rising managers—she was itching to be out on her own. Knowing that she'd have to leave IBM if she was to become a CEO, she took a hard look at the track record of others who had gone from leading divisions to leading companies, and realized that many of them floundered. She figured it would be wise to acclimate to a smaller, fast-growing company before aiming to lead one. "I'm an African American female, and I don't think I get too many swings at bat," says Archambeau. "I try hard to minimize my failures. How do you do that? You make sure you have the right experiences and supports. Officer-level jobs would help me really understand the dynamics of being a CEO at a growing company."

Archambeau left IBM to lead Blockbuster.com, the chain's first online foray. That landed her "a seat at the table." Reporting directly to the CEO, she had secured a place in the top echelon of the company's leaders. "It was a chance to do something new and growing, but still under the umbrella of a big company. It was the right transition," she says. Scanning the start-up landscape, she realized that she needed to become a known quantity to the Silicon Valley venture capital community. She made another lateral move, to executive vice president of sales for Northpoint Communications, trading a seat at one table for a seat at another. When a planned merger disintegrated before she gained the scope of experience she wanted, a Northpoint director referred her to LoudCloud, where she became vice president of marketing and sales. "Then, I was ready. From that job, I was hired by Kleiner Perkins for MetricStream," says Archambeau.

Her path was obvious to her because she plotted it carefully, gaining discrete skills and experiences that rounded out the CEO profile she was assembling. It didn't appear random to others because Archambeau carefully delineated her plan for them. "When people asked me what I wanted to do, I told them: 'I want to run a company,'" says Archambeau. She met her own goal of pulling together the right set of elements within four years, even though it took one position more than she'd anticipated.

Not surprisingly, Archambeau's measured approach has shaped her philosophy of managing talent at MetricStream. She likens the development of executive talent to developing athletes: similar to an athlete who develops muscle memory for a new move, once a manager has mastered the ability to adapt quickly to new responsibilities, he is fit to take on nearly any challenge that emerges. And Archambeau believes that it's important to have a slate of senior executives who have had hands-on experience outside their core competencies. Not only does that help them operate their own arenas with the entire organization in mind, but it also gives them perspective for collaborating and advising each other. "When you're bringing a vice president of finance on board, you want someone who has managed operations, who has business development experience," she says. "If you have a team of people who can do multiple things, you can shift them around. When hiring, I look for skill sets that have breadth and adaptability. Applying your skills to different business conditions and challenges is a business skill that's developed through lateral moves. It's all about how you gain those experiences."

Amidst all the talk of networking in all its variations, Archambeau believes that those who are aiming for top jobs sometimes overlook the most important qualification of all: delivering results in the job they currently have. "Networks and sponsors are all great. But you have to deliver results," she says. In each position, she has counted on a halo of advisors who helped her get that job accomplished, thus creating champions who were ready to back her when she decided to pursue the next position. "Your reputation," she says, "is built on the steps you've taken." Figure 7-1 shows Shellye Archambeau's lattice.

THE LATTICE GOES both over *and* up. Without an eventual promotion, lateral moves become nothing more than a merry-go-round. Chapter 7 explains how latticing has propelled leaders into top spots at major companies—and how they are replacing ladders with lattices for the next generations of leaders. But because the ladder is still the dominant image of advancement, today's leaders must provide messages that reinforce the value of the lattice (which works for the upcoming generation of leaders) while reconciling those messages with their own success stories, which are likely to feature the ladder.

Grow or Go

Top performers expect and want to continue growing. When their employers box them in or block their opportunities to grow in all relevant directions, their loyalty is undermined, and they are more likely to look for opportunities elsewhere. Especially in the slow-growth economy that is expected to characterize this decade, upper-middle and senior managers have reconciled their expectations with reality: nearly three-fourths of senior executives are looking for new positions, but 65 percent of these executives say that they expect to stay in their current positions for the next three to five years, according to a 2011 survey conducted for executive career management service BlueSteps. The majority believe that any move will be a lateral one. In 2009, the same survey had found that 53 percent of executives expected to move on in no more than two years.[2]

Figure 7-1   Shellye Archambeau's Lattice

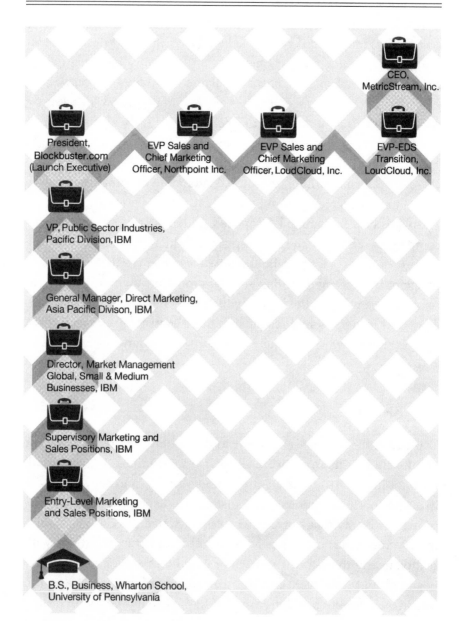

CEO,
MetricStream, Inc.

President,
Blockbuster.com
(Launch Executive)

EVP Sales and
Chief Marketing
Officer, Northpoint Inc.

EVP Sales and
Chief Marketing
Officer, LoudCloud, Inc.

EVP-EDS
Transition,
LoudCloud, Inc.

VP, Public Sector Industries,
Pacific Division, IBM

General Manager, Direct Marketing,
Asia Pacific Divison, IBM

Director, Market Management
Global, Small & Medium
Businesses, IBM

Supervisory Marketing and
Sales Positions, IBM

Entry-Level Marketing
and Sales Positions, IBM

B.S., Business, Wharton School,
University of Pennsylvania

Staying does not mean stagnating. A trio of researchers affiliated with the Accenture Institute for High Performance and the Wharton School of Business found that executives are hungry for more growth experiences than they believe their organizations are giving them.[3] Paradoxically, greater opportunities for strengthening marketable skills fueled greater loyalty. The executives surveyed put top importance on:

98.3 percent	Taking on responsibility
94.9 percent	Working on challenging tasks
89.1 percent	Developing diverse competencies
84.8 percent	Building a professional reputation
83.3 percent	Accumulating marketable skills
72.5 percent	Expanding professional networks

All of these goals are handily addressed by thoughtful lateral assignments.

There is no doubt that the slow-growth economy is prompting CEOs to accelerate lateral moves among their top ranks.[4] An executive who moves internally combines many of the advantages of a newcomer—reviewing operations, problems, and possibilities with a fresh eye—with the confidence of a veteran who is already grounded in the organization's culture.

Innovative employers are using four types of lateral moves to propel leaders up the lattice:

► Expanding current responsibilities with no change in title
► Shifting proven managers to different positions for a medium- to long-term assignment
► Moving rising leaders through custom-designed stretch assignments to equip them with the range of experiences needed for higher-level management
► Leveraging short-term assignments for "try before you buy" fittings

Growing in Place

"I have little time for conversations that start with, 'What do I have to do to get to the next grade level?'" says Yolande Piazza, managing director of global consumer technology for Citigroup.[5] "I look for people who come to me and say, 'I see a gap, and I want to fill it.' I'm not defined by my job description, but by the problems that we as an organization have to solve." As she has risen at Citi, Piazza has consciously shifted her staff's expectations from the technical ladder to a multiskilled lattice.

Her point of view is informed by her own experience—and validated by the fact that it works. "Any reward in my career has always come after I have made a lateral move. It has always been an expansion of a role, solving a bigger problem, or taking over an adjacent space, and then being recognized. I've applied for only two roles with expanded responsibilities," she says. "The rest have come from identifying opportunities and then moving on to solve those problems."

Shortly after joining a division of Citi in 1988, Piazza took on the challenge of learning computer coding. Later, as a senior leader, she realized that her knowledge of that technical skill allowed her to challenge her technical teams. "With that breadth of experience, if I am sitting in front of a customer and am committed to delivering something, I know exactly what I can promise and what it takes to deliver it," she said. Her tactic worked, and she has been using it ever since.

By alternating lateral assignments with challenges to find and own orphaned problems, Piazza has uncovered leadership talent in unexpected places. In the mid-2000s, one employee on her staff was an administrative assistant. Through escalating assignments—starting with a small project—and complementary training, that employee is now running a major global program.

The recession and its fallout for financial institutions forced Citi to reexamine who did what and "forced conversations about people acquiring different skill sets," says Piazza. "We're in a better position now, but we have retained that mentality. Now, we look at candidates' lateral experiences to see if they would be successful in new roles. We look at how people demonstrate that they have breadth in their roles, and how we give them experiences that set them up for an upward move."

The painful truth that titles do not confer competence has spurred Piazza to inventory both the titles and the actual skills possessed by the members of her staff periodically. Tagging skills accurately and working through the implications for emerging talent needs enables Piazza to start moving the right people into place even as new positions are being formulated.

"It's rare in IT to find someone who is a leader at a senior level who doesn't have more than one arrow in his quiver. We're trying to make that an understood part of the career road map: that if you are trying to move up in IT, you may have to make a few moves sideways before you qualify to move up," says Corey Woods, managing director of human resources, global consumer technology, for Citigroup.[6]

Citi's talent management system allows each employee to shape her own skills profile. That forms the basis for her development plan, which is a combination of what the employee thinks she needs and what her manager thinks she needs. The next steps evolve by blending the business skills, relational/creative problem-solving skills, and technical skills required to achieve the target position.

Woods has seen attitudes toward lateral moves warm considerably in the past five years. "As people mature in the workforce and understand the dynamics of the labor market, they understand that there may be fewer upward positions than there used to be. What motivates them can then be a challenge," says Woods.

Shift Gears to Accelerate

When Laure Nordholt started as a salesperson, Time Warner Cable was a traditional, laddered organization. But a few years later, when she was the vice president of sales for the Columbus, Ohio, area, the culture of advancement started to shift in sync with the organizational structure. The next step in her career, regional sales vice president, became more of a stretch when the eight regional sales positions were condensed into five. Nordholt inherited another state (Wisconsin) and had to take stock of her career assumptions. The ladder was collapsing around her. How would she continue to advance?[7]

"I realized that to continue to be successful, you have to be extremely nimble and help lead change," she says. Simply driving for a title and focusing on what she thought she deserved was not going to be a worthwhile ambition. Instead, Nordholt doubled down on developing leaders at every level in her expanded operation. Streamlining operations across cities as seemingly similar but actually diverse as Cleveland and Cincinnati taught her how to win buy-in from her new teams to adjust growth goals and strategies to fit each metro. Managing Wisconsin helped her fine-tune her communication style through remote leadership to minimize confusion and maximize her voice.

Now, as senior vice president for the central region's media division, Nordholt oversees Texas as well. Time Warner Cable now has only three official regions. Since there are fewer chances for upward mobility for the 630 people who ultimately report to her, Nordholt has concentrated on helping them understand how to grow laterally—just as she did once she achieved the regional management level. "If you get your skill set in the right place, just as my influence has expanded, yours can, too," is Nordholt's message.

Employees who feel stuck often need a change of responsibilities and venue if they are to reengage. "I tell them, 'You've been good at this position, but I think that if you move laterally to this other position, you'll have success at a higher level,' she says. For example, one general manager overseeing a metro market had a highly disciplined, structured style, but felt stymied by the apparent lack of opportunity. He was a top-notch trainer, so Nordholt appointed him director of training, overseeing the training function for the entire division. It was a lateral move that gave him a sphere of influence instead of a chain of command. "He was disappointed initially, but I told him, 'We have to do this for the business, and I know you are going to be happier in this position. You are going to have more success,'" she recalls. The tactic was successful, and the division gained an in-house training expert while opening an advancement spot for an employee who was better suited to the trainer's previous job.

Lateral for Liftoff

"My career has been a lattice all the way," says Kerry Hester, senior vice president, operations planning and support, at US Airways.[8] In fact, her path has been a symmetrical waltz: up and over, up and over, up and over.

Lateral moves were the furthest thing from Hester's mind when she joined then-Northwest Airlines in 1996 as a pricing analyst. Happily analyzing away, she was surprised when her manager recommended her to fill his position in the wake of his own promotion. Just 18 months later, the head of the marketing department urged her to take on a position that she was barely aware of: manager of route planning. "I said, 'Why would I do that? I love pricing!' and he said, 'It will make you a better contributor if you can see the other side of the business,'" she recalls. "I saw when I moved over that pricing was not the center of the universe, which was a surprise to me. After that, I saw the value of lateral moves and started aggressively pursuing them."

A quick cost analysis of climbing the traditional ladder illustrates the futility of trying to go straight up. "If you are ambitious, the pyramid is pretty steep," says Hester. "Every move that you make, there is more competition to get those jobs. By taking more jobs at each level, you can improve your chances of advancement. If you only work in finance, you can be a good candidate for vice president of finance, but not for another job."

After wading into route planning and network planning, Hester was boosted to director in the planning group, then took a lateral move to the operations group. "It was not a typical move. I was moving to operations and leaving the umbrella of an important mentor. But I was ready for a new challenge, and the organization I was in was clogged with a lot of talented people. I knew the view was that there was a lack of bench strength in the operations group. And they wanted that analytical talent—that was why they chose me." She shuffled next to oversee reservations, for the first time picking up responsibilities for a frontline, consumer-facing operation. After gaining some additional experience in human resources, Hester landed her current position, which rolls up all of her planning, operations, and analysis experience.

Hester champions lateral moves early and relatively often—every 18 to 36 months—for emerging leaders. The more operational experiences they can capture early in their careers, the better positioned they will be to settle into a few straight-up steps later in their careers, she says. Traditional rotational programs are too rigid to prepare the highest-performing candidates for rapidly shifting business conditions, Hester believes. "For the high performers, you need more flexibility in when and where those moves come—not because it's 'time for a move,' but because the person has been identified as a potential key contributor for the new opportunity."

"Not one of our executives has gone straight up," says Alison Smith, managing director of human resources operations for US Airways.[9] 'They've taken lateral moves, and that enables them to understand how their decisions affect the company."

Many of the company's employees start in operations at one of its airports. Those are great positions for gathering horizontal knowledge of airport operations, from scheduling flights to dealing with passengers to coordinating with federal authorities. But when it's time for them to move up to headquarters, many of them find that their locally acquired experience is too shallow to sustain another promotion. Around they go again to deepen their key skill sets and gain greater context for decisions that must take the entire organization into consideration.

To drive home the point that lateral rotations are the spiral of success, US Airways executives have been increasingly spelling out the exact steps that they took to gain career altitude. "We call it right out," says Smith of the panel discussions that are routinely held at divisional meetings. "We ask, 'What do you say to someone who thinks that a lateral move is detrimental?' That shifts the discussion to the purpose of lateral moves—gaining competence in enough essential skills to qualify for any of several potential promotions."

US Airways has also been reinforcing the power that employees have over their own career paths. "They have to understand that just as we look at our operation critically, they have to look at their careers critically," says Smith. "They are responsible for seeing that they get those experiences and pursue their focus."

Since the recession, discussions about lateral moves among top leaders have dominated succession planning, says Elise Eberwein, executive vice president of people, communications, and public affairs for US Airways.[10] "Before, it was always about who was promoted. In the past 12 months, we have also focused on lateral moves." Regular rotations are proving to be key to serving up fresh growth opportunities so that top executives are engaged.

Learn and Return

By deploying midlevel managers to fill lateral positions on a short-term basis, Cox Communications has created a new developmental platform for rising leaders. Cox has long had a full roster of leadership development opportunities, but it has particularly expanded its lateral programs to ensure that it has midlevel talent ready to take on new challenges in a rapidly changing business environment. About 10 percent of Cox's roughly three hundred midlevel managers are assigned to short-term assignments that arise as a result of key openings and a changing operating model.

Erin Hand, vice president of talent and development, emphasizes that the temporary assignments enable managers to try out new roles and work with teams that they otherwise would not have a chance to collaborate with. "For a developing leader, a temporary assignment provides a different perspective and real-life learning experiences that we cannot create in the classroom. It offers a chance to grow through leading a project and to stretch leadership skills, and it is typically at a high level of leadership," she says.[11] Temporary assignments enable midlevel managers with strong business skills to apply those skills in a new setting; meanwhile, the manager's temporary absence enables members of his home team to step up to cover his duties.

The talent development team is prepared for requests for temporary assignments by having a list of interested midlevel managers, including their skill sets and the type of developmental assignment each prefers. When a request comes in, the team matches it with a likely candidate, and together, the team and the candidate discuss the development goals that are likely to be achieved during that rotation. Through trial and error, Cox has learned that the most productive temporary assignments have had defined learning objectives and have given leaders the opportunity to demonstrate untested leadership skills. Its practice is to open the assignment with a specific goal, which could be learning a new skill or testing leadership abilities, and then debrief the progress made toward that goal when the assignment concludes. Temporary assignments are a low-risk way to discover that a job isn't a good fit for an employee.

Although lateral moves are not a prerequisite for advancement at Cox, they are now granted the same credibility as traditional vertical promotions, says Hand. This represents a significant shift in culture. As rising leaders experience the benefits of lateral moves—both temporary and permanent—they look for ways to replicate those opportunities in their own departments.

Legends of the Lattice

The definition of career success is shifting. It has to. Employers' frustration with the difficulty of finding top-notch employees continues to rise, according to ongoing research by Towers Watson.[12] In late 2011, 59 percent of employers were having trouble finding employees with "critical skills"—more than double the number in 2009. Furthermore, once they land those employees, employers can barely hold on to them. Add in longer hours and employee exhaustion, and it's probably good that 66 percent of the employers surveyed claimed to be overhauling their talent management strategies and related human resource practices.

Lateral moves pace advancement, enabling employees to soak up experiences and master skills, coalescing their achievements instead of always skipping ahead to the next shiny opportunity. But today's top leaders face a bit of a communication dilemma: the traditional ladder apparently worked for most of them. Are they inviting cynicism and accusations of hypocrisy when they tout the lattice for the rising generation of leaders? How can they square their encouraging new employees to try the lattice without lapsing into a weak, "Do as I say, not as I did" endorsement?

The solution is to decouple promotion from development. In the past, the two have been nearly synonymous. Now, promotions and lateral moves are equally valuable. Meanwhile, development means ongoing cultivation of one's full range of career skills and aptitudes, so that one is positioned for any type of emerging opportunity. "How far can you grow?" is a totally different message from "How far can you go?"

"Growth usually precedes moving up," says Citi's Woods.[13] "We absolutely look at growth in this organization and upwardly mobile movement as critical. But career growth and moving up are different."

Top leaders lead every successful organizational culture change. Where the lattice is taking root in an organization, leaders spell out for employees the rationale for their own lateral moves, past and current. The CEO of a major consumer food brand got started in brand management, but he got the best training of his career during a midcareer stint not managing a line of business, but as director of strategy, reporting directly to the CEO.[14] The managing partner of a major consulting firm moved from senior manager to chief of staff for the CEO, where he coordinated all the moving parts of the CEO's office, from reviewing and slotting reports from partners in charge of various practices to serving as secretary of the operating committee, which put him on a first-name basis with the firm's 20 senior partners.[15] Walt Disney Company had a high-level lateral shakeup when the head of its park division traded jobs with its chief financial officer. Analysts speculated that the move had submerged implications for the board's succession plan, but CEO Robert Iger told them that it was all about bolstering the bench strength of the C-suite by having the two men each gain a "broader, deeper, different set of experiences."[16]

Authenticity and honesty neutralize cynical observations that the top leaders have pulled the ladder up after them. Recast the legends in all the channels where employees hear messages about the organization's definition of success. Ensure that leaders' personal stories are aligned with the organization's talent development and succession practices. Choose the language for career moves, lateral moves, and career pathing, and then be consistent with those terms across all media.

These proven and promising practices illustrate how to energize career lattices as a concept, as a plan, and as a personal path:

Personal stories are compelling. Panel discussions, "town hall" meetings, and similar channels are perfect settings for sharing personal narratives. It is heartening to hear how a top leader was at first skeptical when she was faced with a lateral move, but then learned invaluable lessons from it. Midlevel managers who have had to make the transition from laddered to latticed career paths are perfectly positioned to talk about how they shifted their perspectives and how they have navigated the cultural change. Find the universals in the lattice stories—often, taking charge of one's career and not waiting to be "tapped on the shoulder" for the next move—and make those universals recurring themes in the narratives of leaders at all levels.

Congratulate employees on taking lateral moves. Use the same consistency, depth, and enthusiasm as you use for those who are being promoted. Explain the new role and how that employee earned it. This will negate the perception that lateral moves are random dead ends.

Spell out the specifics. How did midlevel employees and professionals pick up adjacent responsibilities and create their own opportunities? "Managing up" is important on the lattice earlier than it is on the ladder because employees must envision target positions that might not yet exist. Be sure to showcase employees at all levels who have identified, pursued, and won lateral moves in ways that are consistent with your organization's values and culture.

Shine a light on your stars. Integrate career-pathing direction with high-profile projects and growth priorities. "Your core constituency—leaders, talent executives, and human resource executives—have to embrace this idea that moving up is not the only way, and often not the best way, to grow your talent. There are numerous ways that can be done, to embrace that as a business model," says Citi's Woods.[17] Citi's consumer technology staff is involved in an ambitious effort to put the bank's global operations on common information technology platforms, complemented only as necessary by components that are tailored specifically for each country. It's the perfect chance to train and transfer high-performing employees from one type of critical role to another. "This initiative is changing the way we approach our technology products, and in some cases creating roles that didn't exist. We are developing product management roles for a global operating model," says Woods. "Some of our program managers are now taking on roles as product experts. Occasionally we have to hire outside experts from major software companies, but frequently, lateral moves can get many of our strong people into these roles."

Encourage generosity with talent. Reward managers for their willingness to let high-performing employees take moves away from their teams. Managers who champion the success of rising leaders need to know that their investment in the overall organization's talent pool will be returned to them. Cast talent development as a marketable skill that equips managers themselves for leadership.

Convert skeptics laterally. Besides training and coaching managers in the new wisdom of latticing, you can convert skeptics directly by giving them developmental lateral moves. When their own future is reshaped under their feet, they will not only grasp the theoretical advantages of lateral moves, but also be able to empathize with employees who are grappling with new rules and realities.

Listen, listen, listen. "I talk with them about defining the future," says Time Warner Cable's Nordholt.[18] "We have to constantly look at how people realize the new career-pathing opportunities." She asks employees who are feeling stuck to envision their ideal position. When the employee has identified a few areas of mastery, she finds a way to expand the employee's realm of influence in those areas. "I do a lot of initiation of lifting them up from managing a particular function, to expand their influence across all the markets so they get exposure across the region," she says. You need to loop in human resources and talent development staff as needed so that employees can find the best sounding boards for their aspirations. And, you need to link employees' hopes to the organization's growth goals. Help them find several potential target jobs and sketch out several lattices to those goals.

"Several times, I've asked people to take a job, and we've talked through the benefits. These people were chosen for those jobs because I saw that they would add a lot of value there. That's a perspective that they might not have," says US Airways's Hester.[19] "And they earned some loyalty from me, because they did what the organization needed them to do. For the ones who said yes, it was a good lesson because they demonstrated that they could be successful in a variety of positions—and that builds your stock and credibility."

Showcase lateral growth and self-directed career pathing in recruiting materials, events, and conversations. From internships to MBA interviews, infuse the conversation with case studies and examples of how employees find growth in different ways at each level. Citi has realigned its university technology leadership recruiting messages to emphasize global opportunities, not simply a road map to becoming a chief information officer. "Now the message we put forward is, 'You will get experiences here you won't get anywhere else,'" says Woods.[20] "You might be working in Asia on your first rotation. It's a whole different conversation from what we were having just a few years ago."

Ideas are currency; execution is the economy. Provide forums that enable employees to practice career self-direction, such as Turner's KEYS program outlined in Chapter 4. Employee resource groups are tailor-made for low-risk, high-return experiments in self-direction. Increasingly (as noted in Chapter 5), employee resource groups are becoming invaluable channels for reaching large groups of employees who want to gain experiences outside the norm of their daily responsibilities. Companies are increasingly using these self-nominated groups to both communicate and reinforce the organization's career-pathing expectations, but also to use the operation of the groups themselves for skills training.

A study by human resources consultant Mercer[21] found that leading companies used ERGs for the following:

75 percent	Coaching and mentoring by diversity staff
58 percent	Leadership training
38 percent	Mentoring by a business manager (cross-functional mentoring)
25 percent	Business fundamentals training
23 percent	Facilitator training
23 percent	Project management training

And, 72 percent of the ERGs in the study were expected to align their own goals with the organization's talent development goals. At many organizations, ERG leaders' responsibilities for the group were folded back into their overall performance evaluations. And at the majority of the organizations—76 percent—ERG leadership was a driver for career advancement.

Ladies Who Lattice

A recent study by the consulting firm Booz Allen Hamilton found that employees gravitate toward leaders who are team-oriented, participative, and humane. Those surveyed put less trust in people with leadership styles that are grounded in autonomy and hierarchy.[22]

Latticing is one tool for retaining women during their high-demand midcareer years, when parenting responsibilities threaten to derail their careers (as outlined in Chapter 8). But strategic lateral moves are also essential for ensuring that women gain operating experience, which is a prerequisite for executive leadership.

Numerous researchers, including those at consulting firm McKinsey, agree that women traditionally embody the characteristics necessary for global leadership: the ability to inspire, participatory decision making, and setting expectations and rewards. And McKinsey's Centered Leadership research indicates that "women often stay put in jobs if they derive a sense of meaning from the work."[23] Meanwhile, cultures and traditional organizational structures often prevent women from applying their leadership styles to operational roles effectively.

Strategic lateral moves are the answer. Rotating women from their traditional realm of staff jobs to operational positions that give them the reins of a business unit—and the consequent accountability for results—ensures that women get the experiences that will qualify them for the C-suite. In the process, women will expand their internal networks, and will have more chances to win sponsors who can advocate for their advancement.

Marti Barletta, CEO of the Trendsight Group and the grande dame of marketing consultants who explain what women want, has found that women at all levels assume that the natural peer group is the "we." Men, on the other hand, see the natural unit as an individual, and intuitively slot those individuals into hierarchies.[24] The male mode reinforces the ladder, while the female mode reinforces the lattice.

For men, says Barletta, the captain of a team defines the vision, and the role of team members is to know what they should contribute. Men put a priority on:

▶ Hierarchy
▶ Moving up
▶ Competition
▶ Differentiation
▶ The idea that status symbols signal success
▶ Testing and challenging
▶ The best idea wins
▶ Respect (look up to someone)
▶ Credentials = respect
▶ Being proved right

The female mode reinforces the lattice. For women, says Barletta, a team is a circle of near-equals, and leadership is conferred by consensus. Women put a priority on:

► What they share with other team members
► Achieving a personal best
► Having a pool of talent
► The wisdom of the group
► Trust built through vulnerability
► Full disclosure
► The process of discovery
► Identifying several good options

These dynamics explain why the ladder feels foreign to many women, and how the dynamics of the lattice can dissolve institutional barriers. The lattice is a model that women buy into, because it's how they've always thought career advancement should work.

Benita Fitzgerald Mosley: In It to Win It

"I had to be a track star to do this job," says Benita Fitzgerald Mosley, chief of sport performance for USA Track & Field. She's not kidding. Mosley oversees the programs that train American track and field athletes.[25] She has brought home the gold herself, as the 1984 Olympic gold medalist in the 100-meter hurdles.

Hurdles, which combine sprinting with jumping, are an apt metaphor for Mosley's career. Her degree in industrial engineering established her analytical and organizational skills, but her career path has been just as much over as up as she assembled the operational and business skills that she now uses to help lead the organization that sends U.S. track and field athletes to international competitions, including the Olympics.

The world of engineering quickly wore thin for Mosley, so when her athletic connections served up an invitation to apply for a job as regional director for Special Olympics International, she did . . . and landed it. In short order, she gathered additional experience in sports marketing for first the Special Olympics and then the Atlanta Committee for the Olympic Games. Managing the complex relationships between sponsors and sport governing bodies solidified her negotiating and communication skills. Mosley then moved sideways to direct one of the four U.S. Olympic Training Centers. "It was like being athletic director of a small university," she says. "I oversaw a 152-acre facility, and I finally had a staff, and managed all the programs and big events hosted on site, from budgeting to staffing to food service."

From there, she vaulted to overseeing all the training centers—which served 50,000 athletes annually and had a $15.5 million budget—and to directing the Olympic Committee's public relations programs. She seemed to be on track to be CEO of a sports organization. At least, that's what others were telling her.

But instead, Mosley was recruited (through her connections as a board member of a women's sports nonprofit) to become CEO of the trade group Women in Cable and Telecommunications. It had 17 employees and an annual budget of $5 million, but Mosley was in charge. She also went from knowing nearly everyone in the very large world of international track and field to knowing almost no one in the relatively small, clubby world of cable television.

Mosley had taken the job for the chance to develop and execute strategy and see the results play out. She dramatically increased the organization's membership and revenue. Eight years later, when she moved to her current position, she knew how to assess the organization's weaknesses, how to frame the solutions, and how to align operations to achieve the needed improvements. She created sports performance workshops where athletes and trainers could gain cross-disciplinary insight into boosting performance. She firmed up the criteria and responsibilities for top-tier athletes.

"It was a brand new approach," says Mosley. Some people in the organization were skeptical that her businesslike approach would work. "But a year later, we'd won 25 medals in the world championship, 15 percent more than in the last championship, and 10 percent more USA T&F athletes ranked in the top 10 in the world in their events. We tied those medals to how those athletes achieved those medals, and suddenly people saw how the plan worked. We were able to make things happen collectively that we couldn't make happen independently."

Mosley both immersed herself in each position and refused to be defined by each position. "I might not yet be plotting my next step, but I take full advantage of the experience to be ready when the next opportunity presents itself," she says. "When I took over the first training center, I knew Olympic sports and the people who ran them, and I knew I had the core skills to build from. The rest, I knew I was smart enough to figure out—with the counsel of others."

And, she never hesitates to "take myself out of that comfort zone and into another arena. As an athlete, you're always going into uncharted territory as you move up to higher levels of competition—but that's what you're in it for."

Lessons of the Lattice

▶ Meaningful lateral moves help to retain top performers, because those performers are oriented toward continual growth. (That's one reason why they are top performers.)

▶ Unlike old-school "fast track" lateral rotations and structured lateral assignments, the lattice is democratic and self-directed.

▶ Executives who climbed the ladder or who experienced traditional structured lateral moves can champion the lattice by sharing their own stories of self-directed development and by personally investing in employee resource groups and other programs that cultivate lattices and democratic lateral moves.

▶ Celebrate all forms of career growth—both lateral moves and promotions.

CHAPTER 8

LATTICE AROUND MIDCAREER AND MIDLIFE CHALLENGES

What is Melissa Randall, a family studies major and licensed clinical social worker, doing at Rothstein Kass, a large accounting firm that specializes in serving high-stakes financial services clients?

Managing its LIFE program, that's what . . . and serving as her own best case study for midcareer professionals who wonder how they can recalibrate their career paths to make more of their core strengths.[1]

As the program manager for the Office of LIFE (the Rothstein Kass women's initiative; LIFE stands for Leadership, Inspiration, Family, and Empowerment), Randall wins leadership support for programs that advance women and foster a work-life blend—both of which are pressing topics in the accounting profession. Balancing the demands of an intense career with the equally insistent priorities of rearing a young family has thrown many women accountants' careers off track; Randall is in charge of reversing that professionwide problem at Rothstein Kass.

To design and implement programs that actually solve problems, Randall has to understand what those problems are. That is where her social work background comes in; in fact, her social work skills of listening, interpreting, and creating action plans based on what she hears have kept her career moving forward.

After graduating from Fordham University, Randall took a traditional first job as a hospital staff social worker. While getting her master's in social work, she ran successive programs for children, AIDS patients, and mental health patients and worked with at-risk youth. It was her understanding of substance abuse that enabled her to segue to a position at an employee assistance program, coordinating referrals from enrolled employers who were worried about workers who exhibited worrisome behaviors.

"The EAP is where I got most of my growth," says Randall. "I saw gaps that I could fill in for it. I asked for the additional work. I didn't get paid any extra, but I took on a lot of extra work outside my official job responsibilities." She worked directly with human resources staffers, then applied her ability to design and run programs to expand her company's client services. She learned how to develop and present proposals, and how to win and manage corporate clients. She designed training programs for human resources staff and managers at the EAP's client companies. A major accounting firm was so impressed with Randall's work that she joined its workplace solutions team to develop its work-life benefits. "That was a mirror image move—with a different title but the same skill sets," says Randall.

Once her own family arrived, Randall cycled out of the workforce, but not for long. She took a position as a home-based executive recruiter. Conducting interviews with candidates and employers was a perfect, if unexpected, application of her social work skills. That lasted until the recession started; the recruiting business was walloped, and Randall's position evaporated.

Just a few months later, an acquaintance from her recruiting days reconnected with her via Facebook to suggest that Randall look into a part-time position at Rothstein Kass. She got the firm's attention because of her stint at the major accounting firm and the master's degree in organizational behavior that she had picked up. But it was Randall's ability to listen intently and translate what Rothstein Kass knew it wanted and didn't know it wanted that won the firm's trust. "For me, the women's initiative brings together organizational work, social work, and relational skills in a corporate environment. I get to help other women succeed, which is so social work," she says. "You're always looking for the client to succeed."

Figure 8-1 shows Melissa Randall's lattice.

Figure 8-1

Melissa Randall's Lattice

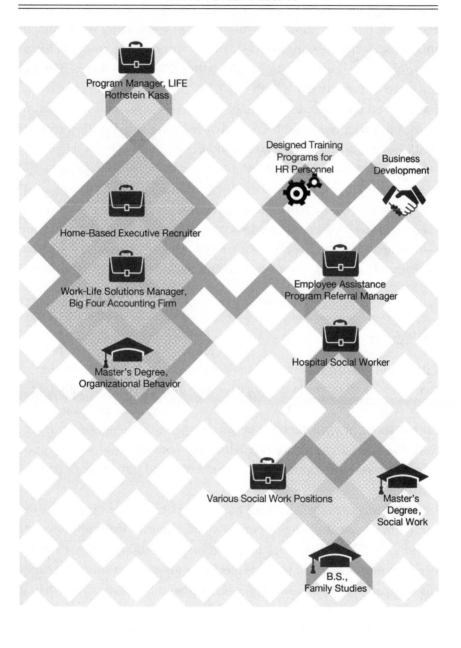

IN SOME OF ITS INCARNATIONS, the career lattice has been promoted as a way to train and retain employees, as a way to equip workers with the most basic education and credentials for self-supporting work, and, in this book, as the sustainable mode of advancement in an era of team-centric, flattened organizations. The lattice is all those things, but it is not a panacea for dealing with work-life conflict. Some organizations have seized on lattice terminology to describe an enhanced vision of work-life programs. The truth is that latticing is a solution to *some* work-life pressures at *some* points in *some* people's careers. However, while resilient and malleable, the lattice will not eradicate work-life conflicts for all employees at every point in their careers. In fact, latticing can exacerbate work-life conflicts when employees need to take on intense stretch assignments to position them for promotions that are within near reach. Chapter 8 shows how career lattices can reinforce and amplify well-designed work-life programs—and when they can't.

Don't Stop Now

Little kids. Aging parents. Yoga. Volunteer work. College tuition in five years. Retirement in thirty years. The desire to occasionally take a drive that isn't an errand. Vacations that are too short. Deadlines that are too short. The creeping sensation that you're missing something. . . and that you might figure out what that something is if you could minimize your job commitments for a while and put yourself first for a change.

In American culture, job and family responsibilities escalate at the same time, typically from a person's late twenties through her mid-forties. Just as proliferating personal responsibilities ratchet up the need for more time and more money, employees gain sufficient experience to aim for key promotions. It happens all at once. Can latticing relieve the pressure?

In a word, no. Career lattices can reinforce and coincide with work-life programs, such as flexwork, telecommuting, job sharing, and alternative work schedules. However, today's solution might not work when a new project lands tomorrow. Reconciling work-life tensions is never quite done. It's always in process. Children's needs change as they grow. Personal commitments blossom. Business growth and economic trends have their own trajectories. It is possible to negotiate a lateral move to a lower-stress position to briefly minimize direct work-life conflicts—and that is one type of lateral move. But latticing is a career-path system that often creates its own work-life collisions.

The great advantage that latticing brings is the chance to take a couple of lower-intensity developmental opportunities to pace growth—as long as those moves are part of a clearly mapped plan. This can be invaluable to employees who might otherwise have felt that their only choice was to step out of the workforce altogether. Even the few workers who can afford to walk away from their jobs for a few years are coming to realize that if they stop, they may never restart. In a slow-growth economy, it is much easier to change your pace than it is to get back in the game.

Employees know this. In a survey sponsored by talent agency Aquent, Dartmouth's Tuck School of Business, and the work-life consulting firm Work + Life Fit, Inc., 25 percent of respondents cited fear of losing their skill sets as one of the top reasons for not taking a career break.[2] (The other top reasons were losing income, not being able to find a new job, and losing their professional networks.) Their fears are justified: 61 percent of hiring managers put a top priority on having an updated, current skill set when considering hiring employees who had temporarily left the workforce. The same survey asked employees how they would "break the traditional workday arrangement and career-path model" (apparently mixing its message in its questions). Participants most wanted daily flexibility, with 20 percent desiring telecommuting and 17 percent expecting that project-based consulting work would relieve workday stress.[3]

But nearly half of the surveyed hiring managers were less impressed with flexibility as a means of managing both talent and the flow of work; just over half chose these solutions. The incorrect perception that lateral career paths will address work-life conflicts is perpetuated even by one of latticing's greatest proponents. Deloitte, the giant accounting and consulting firm, has adopted "mass career customization," which it also calls "the corporate lattice." This system allows employees to "dial up" and "dial down" their work hours and responsibilities in tandem and links the lattice to the strategic goal of employee engagement. But at any given moment, only 8 percent of Deloitte employees take advantage of this program.[4] Most of them stay on the traditional career ladder.

Employers face numerous challenges in retaining overcommitted, overworked midlife employees. The members of generation X (those born between 1966 and 1978) are today's midlevel managers and tomorrow's executives. But if generation Xers see no hope for advancing, they will leave. Working parents seek ways to balance their full plates; work-life programs must move in sync with latticing to enable employees to engage fully in both their careers and their personal responsibilities. And employees of all ages and genders expect to take advantage of flextime, telecommuting, and other productivity perks . . . without derailing their careers. Latticing can complement and strengthen work-life programs, providing support and accommodation for all. But it is primarily a career development tool, not a work-life logistics panacea.

Gen Xpectations

In *The X Factor*, the Center for Work-Life Policy lays out the squeeze on the members of generation X:[5]

- ▶ 41 percent of generation Xers are unsatisfied with their current rate of advancement.
- ▶ 49 percent feel stalled in their careers.
- ▶ 74 percent say that their credit card debt keeps them working; 43 percent say the same about their student loans.
- ▶ 45 percent of fathers of young children are now worried about work-life conflict, compared to 34 percent in 1977.
- ▶ 91 percent of generation X women and 68 percent of generation X men are part of dual-career couples.
- ▶ 64 percent of generation X college grads are women and minorities.

Baby boomers aren't moving on. Millennials are riveting employers' attention with their tech-driven mindset, not to mention their entitlement mentality. Meanwhile, generation Xers soldier on. They have to. They carry significant financial responsibilities. They must continue earning as much as they can. A Columbia University study found that established workers laid off during the 1980–1981 recession never regained their prior earning level.[6] For the next two decades of their careers, they earned 15 to 20 percent less than they would have earned if they had not been laid off. No generation Xer can afford that. (Nobody at all wants that, but millennials generally have fewer financial responsibilities, and so presumably could absorb the blow with more resilience.)

ManpowerGroup reports regularly on the shortages of skilled workers—those who would be expected to be midcareer professionals and managers rising on the basis of a decade's worth of experience. When it comes to engineers, managers, accounting and finance staff, and information technology staff, 52 percent of American employers say that they have trouble filling these jobs, up from 14 percent in 2010.[7] Yet, according to the Center for Work-Life Policy, generation Xers feel overlooked and underappreciated. Many think that they'd fare better on their own. The center reports that 40 percent of generation Xers cite "lack of career progress" as their primary reason for leaving a company.[8]

Work-life programs don't solve these issues. Such programs were pioneered in the late 1980s by activist-minded boomers who wanted to make workplaces more family-friendly. On-site child care was considered the highest level of corporate commitment to moms who were balancing a toddler on one hip and carrying a sheaf of papers on the other (notebook computers not having been invented yet). Had it not been for the persistence of these work-life advocates, we would not now have widespread flexwork, telecommuting, and company-supported family benefits and family leave. However, work-life programs were inevitably cast as concessions to working parents—mainly working mothers.

Just as these programs became widely adopted, however, boomers' childbearing tapered off. And guess what? Only 57 percent of generation X women are mothers, and only 68 percent of generation X men are fathers.[9] The notion that family-framed benefits are relevant to employees of a certain age is simply not true. Yet, parental preference is baked into work-life benefits. That puts the childless 43 percent of generation X women and 32 percent of generation X men on the defensive when it comes to accessing benefits that are purportedly available to all employees, according to the Center for Work-Life Policy. Flexwork and telecommuting help retain midcareer employees, if they don't have to line up behind parents to access these benefits. One silver lining to the Great Recession was that many employers adopted flexwork and telecommuting to offset stagnant or reduced wages; the Society for Human Resources Management found that currently, 53 percent of employers offer flextime, and 20 percent offer full-time telecommuting.[10] As welcome as these developments are, they cannot replace career advancement.

Work-life programs, as currently conceived and applied, are not universally relevant to generation Xers and can even alienate childless top performers. Employers must ratchet up career pathing to prove that they are committed to retaining and advancing generation X.

Build the Business Case

Do more with less? At Cornell University, lateral skills development equips staff members to do more by gaining more skills. More skills mean that more people are qualified to step into opportunities created by growth or cutbacks. Either way, the university's rapidly evolving lateral development program is reorienting its culture from hiring the latest talent to growing it. "We want to increase our 'ready now' internal candidates, and for our high potentials and high performers, we want to create as many opportunities for growth as possible," says Maria Wolff, program manager for career planning and development.[11] By realigning their midlevel career paths with the university's overall growth plans, employees can see several steps ahead for their personal lives, too, making it easier to plan and pace their work-life arrangements.

The Rotational Assignment Program (RAP) bubbled up in 2007 in the university's facilities management department. Supervisors and managers there wanted more ways to cultivate the talent and ambition of their staff members, so they started informally swapping information about short-term needs that could serve as developmental opportunities. Their seedling grew so quickly that it soon moved from the hothouse to the university's department of organizational effectiveness, which formalized the process and delineated two types of lateral tracks: gaining adjacent skills within one's functional area (such as administrative support) and taking on challenge assignments in readiness for promotion:

▶ "Talent discussions" held with supervisors help employees identify complementary skills that would enhance their current skill set and position them for lateral moves or promotions.
▶ Employees outline the type of skills they would like to gain, and why.
▶ Supervisors outline the type of growth opportunities they have on their teams, what the responsibilities of each position are, and what they think a newcomer might learn by filling each spot.
▶ The goal is to establish "career mapping groups" for each of the university's 14 "career families" (or functional categories). For skills development, these are typically within the same pay band or level.
▶ Benefits and expectations both for the participant and for the host and the home supervisors are spelled out.
▶ The supervisors and participants set dates for checking in (for longer-term rotations) and for debriefing when the rotation is over.

Some employees gained so many new skills that they were moved to new positions instead of being laid off when the university had to cut back during the recession, says Wolff.

For leadership development, the university uses lateral and short-term assignments to let people try out stretch roles, including first-time leadership. One popular rotation, for instance, is project management, which requires some supervisory responsibilities but a whole lot of influence, coordinating, time management, and presentation skills. "For someone who is interested in project management as a next career step, having the opportunity to oversee a special project gives her great experience, exposure, and networking, and, because she's working in a different environment, the chance for others to experience [working with] her," says Wolff. Most important, the short-term rotations are a low-risk way to validate career direction. "If they find out it's not a good fit, they're not locked in. The end of the rotation comes and that's a relief, and the hiring manager finds out that he needs to look elsewhere to fill that job, or maybe even change the job description a bit," explains Wolff.

The rotation programs have become part of the foundation of a gradually coalescing succession and talent pipeline plan. The plan is to reorient the organization's talent economy so that managers are willing and amenable to train and coach employees who are on temporary assignments because they are confident that other managers will return the favor. Next steps include developing a management academy for hands-on leadership, stepping up communication about how individuals and the university both benefit from lateral rotations, and illustrating lateral-driven career paths and those who earned promotions on those paths. The university has developed a "career curriculum" that equips employees with the common language and goals for advancing through latticing.

"We are really trying to get supervisors and senior leaders to be open and transparent about expectations and about what they are looking for in terms of high performance and high potentials," says Wolff. "We want a clear message that to be considered for career opportunities, these are the kinds of things that you need to be doing. What critical positions will we need to fill in six months or two years? How are we readying our people to take on those roles and challenges? Lateral rotations can fill those strategic needs. One of the metrics we are developing is how many 'ready now' candidates we have for positions that are not even fully realized."

Don't Count Yourself Out

The emerging story of the 2010s is the economic power of women. Numerous studies—including many produced by Wilson-Taylor Associates, the author's firm—document the importance of including women. As researched by Catalyst, higher proportions of women in board leadership are correlated with greater profits as a percentage of revenue, greater return on assets, and greater return on equity.[12] The widely recognized "female" style of leadership—collaboration, consensus, and communication—resonates with the democratic decision-making styles strongly preferred by generation Xers and millennials. Women outrank men—as rated by their superiors, peers, and direct reports—on key executive competencies, including adaptability, developing talent, influencing and negotiating, leading improvement, driving execution, and shaping strategy.[13] Yet, women continue to evaporate from the leadership pipeline at midlevel.

At the December 2010 TEDWomen conference, Facebook chief operating officer Sheryl Sandberg made an impassioned plea for women to not talk themselves out of success.[14] In a speech that instantly became a rallying point for women around the world (thank you, YouTube!), Sandberg outlined three changes that women can make, on their own, to stay the course and position themselves for top leadership jobs. She challenged women to own their own successes, not downplay their accomplishments, and not coast in anticipation of transferring to the mommy track, thus virtually ensuring that the job they leave isn't worth coming back to.

Sandberg set up her points by setting aside the value of women's initiatives, flexwork, and other well-intended programs with erratic track records. She essentially said that the big picture will change only when each woman changes her own picture. In sync with what Wilson-Taylor reported in its 2011 Accounting MOVE Project Report, Sandberg said that women consistently slow-track themselves well before they have a baby or are even pregnant.[15] They look ahead, look around, and draw conclusions from what they observe: mothers frantically arranging last-minute daycare pickups so that they can stay at meetings that are running long, the quiet evaporation of women at higher levels in the organization, and the apparent acceptance of that as the norm. Too often, young women draw conclusions from these observations about how their own careers might unfold, without initiating a discussion of their career direction with their managers, mentors, or sponsors. They assume that what they see happening for others will be their reality, too. But when they disengage from their career aspirations, or leave for a position that they believe will be more accommodating of their expectations for both their career and their personal life, they inadvertently abandon conversations that are waiting to happen.

Sandberg's point was that it is up to each woman to "raise her hand" and push for development, ask for career-building assignments, and take the personal risk of discussing how her employer might clear the way for her to achieve both her personal and her professional goals. The Center for Work-Life Policy validates Sandberg's perceptions: its research found that 54 percent of "highly qualified" women (that is, those with at least college degrees who are advancing swiftly) who voluntarily left the workforce did so without even discussing flexible work options with their managers.[16]

It is not hard to see why women conclude that their career stories will not differ from the stories of those who are a bit further along. The statistical record is daunting. Catalyst, the nonprofit that advocates for women's advancement, reported in late 2011 that women made up only a little over 14 percent of senior executives at Fortune 500 companies, although women hold over half of all management and professional positions.[17] The 2011 Accounting MOVE Report, authored by Wilson-Taylor Associates, Inc., the author's firm, provides a nuanced view of that profession: women are 51 percent of accounting firm employees, 38 percent of senior managers, and only 17 percent of partners and principals.[18]

Employers need to retain and advance women who are in midlife—just when many women are handling increased personal responsibilities and priorities. According to consulting firm McKinsey, 83 percent of women in early to middle management want to advance.[19] But work-life programs are only part of the solution, part of the time, for part of the workforce. They are not fully effective unless they are blended with innovative career pathing. Lattices help retain tomorrow's leaders and today's women because they offer what work-life programs do not: multiple avenues for continual advancement, with the choice to pursue the avenue that best dovetails with the employee's current work-life arrangement.

Work-life programs can neutralize logistical barriers to productivity. They provide tactical support to caregivers so that those caregivers can fully participate in delivering business results. A lateral move also can be a tactical solution, especially when it is used in tandem with work-life programs. For example, a parent of a small child might deliberately choose to stay in his current job and gradually build out several business skills, in the context of career-pathing conversations with a coach or manager indicating that this decision is not a permanent derailment of his long-term aspirations. Danielle Schaeffer, profiled in Chapter 3, paced her pursuit of a nursing degree, then healthcare managerial responsibilities, around the needs of her children and her husband. She stayed the course by making the most of distance learning and Good Samaritan's custom-scheduled on-site clinical rotations.

The vision of the lattice is lifelong career growth—a flexible blueprint that evolves along with the employee's expanding qualifications. Lattices are supported by work-life programs, not vice versa.

Some lattice moves require significant work-life accommodation. For example, one Fortune 500 regional vice president was only a couple of years from retirement. Her original lattice plan had been to work on special projects as an internal consultant and to take on extra protégés in the company's mentoring program. Instead, a different region hit a rough patch, with several executives abruptly leaving and operations in a shambles. The company's top brass wanted her to sail to the rescue—literally, by moving 900 miles to that region for a six-month assignment. As a single woman, she did not have the classic work-life conflicts—she had no dependent children, she was healthy, and she did not have the complication of a working spouse. However, she did have an elderly, ailing mother who lived on the opposite coast from the region in distress, whom she was visiting increasingly frequently.

Her lateral assignment was on a collision course with her personal responsibilities.

The solution: a combination of extreme commuting and extreme tele-commuting. The vice president camped out at her mother's house and managed the crisis remotely. Twice a month she flew to the region and conducted marathon meetings for several days. It was a tiring stretch, but the combination of latticing and flexible work arrangements came through. She guided the region through its rocky stretch, oriented its new permanent managers, and was still able to personally attend to her mother.

Latticing Fosters Engagement

The intense demands of career and family can make both feel like a slog. On the lattice, employees can see that they are continuing to make progress toward their career goals, even if they must plateau for a while to concentrate on personal responsibilities. In the laddered culture of major promotions, it's easy to understand why many managers chronically underestimate the importance of "small wins," or accomplishments, for job satisfaction and engagement, according to Harvard Business School professor Teresa Amabile. In her studies of midcareer professionals and managers who are handling complex projects, she has found that job engagement is strengthened by gaining new competencies, successfully collaborating with coworkers, and making incremental progress that rolls up to accomplishing larger goals.[20] These characteristics are intuitively woven into the following best practices.

Discovery's MentorNet

Discovery Communications, LLC, is legendary for its banquet of work-life supports. Just as important is its culture of continual growth for employees at all levels. "Good managers take interest in lateral moves as a sign that employees are ready to widen their scope of work and take on new projects," says Evelyne Steward, vice president of wellness and work-life strategies. "What promotes latticing is the culture, not the programs."[21]

Discovery uses programs to reinforce and structure its culture and to show employees—especially new hires—how they are expected to plot their career moves and draft their own career grids. The main program that spells out and perpetuates career lattices at Discovery is MentorNet. It works because employees request to be included; they are mentored by the divisions that they believe they would like to work in; and all communications and training materials reinforce the language of latticing, which in turn strengthens all employees' shared understanding of career management.

"The goal is the lateral moves," says learning and development program manager Jessica Banks Poawui.[22] "It's an opportunity to break away. They gain exposure in departments they would like to be in so that when positions are available, they are top of mind. We don't guarantee the promotion or the move, but we provide the exposure." Discovery benefits because employees branch into adjacent skills and become more qualified for a range of potential positions.

The process starts every spring with a companywide invitation to participate in MentorNet. In their applications, employees spell out what they want to learn. For example, an employee in a department that produces television shows might want to learn more about developing show concepts. A half-day course (available to all employees, whether they are involved in MentorNet or not) spells out the company's expectations for self-directed latticing and career development. "We want them to articulate the skills they'd like to develop," says Poawui. "In their career development workshop, they learn how to speak in terms of transferable skills so that they can see the skill sets they have and what they could transfer to with those skill sets. They talk about champions and others who can speak for your performance beyond your manager, so your name comes up when there is a chance for cross-team collaboration." The class also includes practice at informational interviews. One popular track: finding out how to get in on Discovery's international careers.

Once they have figured out what they have and what they can do with it, potential protégés complete their applications, which ask them to explain what adjacent experiences they want to have and why. "You can't just say, 'I want development,'" says Poawui.

Protégés must have been with Discovery for a year and perform well before they can participate in MentorNet; potential mentors must have been with the company at least six months. Mentors must be at least two reporting levels above their protégés, and outside the protégés' chain of command—in other words, a protégé cannot be mentored by his boss's boss. That ensures honest discussions without upsetting day-to-day relationships. Poawui makes the matches; with three times as many potential protégés as mentors, the skills represented by the mentors determine which protégés are matched. In 2011, there were 117 MentorNet pairs. Those who didn't get chosen rise to the top in the next year's round, ensuring that everyone gets a chance.

Piloted by a Discovery employee resource group in 2005, MentorNet quickly became so popular that just two years later, it was adopted as a program managed by the human resources staff, winning staff resources. One distinction that Poawui makes is that what happens in MentorNet stays in MentorNet. Feedback is not integrated into the protégés' performance records; their managers don't know what happens in the mentoring sessions.

The annual MentorNet launch is one of Discovery's annual spring programs on career development. Other components include employee skill self-assessments, presentations by company leaders about Discovery's direction, and panel discussions that show the variety of skills and positions in the company's divisions, from creative to finance. The programs let employees see different ways in which they can mix and match their skills to lattice within Discovery. Leaders talk about their own career paths, including how they have benefited from lateral steps.

A high comfort level with rotating among lateral positions is a core career skill as employees advance, says Poawui. "There's a lot of movement among New York, Los Angeles, and Silver Spring [the company's headquarters]. As we adapt to business conditions, vice presidents have the opportunity to manage different groups, and there's a lot of movement among those divisions. They might lead teams within larger divisions and then take those skills to emerging networks so that they are applying different perspectives and understanding the entire company," she says. As business needs shift, generalists might need to become specialists, and vice versa. And with a commonly held perception of latticing, employees know how to present their lateral moves when it's finally time for them to apply for a coveted destination job. Managers interviewing internal candidates ask them to explain the logic behind their lateral moves, what they learned by making lateral moves, and, if the position they are applying for is also lateral, how it fits into the employee's self-directed career plan.

Four Hands on the Wheel: Ford's Job Sharing Lattices Midcareer Engineers

Job sharing is more admired than adopted, but when this little-used work-life technique is blended with lateral career development, it can keep two mid-career employees on track. On the spectrum of flexible work options, from flexible hours to telecommuting, job sharing is one of the least used. As few as 2 percent of all workers have arranged to split the duties of a full-time job between two coworkers.[23]

Leave it to two engineers to crack the code.

Julie Rocco and Julie Levine were, together, the product manager for the 2011 Ford Explorer product team. They're the ones who make sure that all the elements of the product development process are on point and on time. They coordinate the product concept, product strategy, development, design, prototype, and ultimate launch of the product to the public.[24]

It's a big job and a big commitment: half of that job is still a 40-hour week jammed into three days, plus evening hours spent updating each other. Both women are mothers of young children who realized in 2007 that they weren't willing to sacrifice either time with their kids or career advancement. They found each other by networking internally and then, well, engineered the collaboration.

They immediately agreed that they'd each work three days a week, overlapping on Wednesdays. Also, their shared top priority was to make their arrangement seamless and invisible to their colleagues. They accomplish that with nightly one-hour briefings that ensure that the Julie du jour walks in with everything she needs to know to keep the balls in the air. Key meetings are held on Wednesdays.

One point of unity: they share responsibility for each task and don't divide responsibility. "People naturally want to divide up the work, meeting with one of you or giving one thing to one of you," says Julie Levine. "But that doesn't work. Either of us has to know the answers to any question we get whenever we pick up the phone."

They have discovered some unexpected advantages. Together, they've nearly doubled their internal networks, so that they save time finding the right contacts in other departments. The nightly briefings include interviewing each other, a process that often uncovers problems and evokes solutions more quickly than if each were flying solo. They swap favorite techniques for getting through key tasks, multiplying efficiency.

A critical test came when a new director inherited the duo's year-old arrangement. He was skeptical at first. One day, after hours of collaborating on a critical presentation to Ford brass, the director anxiously asked Julie Levine, "You'll be here, tomorrow, right?" Her response: "Julie's here tomorrow. You have to trust us." The next day, Julie Rocco coached him page by page through the last-minute changes to the presentation. She didn't miss a beat, and neither did he.

"We can tell we're seamless when people say, 'I met with one of the Julies, I don't know which one,'" says Julie Rocco. "We are extremely grateful that we work for a company like Ford that is progressive and supportive enough to allow management to job-share."

Latticing Will Develop as Flexwork Did

Flexible working and telecommuting were revolutionary 20 years ago. Now, they are so common that some companies consider mobile work their default. The adoption of career lattices is following the same pattern, so it is not hard to predict lattices' arc of acceptance.

Then: Flex was the exception, used only in situations that were business-critical or dramatic (someone recovering from an injury).

Now: At leading companies, flexible work schedules are the norm.

Lateral lesson: Make lateral moves the norm for everyone—a routine and anticipated part of employees' career development.

Then: Flexwork was a closet practice, with people getting permission behind closed doors from sympathetic managers and entering and exiting quietly so as not to tip off their coworkers who were working 9 to 5.

Now: There's no more closet. Flex hours are widely accepted because the majority of employees use flex schedules as intended and ensure that flexibility reinforces their productivity and responsiveness.

Lateral lesson: Neutralize any lingering doubts about the value of lateral moves by recognizing and rewarding the success of these moves in team meetings, organizational communications, and communications that define and frame success. Weave training, development, and organizational success into the narrative about lateral success so that employees gain a 360-degree understanding of how personal growth unfolds.

Then: It was assumed that flexwork would retain highly valued employees, but there were so few of them that it was impossible to prove the business case.

Now: Numerous academic studies have validated that gaining control over something as simple as when and where they work—even for part of their workweek—measurably increases people's engagement, productivity, and job satisfaction. Flexwork correlates with greater retention, with more corporate innovation, and even with higher returns.[25]

Lateral lesson: Engineer measurements of lateral success from the start so that the investment in training, coaching, and tracking employees is quantified. Common quantifiers include retention, engagement, and reduced layoffs.

Then: Flexwork was cloaked in broad assumptions about productivity and retention, but the lack of management training reduced many

early efforts to a sad reality of high school politics run amuck. Too
often, winning support for flexwork depended on the largesse of
individual managers and the tolerance level of teammates.

Now: Widespread use of flexwork "contracts," regular reviews of
flexwork arrangements with supervisors, and, at leading employers,
shared team responsibilities that call on everyone's willingness to
flex to deliver top-notch processes and results have transformed
flexwork to a democratic productivity driver.

Lateral lesson: Simple, easy-to-manage structures and mutual accountability ensure that lateral moves deliver results for individuals,
teams, departments, and organizations. Well-designed lateral
systems become self-sustaining.

Plot Your Midcareer Lattice

Centrifugal force can spin careers off course in midcareer. These tactics
can keep yours on track.

One-on-one conversations are a nearly universal but underappreciated
element of strong lateral development programs.[26] Managers chronically
underestimate the effect of investing time and thought in discussing not
performance, but career direction. First, find out if your organization has
career-planning tools and competency models for employees at the level
at which you are currently and the level at which you would like to be. If
so, use them as an outline for your discussion. If your organization does
not offer such plans, career coaches, or regularly scheduled career conversations, ask for such a conversation with your manager. Use the tools
in Chapter 2 to plot the points you want to cover. Focus less on what it
takes to get to a specific level or job, and more on what competencies and
experiences you can gain in the next six months to round out either your
current array of capabilities or those that lead into categories that you
would like to move into. Explain how doing so will return short-term
value to your team and your department.

Separate from your performance review, take stock of how well
your job fits your current skills, experience, abilities, and personal

responsibilities and aspirations. Just because you are competent and confident at your current job does not mean that you should be doing it forever. What changes do you anticipate in the next six months that you might want to start planning for now? Do you have greater bandwidth or energy for a high-stakes assignment now than you might have had a few months ago? Do you need a short breather to integrate things that you've recently mastered? On what area—technical skills, business skills, or relational/creative problem solving—do you next want to concentrate? Your manager can't read your mind. Make sure you can read your own mind before you launch into a conversation about your next career steps.

Downsizing, reorganizations, and rapid growth all have one thing in common: they all leave bits of work unclaimed. Look over the leavings and figure out which tasks fit into your career plan. Zero in on those that will give you a platform, no matter how slim, for connecting directly with those higher up who can become sponsors or otherwise give you a hand to the next step on your lattice. For example, if you take over the task of compiling a routine weekly report that goes to the division manager, you have an opportunity to meet with him to find out how the report format and metrics could be updated to better capture emerging trends. Such opportunities give you a chance to show in real time how you take ownership of tasks that are low in glamour but essential. Of course, document your process, improvements, and results.

Track your lateral moves just as you would promotions. Benchmark the situation you inherit, document your strategy and tactics, and measure your results. Build short business case studies to justify any of the moves that might come your way—lateral, promotion, a training investment, a bonus, or a raise—or, in the event that none of these comes your way, your job search.

Business conditions realign revenue and profit expectations, and that ripples down to reshape the definition of success for departments and individuals. As conditions shift, the currency of advancement might favor lateral rotations one year, training the next, then, if there is a burst of revenue or profits, a shift to bonuses and promotions. Sniff out these trends as they crystallize by reading company financial reports, tracking analysts' reports on your company, and observing how known top performers are being treated. This can help you keep your development pitch in sync with the new normal—whatever that is.

Lessons of the Lattice

▶ Work-life programs are not synonymous with career lattices because such programs are rarely integrated with career advancement.

▶ For midcareer employees with significant personal responsibilities, lattices work best in the context of continual communication. That way, employees and managers can explore how to address all the "moving parts" that play into a career decision.

▶ Lattices fuel job satisfaction and engagement by supporting ongoing measurable progress. It is impossible to overestimate the importance of feeling that one has not become hopelessly mired in the ever-changing responsibilities of midlife.

▶ Structured mentoring and cross-training are two components of lattices that are flexible enough to accommodate the demands of midlife.

nationally through major retailers and specialty stores. And Crevin's ability to start and grow a million-dollar business from scratch sped her advance within Microsoft, where she served on the human resources staff for the games division until December 2010. Because Xbox is "the sexy place to be in Microsoft," she found that her entrepreneurial experience made her even more qualified to detect strong job candidates and to reinforce the division's culture.

Many people would think that Crevin had three full-time jobs—her staff job at Microsoft, running Booginhead, and co-parenting two young sons. How did she make it all happen? The end of her Microsoft day was just a dinner hour away from the start of the next day in China, enabling her to talk with Booginhead contractors in the evening. Crevin also developed a virtual staff for marketing, accounting, supply chain, legal help, and public relations, freeing her to focus on new product development and strategy. Though Crevin has again cycled out of the corporate world, she's now head of a multimillion-dollar business that offers a whole new way to apply her big-company experience. Sari Crevin's career lattice is shown in Figure 9-1.

THERE ARE A DOZEN good reasons to leave full-time work: to spend time with young children, to pursue a personal passion, to take a year off to travel, or to give entrepreneurship a shot. Leaving is easy and exciting. Returning, however, is difficult and frightening. Resilient career lattices can accommodate many of the urges that tempt employees to leave the workplace, retaining valuable talent, forging new ways to grow, and keeping earnings on track.

Ramps, Exits, and Shoulders

In 2005, the Center for Work-Life Policy published *Off-Ramps and On-Ramps: Keeping Talented Women on the Road to Success*.[2] Focusing on women because it is socially more acceptable for women to pause or abandon their careers than it is for men to do so, the study found that 37 percent of "highly qualified" women voluntarily leave their jobs for six months or more. Furthermore, two-thirds of the women in the study took an alternative career path for a stretch, most typically in midcareer.

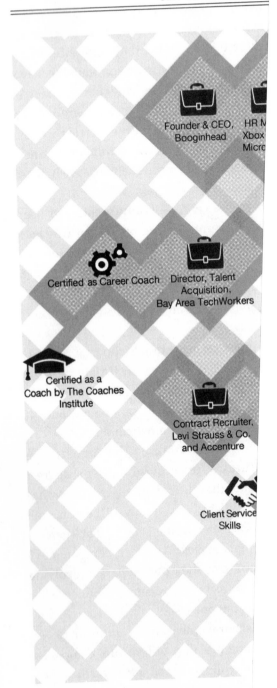

Figure 9-1
Sari Crevin's Lattice

Founder & CEO, Booginhead

HR M...
Xbox
Micro...

Certified as Career Coach

Director, Talent Acquisition, Bay Area TechWorkers

Certified as a Coach by The Coaches Institute

Contract Recruiter, Levi Strauss & Co. and Accenture

Client Service Skills

A fo...
of the r...
on pur...
difficul...
departe...
26 perc...
percent...
but not...
had ste...
In fact, t...
of chron...

Near...
working...
to full-ti...
23 perce...
employ...
years, th...
their ear...

No m...
of highl...
those th...
wanted...
percent...

Other...
well-inte...
in busin...
the diffic...
advocate...
of wome...
percent...
door. The...
no better...

Leavir...
harder.[6]...
of the sar...

especially if they are fortunate enough to retain the same title or level of responsibility.

The Center for Work-Life Policy picked up early on people's desire to deliberately take an extended break. Nearly two-thirds of respondents of all ages and career stages want to stop work and get off, according to a survey conducted by talent agency Aquent, consulting firm Work + Life Fit, and the Tuck Executive Education program at Dartmouth. Parenthood was the top reason, cited by 63 percent of respondents (and by most women), but pursuing an avocation was cited by 43 percent and was the top motivation for men.[7]

Pulling over on the shoulder doesn't just pause careers. It stalls them. Employees do not recoup their investment in education and the effort they put into their careers up to the point where they left. Household income suffers, and the damage to couples' and women's retirement security is incalculable. Employers lose an enormous slice of their talent pool.

By using the lattice for on- and off-ramping, people can keep their careers at cruising altitude. By building a range of skills and continuing to develop them *without significant interruption*, employees can stay the course. Preserving momentum can take a variety of entrepreneurial forms. Employees might contribute from the outside as a contractor or small business supplier. Either way, employers haven't lost talent when they can continue working with valued ex-employees . . . and former employees leave the door wide open for a potential return to traditional employment.

Right out of college, Brian Leleux and a partner launched an e-commerce company selling specialized fitness equipment. But after 10 years, the partnership was wearing thin, and Leleux realized that he needed a bigger arena in which to grow his career. The barrier: though his title was CEO, he felt that it would be difficult for potential employers to check out exactly what he had accomplished. "My résumé says, 'Managed 15 employees, payroll, taxes, and insurance for number one website for our industry,' but there's no third-party way to verify that," he says. "It is what I say it is, and for a candidate, that's suspect."[8]

And located as he was in Louisiana, and reluctant to move because of his smaller, but ongoing, responsibilities with the e-commerce company he had helped launch, Leleux found himself turning down promising positions for small company CEO jobs elsewhere in the country. He changed strategies, effectively demoting himself on his résumé to general manager and operations manager, which better described his daily responsibilities. That landed him a job as an operations manager with a local manufacturer of pipe and flange protection products. "Whether you off-ramp or on-ramp, there's going to be a deceleration," says Leleux. "I knew I'd have to slow down to change."

Though it proved to be only six months long, his stint at the manufacturing company was enough to validate his skills and experience. Leleux swiftly moved on to his current position as international sales and marketing director for Tech Oil Products, which manufactures oilfield equipment. And in the end, the strategic thinking and creative problem-solving skills he gained as CEO of a much smaller operation have prompted his new boss, the company owner, to expand Leleux's role.

Coordinating all the moving parts of the operation is his favorite part of the job, but, coming full circle, his e-commerce experience is proving essential, too, as he takes over online marketing, managing the company's website, and overseeing its trade show marketing. "A lateral move allows you to broaden your experience so when it's time to move up, you're the one," says Leleux.

Entrepreneurship: One Link on the Lattice

From the outside, entrepreneurship can seem to solve all the problems that drain career satisfaction and slow success. From the outside, it appears that entrepreneurs pilot their own ships, control their time, build their own futures, and trade Manolo Blahniks for bunny slippers. Some of this is true. Owning a business can enable you to reestablish healthy habits and stress management, according to the Gallup-Healthways Well-Being Index.[9] Though business owners answer to everyone from customers to lenders to suppliers, they edged out managers and professionals in overall well-being because they are positioned to make the most of their strengths. The implication is that when your success draws on the best combination of your skills, experience, and creative problem solving, you are less likely to have outcomes thwarted by others in your organization.

This explains why the Aquent–Work + Life–Tuck study found that 35 percent of employees yearned to pursue entrepreneurship.[10] Yet, the same study found that 61 percent of managers list an updated skill set as the most important factor in hiring. Many small businesses fail.[11] In other cases, owners outgrow their own businesses and need bigger horizons. On the lattice, employees approach entrepreneurship as a step on their lattices, not a step off. That means layering onto all their other hopes for entrepreneurship a plan for ensuring that they hone the skills that will enable them to return to traditional employment.

Savvy latticers find ways to build their career skills and their businesses at the same time, making it easier for them to step back into a bigger organization. Marilyn Lunnemann started out as an accountant, became a teacher, then helped launch a financial consulting practice as a part-time partner with a full-time contribution. Even then, she might have found herself in jeopardy when the firm was acquired, had it not been for her steady development of business and relational/creative problem-solving skills through an often-overlooked channel: volunteering.[12]

Planned correctly, taking on nonprofit responsibilities can return immediate career growth to the volunteer and his employer while helping the nonprofit fulfill its mission. And, nonprofits are often the gateway to top-notch training programs offered through foundations, universities, and industry groups—programs that might otherwise be unavailable to workers at small companies.

When she joined the board of the YMCA of Greater St. Louis, Lunnemann thought that she knew networking and knew that she knew consulting. What she did not know was how to run with the big dogs—top executives of large companies. "I was in a small firm, learning from people who were managing small businesses," she recalls. But shortly after joining the Y's operations committee, she was introduced to a rarefied world of leadership development training. Some of her new colleagues were graduates of Harvard Business School, and they approached problem solving from a perspective that was completely new to Lunnemann. She learned new ways to organize brainstorming sessions, new approaches to strategic planning, how to get group consensus, and then, as a board chair, how to set the direction for a $60 million organization. She credits her YMCA training with helping her lead complex projects for big corporate clients. "It has taught me to go beyond my technical skills," she says.

Lunnemann's small practice was acquired by accounting firm Clifton Gunderson. Partly because of her community profile, and definitely because of the professional polish she had gained through her involvement with the YMCA, Lunnemann landed a position as a partner.

Trying It Before Buying Into It

When Brian Kurth opened VocationVacations in 2004, he thought that reinventing baby boomers would be his core market. To his surprise, burned-out generation Xers flooded to his short working vacations that offered immersion in an entrepreneurial venture on a "try before you buy" basis. Since the recession, well over half of the company's clients are frustrated thirty- and forty-somethings who are tired of working overtime with little chance of actual advancement. "The fact that we get so many generation Xers proves the point that we need more latticing from boomers to generation Xers, which ultimately gives boomers the opportunity to pursue their dreams in new, exciting careers prior to retirement," he says.[13]

VocationVacations primarily offers career-switching options like running a dog daycare center—the kind of lifestyle business that makes envious outsiders wonder how you actually get paid for doing work you'd do for free. Nobody turns to VocationVacations to learn how to make the transition from corporate attorney to self-employed mediator, for instance.

But, often to their surprise, career switchers find that their corporate skills are more useful than they'd expected. More than ever, they are ramping up their second careers in their off-hours, keeping their day jobs as long as possible. While exhausting, moonlighting does afford them enough transition time to transfer their business skills to their new ventures.

"It's latticing in the sense that they don't make these changes overnight. They move into their dream careers while still employed. They do find that there are applicable skills," says Kurth. "You might not want to be a financial analyst looking at spreadsheets day in and day out, but you still have to apply that skill set to your new career as an entrepreneur, even if you're doing something that seems to be disconnected, like running a wine bar. You still have to work the inventory, cash flow, and profit and loss statements."

Attorneys (VocationVacations sees a lot of them) find that their ability to negotiate and read contracts positions them to set firm terms with suppliers and employees. Marketing professionals may have to bone up on financial reporting and negotiating, but they can write copy, manage the design and development of their websites and marketing materials, and develop collateral materials.

Small Business, Big Skills

"Jack of all trades" is not a category that's on most corporate résumés. Entrepreneurs who want to leave all their career options open need to cultivate their technical, business, and relational/creative problem-solving skills in a way that recruiters and hiring managers can recognize. It is easy—and wrong—to assume that skills such as managing small business cash flow are equivalent to similar-sounding responsibilities in a larger organization (see Table 9-1). And if the venture is a roaring success, those skills must be recast in terms of top leadership anyway, because investors bet on people and their ability to execute even more than they bet on ideas.[14]

(See Chapter 10 for more on securing contracts from your employer as you make the transition to being a small business owner and supplier.)

The most important skill to capitalize on is your experience in the industry you are entering, according to research conducted by the

Table 9-1

Small Business Skills Translator

Small Business Activity	Big Business Qualifications
Technical skills	Validate through certifications and testing
	Publish client case studies on website (with permission)
Marketing	Identify and vet business growth opportunities
	Negotiate partnerships
	Cite stakeholder metrics
Sales	Win, retain, and upsell clients
	Validate through case studies
Hiring	Talent acquisition and management
	Finding, vetting, and managing contractors
	Qualifying and managing virtual teams
Financial management	Show ROI of business decisions
	Pricing analysis case studies

Wharton School of Business.[15] Having an operational history in the industry you are entering means that you know the industry's needs and can identify what problems you can solve. That means that you are less likely to make mistakes. You also have networks within the industry that can give you advice and guidance in sourcing key materials and expertise. Industry experience also tempers the rainbow of optimism that tends to bias the judgment of all entrepreneurs.

The Wharton researchers found that entrepreneurs overestimate the value of their general business experience. In addition, the fog of entrepreneurship will make it harder than you anticipate to discern your direction. For example, are your clients slow to pay because they are in financial trouble? Because they are dissatisfied with your work? Because the accounts payable staff is incompetent? Or because in your industry, certain types of invoices are paid last?

The Wharton researchers explicitly recommend "deliberately engaging in vocational activity in the industry where they intend to start a new business"—in other words, somehow experiencing what you are getting yourself into.

Viewing entrepreneurship as part of your career lattice can help minimize the risk and maximize your chances of success. While you are still employed, you can challenge yourself to quickly "learn to learn" by latticing into responsibilities that help you gain entrepreneurial skills within the context of your industry. You can replicate your anticipated entrepreneurial activity as much as possible before you leave the company. It will be much easier to diagnose and solve problems as an employee who is concentrating just on that project, without the chaos of small business tasks claiming your attention.

Lattice Over Instead of Out

Like 15 percent of the women surveyed in the Center for Work-Life Policy's "Off-Ramps and On-Ramps" studies, Jennifer Soltesz wanted to change both careers and industries.[16] Instead of coming to a complete stop, or going to school to try to requalify herself for a new field and build a new network, she latticed. Her lattice illustrates one way in which a structured series of bridges can alleviate an entrepreneurial detour.

Soltesz started out in accounting, but she loved the entertainment industry more than she loved auditing. But given that she had no industry experience and few connections, how could she segue both into a new industry and into a position—which position exactly, she wasn't even sure—that was a better fit?

Soltesz used her financial skills as the wedge for a multistep lattice strategy. First, she moved from the accounting firm to one of her client companies—Showtime. That got her from one industry (accounting) to her destination industry (entertainment). As a financial account manager, she conducted financial analyses of deals that Showtime was pursuing with industry partners. Collaborating closely with the sales team, she gained a working knowledge of the industry and company growth drivers, lingo, and career paths. She zeroed in on affiliate sales as the logical route, and she let higher-ups at Showtime know that she wanted to make the transition into that role. "I pointed out that my financial skills would be useful to the team while I developed my sales and client skills," says Soltesz. "Otherwise, you're just saying, 'I like that job; hire me!'"

Technical skills framed her pitch to join the team, and her subsequent performance, which clearly contributed to the team's results, cemented her value. "It's easy to sit back and say, 'I don't have the experience to do that job,'" says Soltesz. "But you need to dive in."

Leaving the Door Open for Return

Employers that hope that valued former employees might return are using alumni networks to keep the door open.[17]

The construct is simple: contact information is collected during the exit interview, along with permission to stay in touch. (Employees who are not welcome to return are simply not invited to join the alumni network.) The "careers" section of the employer's website includes an entry point for returning employees. Inquiries sent through that point are funneled to a recruiter who has access to the former employee's records and who is specially trained to counsel him about his current career aspirations and potential options at the organization.

Some employers actively reach out by sending out regular alumni newsletters with the inside scoop on upcoming hiring, open positions, employee events, and company news. Increasingly, employers are drawing on pools of alumni and retirees for part-time, seasonal, short-term, and contract work. The alumni network corrals opportunities, alumni-appropriate news, and contact data so that the information can be easily managed by recruiting staff.

The Payoff for Volunteering

Volunteering has become a standard strategy for keeping one's skills fresh while one is out of the paid workforce. That works only when volunteering is as strategic as any other career stage. These tactics will help individuals manage their volunteer experiences as part of their larger career lattice.

Take on substantive projects that will yield measureable results. Launching new projects, reorganizing moribund programs, conducting effectiveness audits, and formulating strategic plans can all expand your business and relational problem-solving skills. Before you dive into a project, identify the specific skills you want to develop and ensure that you will be actually gaining those competencies in the course of the project.

Get it in writing. Putting your internship agreement on paper helps both you and your nonprofit colleagues. This ensures that everyone's expectations are clear and also provides legal proof for the organization that it is adhering to U.S. Department of Labor standards for licit internships. For example, it is against the law to fire employees and then "hire" unpaid workers to cover their job duties.

Manage your budget. Some volunteer gigs will require a budget in addition to the labor of volunteers. Make sure that you understand the organization's resource limitations and its priorities for funding. Who signs off on purchases, and who approves any overages?

Starting a new project from scratch is a chance to build a holistic narrative starring your current skills. Document every step you took so that you can explain in detail during a job interview how you conceived, vetted, and executed the project—and show the results.

Not sure where to start? Use your technical skills to join the committee of a well-established, well-respected nonprofit whose members complement your professional network. For example, an accounting manager is a perfect fit on the financial oversight committee of a local museum. A web designer would probably be welcome on the marketing committee of a theater troupe. Once your work has established your credibility, you can lattice within the organization to projects and positions that enable you to concentrate on the skills you need to develop. For example, the accounting manager might want to join the fund-raising committee to sharpen her networking skills. To gain experience in negotiation and business strategy, the web designer might want to join a committee exploring the possibility of merging the theater troupe with another.

Many people who use volunteering to advance their careers aim to land on the board of directors. If you believe that board experience is critical, join the fund-raising committee of a relatively small organization. If you can bring in big money (in terms of that organization's needs and fund-raising history), you will probably not even have to ask to be on the board. Once you are on the board, you can wangle invitations to regional or category meetings of board members, dramatically expanding your nonprofit network. Beware, though: if you have established a reputation for fund-raising, other organizations will naturally expect repeat performances.

Lessons of the Lattice

► Entrepreneurship can be part of a lifelong lattice, benefiting both the latticer and the former employer when their relationship shifts to client and contractor or supplier.

► Entrepreneurship can be a career stage, not a complete change of direction. Business and relational/creative problem-solving skills cultivated as an entrepreneur can make a former business owner a strong candidate for mid- or upper-level management.

► Latticing throughout entrepreneurship notches up self-direction, as the entrepreneur must not only determine his direction but also secure the resources and lattice crew needed to achieve those goals.

► A structured lateral transition from one industry to another is one lattice alternative to making the transition by leaving corporate employment to start a company or go freelance.

LATTICE FOREVER:
To and Through Retirement

Confusing, contradictory, confounding healthcare paperwork maze, you've met your match. "I've spent 24 years in government. There isn't a bureaucracy I can't crack," says Elisabeth Schuler Russell.

She latticed from the U.S. State Department to entrepreneurship. As founder and CEO of Patient Navigator, LLC, Russell calls on all her diplomatic skills to help sick patients and their loved ones sort through healthcare bills, directives, and requirements to ensure that they get the care they need.

"I get asked a lot, 'How can you do this? You're not a doctor or a nurse,'" says Russell. But doctors and nurses don't do what she does—and therein lies her latticing lesson for baby boomers who are wondering how they will translate a lifetime of experience into a retirement position.[1]

Russell already had 15 years as a foreign service officer under her belt when her toddler daughter, Claire, was diagnosed with an inoperable brain tumor. "I needed to get smart on this right away and learn everything I could, so that's what I did," she recalls. Pulling together the right specialists to deal with a catastrophic illness demanded that she work with insurers, a range of providers, hospitals, outpatient care, equipment vendors, pharmacies, and on and on. She learned so much that by the time Claire recovered (she's now a healthy teenager), Russell had her own breakthrough. She realized that her ability to untangle red tape was simply a new application for her abilities to negotiate, research, and communicate quickly, clearly, and with conviction. "It's knowing how to communicate in different environments," says Russell. "It's not that different talking with a village elder or the prime minister of a host country, compared to a doctor's gatekeeper or a charge nurse. The medical world has its own hierarchies, its own protocols, its own culture, and knowing how to figure out a new culture is something you do when you live in a foreign country." And if it worked for her family, why wouldn't it work for others?

In 2004, while she was still at the State Department, she set up Patient Navigator. She helped establish a new trade group for the nascent profession to help establish standards and ethical guidelines. She learned that an hourly fee structure was more effective when it was paired with a subscription service to Patient Navigator road maps, customized for each patient. Her far-flung State Department connections yielded clients close to home. And, her reputation within the State Department for meticulous work quickly branded her as a trustworthy, discreet advocate for fragile patients and their vulnerable families.

Now, Patient Navigator has three contract employees and a growing national reputation. Russell has a thriving career for her second act. "With the demise of the role of the primary-care physician, there is nobody to tie the pieces together. And that is our role," says Russell.

Figure 10-1 shows Elisabeth Russell's lattice

BABY BOOMERS CAN'T afford to retire, and we can't afford to let them. The career lattice remixes a lifetime of learning, skills, relationships, and accomplishments for a final phase of life that is already redefining retirement. The lattice addresses the biggest fear of many boomers: living obsolescence. Instead of coasting over the finish line, latticing enables near-retirees to downshift with purpose, while the lattice affords employers new ways to make the most of their investment in their workers. Call it what you will (third stage or encore career), it's an unprecedented opportunity for both employers and individuals to create a new configuration for a new stage of life.

Figure 10-1

Elisabeth Russell's Lattice

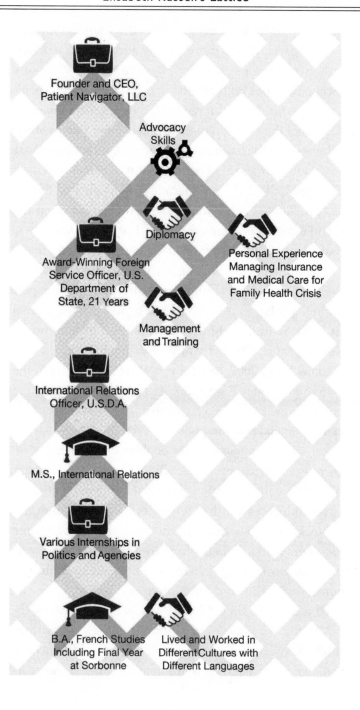

The Finish Line Moved

The famed demographic bump that is the baby boom generation probably has precipitated more utterly foreseeable workforce predictions than any prior generation. But the boomers' equally famed self-preoccupation has both created and solved a realignment of their retirement expectations. Until recently, they couldn't imagine leaving a workforce that they couldn't imagine could get along without them. Now, in the wake of the financial implosion, many boomers are hanging on as much out of financial necessity as out of career narcissism.

The economic jolts of the past decade have desiccated the retirement resources of millions of Americans.[2] Home equity, retirement accounts of all sorts, and most investments shriveled. Businesses failed, wiping out decades of sweat equity. Many boomers borrowed from their future—from their retirement—by making early withdrawals from what was left in their retirement accounts to pay for basic living expenses and their children's college costs. It used to be that Americans sauntered into retirement with their houses paid off and little to no consumer debt.[3] Not any more. The net worth of younger boomers declined 45 percent from 2004 to 2009, to a paltry $94,200, according to the Center for Economic and Policy Research. Older boomers—those on the verge of retirement—saw their net worth halved, to an average of $159,800.[4]

Standard financial planning wisdom dictates that the earnings peak in the last 15 years of one's career enables empty-nesters to double down on retirement saving, especially once they are out from under their children's college tuition payments. However, the economic fallout from the recession has wiped out that tidy assumption for many boomers. They cannot earn their way back into retirement by age 65. Boomers who lost their jobs in the Great Recession were a third less likely than workers aged 25 to 34 to find work within 12 months. And boomers who did find work often had to accept less than they had earned at the jobs they'd lost, according to a study by the Urban Institute.[5] A 2011 survey conducted by the American Institute of Certified Public Accountants found that 79 percent of financial planners had clients who had delayed retirement because of the economy. A third of the surveyed CPA planners estimated that their boomer clients would have to work one to three more years to recoup their losses; 39 percent estimated four to six more years of work; 10 percent estimated seven to ten years, and the remainder estimated more than ten years.[6]

Even those who are relatively unscathed are apprehensive about their retirement prospects. A 2011 study by TNS, a custom research firm, found that 43 percent of Americans with at least half a million dollars in investable assets worried that the ongoing economic malaise would undermine their retirement plans.[7] The Pew Research Center found that 52 percent of boomers expect to delay their retirements.[8] Not surprisingly, boomers are nearly universally worried about their prospects for staying employed or getting back into the workforce.[9]

Employers are less detectably concerned about the pending departure of boomer know-how, despite ample evidence that the boomers' absence will exacerbate the chronic skills shortage. In truth, employers need boomers to lattice to and through retirement.[10] They need boomers' expertise, experience, and abilities—but they also need to clear the way for rising generation X talent. Latticing defuses the collision course that is looming between boomers and ambitious generation Xers who want their chances at top jobs. Promising practices are already showing how lateral moves create completely new "last lattice" positions for boomers and open meaningful advancement for the next generation. Boomers who embraced latticing earlier in their careers will gravitate toward this configuration; those who rode the last rungs of the ladder to the top will have to reconcile their long-held definitions of success with late-career latticing. Either way, human resources staff and managers have a new architecture for segueing experienced, valued employees into a career stage that has been invented just in time.

Finish Strong

Latticing to or through retirement recalibrates boomers' expectations and offers them a chance to make the transition into retirement from their strengths. Only a few will be able to afford to abandon household-supporting work and take up full-time volunteering. Lat-ticing is the way for boomers to recapture their hopes for a satisfying culmination to their careers. Best of all, several long-percolating trends are converging to build the last lattice.

For years, boomers have been telling researchers that they expected to stretch work into retirement in some way. AARP's research found that only 16 percent of boomers defined retirement as a dead stop from work.[11] They have gradually pushed the official retirement finish line from 65 to past 68; latticing is the way to reconcile the now-urgent need to work with boomers' longstanding assumption that they will continue to use their career skills as long as possible. AARP research finds that preretirement boomers expect to work at least part time for the money (29 percent) or for the fun of it (23 percent); another 7 percent believe that their retirement will consist of switching from one full-time job to another. And 11 percent expect to become self-employed in retirement.[12]

While they want to continue working, in keeping with their per-petual expectation that their arrival changes the rules, boomers expect their last jobs to offer more than money. They want jobs with greater time and place flexibility so that they can have at least a bit more time for their personal pursuits. Many want to blend cultural, community, or other causes with their professional responsibilities.[13] The emerging definition of the "encore career" is one that combines a greater purpose with a challenging and growth-oriented professional opportunity. In a study for the MetLife Foundation/Civic Ventures, two-thirds of respondents aged 44 to 70 wanted to apply their skills and experience to help others.[14] Top causes were addressing environmental issues and working with children and youth.

Of course, not everyone can lattice into jobs with nonprofits (which are typically assumed to have more virtuous missions than for-profit enterprises), and fewer still can establish foundations to support their own encore careers. Through the career lattice, employers and com-munity-minded boomers can create new ways to infuse work with meaning, whether that is within the organization or tied to the organi-zation's greater mission or external stakeholders.

The Lattice Decloaks

Here's the good news: many boomers are already latticing, whether they call it that or not. The Sloan Center on Aging & Work at Boston College runs ongoing studies of retirement trends. Its researchers have found that 60 percent of mature workers are already bridging into their final phase of work.[15] They may not have realized that they were creating a distinct career stage, but that is what boomers are doing as they shift gears not down, but over, to jobs that keep them engaged and earning. Part-time work is currently the most prevalent form of bridging, according to the Boston College analysis. About three-quarters of self-employed boomers took bridge jobs, compared to about half of those in traditional salaried jobs. The researchers also found that bridgers were more likely to be either highly educated professionals or those on the opposite end of the skill spectrum, with minimal credentials and career achievement. The implication for employers is that since lattices are already working for professionals, why should they not also work for technical and support staffers and those at midlevel?

Latticing to Retirement

American employers can't afford to let highly skilled and experienced baby boomers go en masse, according to analysis conducted by the Council for Adult and Experiential Learning (CAEL). Utilities, healthcare, steel, and skilled manufacturing are already struggling to retain a critical mass of top-notch workers.[16] As it collaborates with the U.S. Department of Labor on a multistate pilot, CAEL has blended latticing with new modes of recruiting and redeploying boomers.

Other researchers assume that boomers' desire to blend "giving back" with paid work will primarily be fulfilled by directing boomers to jobs in government, teaching, social service, and nonprofits. However, high government debt, coupled with stagnant investment returns, is likely to suppress hiring in these sectors while the economy gropes for full recovery. Fortunately, private employers are catching on to the importance of romancing boomers with valued skills through lattices that enable preretirees to include at least a bit of the flexibility and community investment that they crave. Just because organizations assume that boomers will stay on the job longer doesn't mean that they have magically solved the talent transition. Boomers will eventually exit; an extended runway represents a chance for them to merge out purposefully instead of simply coasting to the shoulder. These promising practices have been pioneered or recommended by CAEL and its partners.

Career navigators. Boomers who grew up in laddered environments are often at a loss as to how to even begin branching out in a latticed world. Career navigators are trained to interview boomers to understand their career goals and to apply the classic CAEL techniques outlined in Chapters 2 and 3, such as assembling portfolios of their prior learning. The more skills and experiences one has, the more complex the process of consolidating those skills and experiences into a coherent portfolio will be. In collaboration with Indiana University's School of Continuing Education, CAEL is in the process of launching a program to train and certify career navigators with a particular emphasis on working with baby boomers who are reorienting their careers.[17]

"Burst" training. One frustrating training disconnect is that employers often urgently need to fill very specific technical positions, but those positions may or may not lead to career advancement. Intense, short-term training that takes advantage of a mature worker's knowledge and experience with that type of skill, and with that type of workplace setting, can quickly qualify boomers to take those positions. Employers don't need a long orientation phase when boomers can quickly translate skill sets from "not quite" to "just right."

Backfilling technology skills. Boomers whose careers have not demanded significant computer skills are at an enormous disadvantage when trying to reenter the workforce. Training in the basics, from keyboarding skills to using basic word processing software to navigating the cloud, can shore up a résumé that's long on experience but short on skills that workers are now assumed to have.

Internal consulting and special assignments. Cox Communications maintains a list of seasoned executives whose retirement horizon is nearing, who can be tapped for short-term assignments. Parachuting into situations in which their extensive experience is a godsend affirms the value of the "Executives on Demand" and also ensures that they can transfer their know-how to the teams that need it. One executive, for example, spent the last three months of his career troubleshooting difficulties with a business-to-business client in a large, critical market. Executives on Demand both serve as internal consultants and fill in for regional and headquarters leaders who must take short-term leave. The availability of the Executives on Demand provides backup when Cox leadership wants to take advantage of a sudden opportunity to give a rising leader operating experience: the executive can step in and keep things running while the rising leader tackles the short-term growth assignment.[18]

Flextime and flexible places. Employers who are located in retiree-dominant regions—most notably, Florida, Phoenix, and Las Vegas—have the chance to pioneer new types of work time and place flexibility. Some maintain databases of retirees who are qualified to serve as temporary technical and call center staff. The databases include information about the retirees' seasonal living habits (for example, "Bob is in our region from December through April") and their potential for remote access for telecommuting or project work.[19]

One celebrated program is run by pharmacy retailer CVS. Its "Talent is Ageless" program, formally launched in 2003, recruits mature workers from local workforce agencies using CVS filters. Training for new mature workers takes into consideration their hopes for their career with CVS and identifies the experiences and skills that they have gained through prior employment. Flexible work preferences and availabilities are also worked out during the orientation and training. CVS also broke down some elements of its technical training into smaller steps to make it more easily absorbed by applicants and new employees who were unfamiliar with the spectrum of technology used in the job application process and store operations. By welcoming mature workers, CVS has built up its pipeline of hard-to-fill positions, such as pharmacy technician slots that are filled by retrained workers with prior experience in medical fields.[20]

Experts on loan. A number of professional firms offer short-term loans of experts and managers to community groups and even to small suppliers. Ernst & Young, for instance, offers experienced employees the chance to go on volunteer assignments through its Corporate Responsibility Fellows program. Through partnerships with a few international programs that funnel expertise, mentoring, and, in some cases, seed capital to promising businesses in developing economies, the E&Y Fellows parachute in and immerse themselves in high-stakes projects that are intended to get the businesses on a firm operational footing.[21]

Cross-generational mentoring. The needs of millennials and boomers make them a perfect workplace match. Millennials want to share their expertise in technology and to be mentored early and often. Boomers consider it a career legacy to ensure that their accumulated wisdom is embedded in the organization, and they want to keep their operational skills—including technology—sharp to the very end. Put these two groups together and you've got a perfect opportunity for the newest and oldest generations to swap skills. Employee resource groups are the perfect setting for the generations to mingle. Cisco, for example, encourages boomer executives to get to know newly arrived millennials.[22]

After discussions with CAEL, Main Line Health System created the Wise Moves pilot program, which created a new category of part-time positions for mature workers to train and mentor younger employees in both technical and "emotional intelligence" aspects of dealing with patients.[23] The employees mentor nurses, evaluate patient files, and coach employees through the intricacies of counseling patients with directions for their own care after they leave the hospital. These responsibilities can be scheduled flexibly, while the ongoing relationship allows plenty of time for staff protégés to absorb the mature employees' experience, insights, and creative problem-solving expertise.

Bridge to a New Career

When IBM found that many of its preretiree boomers fully expected to pursue second careers that were largely unrelated to their time at Big Blue, it constructed a career scaffold that reinforced its organizational commitment to education while helping preretirees achieve their goals of becoming teachers. IBM has long supported various educational ventures that support science, technology, engineering, and math (STEM) education at colleges and universities. Yet, along with many other technology employers, IBM also realizes that a lifelong pursuit of STEM careers starts in high school. Its "Transition to Teaching" program addressed all these goals. Through Transition to Teaching, IBM employees with at least 10 years' tenure can use their tuition reimbursement and earned leaves of absence to pursue STEM teaching credentials. Administration of the program was absorbed by the human resources structure and the tuition expense offset by other changes, which enabled IBM to offer Transition to Teaching to all qualified employees. The program has been successful enough that IBM is considering expanding it globally.[24]

Lattice Through Retirement

Given the ruthless arithmetic of pensions, retirement savings, and social security, many imminent retirees expect to downshift to a lower-stress job, a part-time job, or self-employment.

The Pew Research Center reports that 77 percent of baby boomers expect to continue earning in retirement, although only 12 percent of current retirees do so. Pew also reports that 16 percent of boomers believe they will never retire.[25]

Latticing while still employed full-time can give retirees a running start on their third careers. Armed with relevant skills and an up-to-date portfolio, they will be able to step from one moving sidewalk to another, maintaining their career momentum. Earning during retirement is especially important for women, who must make lower lifetime earnings stretch over a longer retirement period.[26]

Employers can provide a number of boomerang job opportunities for valued former employees.

Review and revise retirement policies and practices. A tangle of regulations, guidelines, and customary practices can trip up a company's efforts to offer retirees part-time, contingent, or consulting work. Remove logistical barriers and streamline communications so that preretirees are clear on what they will gain and what they must give up if they continue to earn. Employees need to understand how retirement earnings affect social security benefits and the mix of income that they can take from other retirement sources. Retirement income can also complicate taxes. Employee assistance providers might offer special counseling for preretirees that can help them sort through the contradictions that are sometimes invoked by continuing to earn while retired.

Create a pool of contingent workers. Include both retirees and parents who are temporarily outside the workforce. Because they are conversant with the company's practices, policies, culture, and operation, retirees can smoothly rejoin the company to fill temporary gaps and bolster staff during peak seasons.

Bring them back as consultants. This is especially important when retirees have a wealth of technical and client knowledge. Even drawing them back to help a new team get acclimated to a complex project can save full-time staff members time, effort, and distress. Just-in-time training, coaching, and mentoring can extend the payback from the company's investment in a high-performing former staffer. Establish clear parameters for such relationships, including nondisclosure agreements, to delineate the new working relationship.

Source from retirees' small businesses. Entrepreneurial boomers can provide you with a reliable stream of goods and services, and can help the company meet its goals for diverse suppliers. Federal contractors and subcontractors are subject to supplier diversity audits by the Office of Federal Contract Compliance. A few companies have stayed ahead of those demands by providing internal networking that enables entrepreneurial-minded preretirees to get set up with purchasing and supplier diversity staff in advance of their departure.

Train throughout the transition. Include entrepreneurial training and resources as part of the company's financial advisory services and retirement transition programs. Hold workshops with local economic development and small business resource organizations. Host mixers and networking events with local small business suppliers so that retirees can meet small business owners who are already working with the company.

Building a Nest on the Lattice

Tech tools that keep Grandma happy and safe at home? Aging-in-place technologies are an emerging category, and analyst Laurie Orlov knows all about them. In fact, she's practically the only industry analyst who pulls together data and trends about software, services, and gear that make it easier for adult children and medical professionals to help seniors continue to live independently.[27]

She latticed from a high-profile analyst position at Forrester Research to creating and owning the aging-in-place niche on the strength of her content knowledge and her client management skills. Orlov turned her Forrester coattails into a magic carpet that gained her credibility with potential clients. Even so, her apparently seamless transition took several years to gain altitude. "You can't just create a market and expect people to pay attention. Marketing is job one," she says. "Top-drawer communication skills are essential to latticing to a new career. Visibility is hard to get in a crowded universe."

Considering the kind of last lattice typical of many knowledge workers, Orlov wondered if she could translate her 9 years as a Forrester analyst and her prior 24 years as an information technology professional to self-employment. She discovered the eldercare market through her experience in caring for her own mother. Relentless demographic trends will drive the need for aging-in-place supports regardless of the economy, she believes.

Orlov first set up her transition by making sure she was not conflicting with Forrester's plans or infringing on her relationships with its clients. Though she networked with experts and mined LinkedIn, it took her nearly a year to gain paying clients and paying speaking gigs. She priced her services below the rack rate charged by her former employer and similar white-shoe consulting firms. And she structured her workflow and policies to make sure she could make the most of her newfound independence. She has time for water aerobics every day, is accompanied by her husband on her numerous client trips, and has a full roster of speaking gigs—as full, that is, as she wants that roster to be.

The key to her last career switch was to get in early on a market that hadn't quite realized that it was a market. Orlov got there first, staked out her ground, and paced herself for the long haul. In 2008, when she started, "the whole age wave thing had not taken off," she says. "It hadn't caught the imagination of vendors. That's changing now."

Your Last Lattice

It's heartbreaking to read stories of baby boomers who were laid off on the cusp of retirement, after decades with their employers. Forced out of their comfortable jobs, unsure of how to pursue a retirement career, and dismayed at their out-of-touch skills, these reluctant retirees must forge through harsh market realities if they are to regain career relevance.

Whether they jumped or were pushed from corporate life, more and more mid- and late-career adults are striking out on their own. Nearly 23 percent of new entrepreneurs were between the ages of 55 and 64 in 2010, according to the Ewing Marion Kauffman Foundation's Index of Entrepreneurial Activity, up from 14½ percent in 1996.[28]

Latticing into and through retirement minimizes the chances that this will be your scenario. By continuing to sharpen and refresh your skills right up to the moment you officially exit, not only will you decrease your risk of layoff, but you will also be better prepared to shift gears if an economic convulsion rocks you from your position. Lattice to keep growing in whatever position you are in so that you are not perceived as just watching the clock until you hit key retirement transition milestones, such as vesting in certain types of retirement plans. These strategies for individuals will give you tactics for latticing to the last.

Put the pro in nonprofit. Many boomers hope to bless nonprofits with their business acumen, creating a part-time or full-time retirement job that pays them to "give back." Erratic investment income is likely to limit the number of paying jobs that nonprofits can offer, but one thing is for sure: a job that more than pays for itself is secure.

Take a cue from the classic executive transition model of directing the foundation or nonprofit affiliated with your company, industry, or related community group. Several years before you expect to retire, get involved with the group as an ambassador or loaned executive from your company. Use your involvement on the corporate foundation committee to gain key skills and experience that you can use once you have latticed out. For example, get involved with vetting grant applications and writing reports to learn how to shape a winning funding proposal. Take advantage of leadership training for nonprofits while your employer is paying for it. Establish a track record of conceiving and executing fund-raising and operations strategy. Gain operating experience by working on budgets, acting as a liaison with projects supported by the foundation, and filling in the last chinks in your skills and experience. Use your rising profile with the company-affiliated nonprofit to daisy-chain onto the boards of other organizations that you want to be involved in during retirement.

Get sold on marketing. Many internal staff positions are insulated from marketing and sales. Marketing is the art of gaining awareness of your product or service among consumers. Sales is the craft of winning a transaction from a customer. You are not in business for yourself until you are getting paid for what you do. If you intend to become an entrepreneur of any sort, and you have little or no sales and marketing experience, use your last lattice to gain those skills. Get in on the start-up or relaunch of a new product so that you can be involved in the entire process of conceiving, prototyping, and testing a product, as well as identifying the market niche, pricing, testing, positioning, messaging, and launching. The biggest shock to neophyte entrepreneurs is that nearly half their time is taken up by marketing, sales, and customer service. Absorb that shock while you are part of a team so that you can get right to it when you are on your own.

Network with supplier diversity staff and organizations. Many companies try to buy from firms owned by women and minorities, on the theory that those customer populations should benefit as suppliers, too. This is especially true for companies with federal contracts or subcontracts. The Obama administration has strengthened accountability for supplier diversity through the Office of Federal Contract Compliance. By starting your small business before you retire, you have an inside track in introducing yourself and your new venture to the members of your company's supplier diversity and purchasing staff. Internal rules might prohibit them from buying from your company until you separate, but it is much easier to establish the relationship before you go than it is to try to get their attention from the outside.

Ramp up your consulting skills. By taking temporary assignments, mentoring, and otherwise becoming an internal consultant, you can start to build a scaffold for an independent consulting practice. Formulate and practice an "elevator pitch" that crystallizes your expertise, and use that to introduce yourself to new internal clients. Create a portfolio of projects and documented results. Master the technology you need in order to communicate with clients from anywhere (because soon, that "anywhere" will be at home or on the road). In other words, treat your internal consulting clients just like external clients.

Calculating the ROI of Mature Worker Initiatives

Based on the experiences of several corporate clients, CAEL developed the following list of questions that businesses can use to consider the return on investment of potential initiatives.[29]

Value Proposition

► To what extent can strategic business challenges be reasonably addressed through an older-worker initiative?
► How would an older-worker initiative benefit our employees?
► Are the expected benefits limited to older workers only, or would they affect all employees?
► How would such an initiative benefit our customers?
► Would fostering a reputation for corporate citizenship translate into increased customer satisfaction?

Employee Interest Level

► Are our employees interested in older-worker initiatives?
► What percentage of employees would be eligible to take part?
► How many employees would decide to participate?

Operations

► What staffing is needed to implement such a program?
► How much would an older-worker initiative cost?
► Do we have senior management support for an older-worker initiative?
► Are there alternative resources that could be diverted?
► What are the relevant legal and regulatory concerns?
► Are there external factors that could alter the expected benefits?

Future Outlook

► How will the demographic composition of the workforce change in the future?
► What effect will demographic shifts have on access to talent?
► How might demographic changes affect the company's strategic goals?

Legal and Regulatory Considerations

► Pension, healthcare, retirement, and age discrimination laws and regulations can dictate the specifics of programs intended to help employees lattice to retirement.

▶ Consider offering some form of benefits, perhaps on a scaled arrangement, as an incentive to encourage highly productive preretirees to take full advantage of lattice programs.

▶ Regulations vary, but financial planning services are highly valued by employees who are close to retirement.

▶ Some employee counseling services include access to financial counselors, financial advisors, and tools that help preretirees assess the financial effect of continuing to work full or part time.

In addition, a variety of regulations have implications for older-worker programs. Often, companies have to pay attention to the numerous regulations related to pension, healthcare, retirement, and age discrimination that can influence older workers' ability and willingness to work. IRS tax laws currently restrict workers' options for partial retirement, although some important changes have been proposed. Company policies can also pose barriers. For example, one pilot program that targeted people who had already retired had to comply with company policies mandating limits on the number of hours that older employees could work while maintaining both health and retirement benefits.

Lessons of the Lattice

▶ Baby boomers can't afford to retire, and employers can't afford to let them leave without latticing.

▶ Employers can continue to recoup their investment in boomers by creating an "inner circle" of seasonal and consulting positions that draw on ready and willing retirees as needed.

▶ Mutually productive late-stage lattice programs enable near-retirees to learn the skills they need for a retirement career, such as business development and nonprofit involvement, while deploying these employees as internal consultants, trainers, and mentors.

Appendix A

LATTICE AN INTERVIEW

When Job Hunting

Research your interviewer in advance. In reviewing your interviewer's career path and résumé, you might detect key lateral moves or a nontraditional career direction. If these experiences parallel your own, you can link your career progression to his to frame your lateral success story. (Don't overdo it, lest you appear to be a stalker.)

Research the organization. Showcase your awareness of the challenges and growth trajectory of the organization and its industry. Be ready with ideas on how your lateral experience relates to potential new streams of revenue or morphing business plans. Ask about career advancement programs and employee resource groups that foster lateral moves.

What kind of job is it? Employers hire for one of three reasons, according to HR guru Paul Falcone: to increase revenues, to decrease expenses, or to save time. Which one matches the job you are applying for? How does that compare with your past work experience and the lateral moves you want to highlight in this interview?

Less is more. Develop a 30-second summary of the results you achieved through latticing. If you spend too much time trying to justify a lateral move, you might sound defensive. Be sure to present your experience and results for both lateral and upward moves.

Qualifications matter. If you are in the process of earning a certification or validating existing skills that are relevant to the open position, say so. Otherwise, do not bring up a skills gap unless the interviewer does. Clearly she felt that you deserved a second look; you got an interview. Most important, have a plan for acquiring any missing credentials, and make sure you understand why these credentials are required for this job.

Focus on work challenges, not personal ones. Even if your original impetus for a lateral move was to allow for caretaking or a health crisis, this information is irrelevant—and possibly illegal. (Interviewers prefer that you not mention such factors; help them keep their questions within legal bounds.) Emphasize your skill set, your recent results, and the value added of your recent training, and match your personal case studies and stories to the job description.

Point to the bottom line. Quantify how you increased revenues or decreased costs in the positions you've held. Segue from that to a discussion of how you expect your newly acquired lateral experience to deliver a return no matter where you work.

Know your story. Don't speak in generalities. Use examples to explain your strengths and weaknesses. When you look at your résumé, summon up the places and times of your past in vivid color, and try to remember anecdotes that portray the best and the worst of your experiences. Then, use the examples to tell your lateral success story within the overall storyline of your career.

Preview the expectations. Ask what you would need to do in the position to help your new boss earn a stellar performance rating next year. If the hiring manager is vague, mention any potential company problems that your preinterview research revealed. You might also press for specific sales targets or other quantifiable measures of productivity that the manager is graded on. This will give you an opening to discuss the ways in which you believe you can contribute to the bottom line based on your research of the industry.

Outline your sequel. Know the different directions you could trellis to on the lattice if you do achieve the new position. If this doesn't come up in the interview, inquire why the position is open. Was the previous worker either promoted or given a lateral move to build his skills? What kinds of talent development opportunities does the company provide? Keep it low-key; presumably you have much to learn at the new job first. And, your future aspirations should have a direct relationship with the business goals of the company you want to join.

Request feedback before you leave. At the end of the interview, ask directly whether the interviewer has any concerns about your background and experience based on the information that came up in the interview. The interviewer will not bring up any personal issues (which is illegal); therefore, her response will be related to your professional qualifications. This gives you the opportunity to listen carefully to the skill set parameters that the hiring manager is seeking, and hopefully opens a chance for you to respond, right then and there, to any misconceptions about your skill set.

When Hiring

Go ahead and ask about résumé gaps. Candidates who have thought through their career histories and are ready to share their story with you will not be flummoxed by this question. In fact, they should be prepared for it. If the response has only a tangential reference to the job you are hiring for, probe for more information. (And, if the job applicant does not appear to be prepared for this question, that's a useful indicator, too.)

Know your bottom line. Some of the qualifications listed in a posting are essential for success in that job. Others are not. For a job candidate who is making a lateral move or is seeking to apply new skills in a new career path, be clear about what credentials are required. If his résumé landed him the interview, but it is clear that his skills are not yet solid enough to make it likely that he will succeed, be honest. At the same time, if the interview was positive, you might invite the candidate to stay in touch as he continues building his credentials. And, if he is an internal candidate, brainstorm ways to help him achieve his career aspirations.

A day in the life. Ask the candidate to walk you through a day on her current job. See how the routine matches the job description on the résumé. Listen carefully for problem-solving situations, the amount of independent work allowed, and collaboration with other staff members. If necessary, ask about these things, including how much supervision the candidate feels is optimal for success. Lateral moves are not an escape from current responsibilities, but an opportunity to grow in a new direction. You don't want to transplant a hothouse flower.

Ask for a tutorial. Very few jobs consist of individuals working alone on stand-alone projects. To find out how the person might work with direct reports, ask him to teach you to perform a skill listed on his résumé. Notice how he breaks the task into steps and his awareness of potential misunderstandings as he teaches. This will help you assess both his mastery of the task and his enthusiasm for teaching.

Go outside the box. Sometimes, candidates seem to have all the answers. To pop her bubble without a direct attack, ask about a more technical part of the business that is outside the parameters of the job description. See how she deals with ambiguity, and if she is interested in how the many parts of the business fit together. Does she ask intelligent questions? Or does she just get flustered?

Consider coworkers. Even if you are wowed by the candidate and are inclined to make an offer, consider the context of the hire. Are the other employees in this department capable of helping the candidate solidify his new skills? Are they patient with newcomers? Do they enjoy mentoring and cross training? If yes, great! If the answer is no, however, you might ask about the candidate's "lattice crew" (see Chapter 2). Who has been instrumental in helping the candidate make career decisions? How does he expect to solidify his new skill set?

Taking risks. Risk takers are more likely to be successful than the risk-averse. If a candidate is touting a lateral move or a new skill set, ask for an example of a time when she took a risk on the job, and what happened. If the candidate shares a success story, be sure to probe about what she would have done if the risk had ended in failure. After all, mistakes are opportunities to learn, right?

Ask for a wider range of references. Instead of former supervisors, ask for the names of former colleagues, clients, or direct reports. You could even press for persons who were associated with the candidate a decade ago. Positive peer networks indicate that the candidate is a team player and celebrates the success of others. If the candidate has a hard time coming up with any former colleagues who would recommend him, that is an interesting fact in itself. Alternatively, you might ask the candidate to tell you about a former supervisor or coworker whom he would not want you to contact as a reference. What would that person say? Is the criticism fair?

—Kristen West McGuire

Appendix B

LATTICE BEST PRACTICES

Lattice Best Practices by Employer

Aetna: An employee resource group (ERG) for millennials (EnRGY) launches a career (Chapter 5).

CAEL: Light Up Your Future is a series of entry-level lattices that rotate math-minded high school students into job shadowing and paid internships with employers in energy, steel, and other technical industries (Chapter 5).

CAEL: Map to Your Map describes how to design career lattices for your workplace or region (Chapter 3).

CAEL: Mission Verde is an economic development plan that links educational institutions, local businesses, and nonprofits in San Antonio, Texas, to create jobs and demand for green technologies (Chapter 1). Partners include:

Alamo Colleges' Green Job Training Institute
Solar San Antonio
Texas Technology Development Center
Build San Antonio Green

CAEL: A Personal Portfolio helps you inventory your skills and accomplishments (Chapter 2).

CAEL: The Supervisor Toolkit program trains new managers (Chapter 6).

Chubb & Son Insurance: The company's ERGs directly support talent development and structured lateral rotations (Chapter 2).

Cisco: An ERG for older workers encourages legacy leadership (Chapter 10).

Cornell University: The Rotational Assignment Program helps employees gain adjacent skills and try new jobs on a short-term basis (Chapter 8).

Cox Communications: The Executives on Demand Program tracks retirement-age workers and deploys them for short-term assignments (Chapter 10).

CVS Pharmacy: Talent Is Ageless is a program that recruits mature workers (Chapter 10).

Discovery Communications: MentorNet is a structured temporary rotation program that originated in a Discovery ERG (Chapter 8).

Ernst & Young: The Corporate Fellows Program promotes corporate social responsibility (Chapter 10).

Evangelical Lutheran Good Samaritan Society: Growing Our Own is the society's career lattice (Chapter 3).

Ford Motor Company: The company provides an example of successful job sharing (Chapter 8).

Hood & Strong, LLC: The firm involves its young associates in nonprofit community service (Chapter 4).

IBM: Through Transition to Teaching, preretirees achieve their goals of becoming teachers (Chapter 10).

Indiana University: Career navigators help mature workers retrain for encore careers (Chapter 10).

Inforum Center for Leadership: NextUp provides training, coaching, and networking to young women in Michigan (Chapter 5).

Jones & Roth CPAs and Business Advisors: Coaches for Everyone is the firm's employee development program (Chapter 3).

LinkedIn and PricewaterhouseCoopers: The two teamed to develop Career Explorer, which lets college students map career options in a range of industries based on their majors—any majors (Chapter 5).

Main Line Health System: The Wise Moves program provides bridge jobs for mature workers (Chapter 10).

Montgomery County Public School System: The system offers an education career lattice and lead teacher certification (Chapter 1).

Moss Adams, LLP: Forum_W supports women's careers (Chapter 5).

National Coalition for Telecommunications Education and Learning (NACTEL): VIVID Future (VIVIDfuture.org) is an online career-mapping site (Chapter 3).

Pennsylvania Keys to Quality Childcare Career Lattice: a career lattice for childcare workers in Pennsylvania (Chapter 3).

Thrivent Financial: The Career GPS program is a latticed talent development tool (Chapter 6).

Turner Broadcasting: The KEYS (Knowledge Energizing Your Success) program is an internal business plan competition run by the company's senior women's network (Chapter 4).

VocationVacations: This firm provides short working vacations that offer immersion in an entrepreneurial venture (Chapter 9).

Lattice Best Practices by Type

Career Mapping/Lattice

CAEL: Map to Your Map describes how to design career lattices for your workplace or region (Chapter 3).

CAEL: Mission Verde is an economic development plan that links educational institutions, local businesses, and nonprofits in San Antonio, Texas, to create jobs and demand for green technologies (Chapter 1). Partners include:

Alamo Colleges' Green Job Training Institute

Solar San Antonio

Texas Technology Development Center

Build San Antonio Green

Evangelical Lutheran Good Samaritan Society: Growing Our Own is the society's career lattice (Chapter 3).

LinkedIn and PricewaterhouseCoopers: The two teamed to develop Career Explorer, which lets college students map career options in a range of industries based on their majors—any majors (Chapter 5).

Montgomery County Public School System: The system offers an education career lattice and lead teacher certification (Chapter 1).

National Coalition for Telecommunications Education and Learning (NACTEL): VIVID Future (VIVIDfuture.org) is an online career-mapping site (Chapter 3).

Pennsylvania Keys to Quality Childcare Career Lattice: a career lattice for childcare workers in Pennsylvania (Chapter 3).

Thrivent Financial: The Career GPS program is a latticed talent development tool (Chapter 6).

Employee Resource Groups

Aetna: An ERG for millennials (EnRGY) launches a career (Chapter 5).

Chubb & Son Insurance: The company's ERGs directly support talent development and structured lateral rotations (Chapter 2).

Cisco: An ERG for older workers encourages legacy leadership (Chapter 10).

Discovery Communications: MentorNet is a structured temporary rotation program that originated in a Discovery ERG (Chapter 8).

Moss Adams, LLP: Forum_W supports women's careers (Chapter 5).

Turner Broadcasting: The KEYS (Knowledge Energizing Your Success) program is an internal business plan competition run by the company's senior women's network (Chapter 4).

NOTES

Chapter 1

1. Andrew Madison, telephone interview with the author, October 18, 2011.
2. See Frieda Reitman and Joy Schneer, "Enabling the New Careers of the 21st Century," *Organization Management Journal*, vol. 5, 2008, pp. 17–28; and Nancy M. Carter and Christine Silva, *Opportunity or Setback? High Potential Women and Men During Economic Crisis* (New York: Catalyst, 2010), p. 3.
3. Henry DeVries, telephone interview with the author, July 27, 2011.
4. Anthony Carnevale, Nicole Smith, and Jeff Strohl, *Help Wanted: Projections of Jobs and Education Requirements Through 2018* (Washington, DC: Georgetown University Center on Education and the Workforce, 2010), p. 13.
5. James Manyika et al., *An Economy That Works: Job Creation and America's Future* (Boston: McKinsey Global Institute, June 2011), p. 6.
6. Paul Taylor et al., *Is College Worth It?* (Pew Research Center in association with *Chronicle of Higher Education*, May 15, 2011), p. 76.
7. Thomas Friedman, "The New Untouchables," *New York Times*, October 20, 2009.
8. Norbert Büning et al. "Solving the Skills Crisis" in *Accenture Outlook*, 2011, No. 3) http://newsroom.accenture.com/news/accenture-study -finds-us-workers-under-pressure-to-improve-skills-need-more-support -from-employers.htm.
9. Society for Human Resources Management, *2011 Employee Benefits* (Washington, DC: SHRM, 2011), p. 51.
10. Lowell Bryan, "Strategy and Leadership in Turbulent Times," *McKinsey Quarterly* (first quarter, 2010), p. 6.
11. Carnevale et al., *Help Wanted*, p. 16.
12. WorldatWork in conjunction with Towers Watson, "Creating a Sustainable Rewards and Talent Management Model Results of the 2010 Global Talent Management and Rewards Survey," 2010, p. 2.

13. Ibid., p. 5.

14. Ibid., p. 6.

15. Ibid., p. 8.

16. Mercer Consulting, "Inside Employees' Minds: Navigating the New Rules of Engagement," June 2011, p. 2.

17. Fran Dory, *Career Ladders and Lattices* (New York: CUNY and Queens College Career Opportunities Program, 1975), p. 2.

18. Montgomery County Public Schools in conjunction with the Maryland County Education Association, "Career Lattice Design Team Report" (Montgomery County, Maryland, 2007), pp. 3–4.

19. Harris Interactive in conjunction with CareerBuilder, August 2011; www.careerbuilder.com.

20. Towers Watson, "The New Employment Deal: How Far, How Fast, and How Enduring," Towers Watson Global Workforce Survey, 2010, p. 3.

21. Ibid.

22. Ibid.

23. Nancy M. Carter and Christine Silva, "Opportunity or Setback? High Potential Women and Men During Economic Crisis," *Catalyst*, (August 2009) p. 3.

24. Spherion Staffing Labor Day Workforce Study, 2010; www.spherion.com.

25. John Bridgeland, Jessica Milano, and Elyse Rosenblum, "Across the Great Divide: Perspectives of CEOs and College Presidents on America's Higher Education and Skills Gap Executive Summary," Corporate Voices for Working Families, 2011, p. 4.

26. Michael Vasquez, "Study Less—Earn More, at Least in the Beginning," *Miami Herald*, January 1, 2011.

27. Alexandra Kalev, "Cracking the Glass Cages? Restructuring and Ascriptive Inequality at Work," *American Journal of Sociology*, vol. 114, no. 6 (May 2009), p. 1592.

28. Ibid., p. 1596.

29. American Institute of Certified Public Accountants, "Annual High Net Worth Survey (2010)"; www.aicpa.com.

30. Council on Adult & Experiential Learning, "Building Green Skills—Mission Verde: A Green Jobs Program for San Antonio" (Chicago: CAEL, May 2009).

31. Anson Green, telephone interview with the author, July 28, 2011.

32. Lanny Sinkin, telephone interview with the author, August 18, 2011.

33. Randall Goldsmith, telephone interview with the author, August 9, 2011.

34. Anita Devora, telephone interview with the author, August 15, 2011.

35. W. Laurence Doxsey, telephone interview with the author, August 18, 2011.

36. Bruce Leslie, telephone interview with the author, August 17, 2011.

37. CAEL, "Building Green Skills."

38. Mac Rattan, telephone interview with the author, August 23, 2011.

Chapter 2

1. Sabrina McCoy, telephone interview with the author, July 27, 2011.

2. Henry DeVries, telephone interview with the author, July 27, 2011.

3. James Manyika et al., *Big Data: The Next Frontier for Innovation, Competition and Productivity* (Boston: McKinsey Global Institute, May 2011), p. 10.

4. Ursula Burns, telephone interview with the author, March 1998.

5. J. Xie et al., "Social Consensus Through the Influence of Committed Minorities," *Physical Review E*, vol. 84, 011130 (2011).

6. ManpowerGroup, "'Manufacturing Talent for the Human Age 2011 Talent Shortage Survey Results" (Milwaukee, WI: Manpower, 2011), p. 1.

7. Ibid., p. 2.

8. ManpowerGroup, "Silicon Valley in Transition" (Milwaukee, WI: Manpower, 2010), p. 2.

9. Cristian L. Dezso and David Gaddis Ross, "Does Female Representation in Top Management Improve Firm Performance? A Panel Data Investigation," Robert H. Smith School Research Paper No. RHS 06-104, March 9, 2011; available at SSRN: http://ssrn.com/abstract=1088182.

10. Wilson-Taylor Associates, American Society of Women Accountants, and American Woman's Society of Certified Public Accountants, "2011 Accounting MOVE Project Executive Report" (Chicago: Wilson-Taylor Associates, May 2011), p. 3.

11. Star Fischer, telephone interview with the author, August 8, 2011.

12. Council for Adult & Experiential Learning, *Employee Guide to Self-Assessment* (Chicago: CAEL, 2010), internal document.

13. David B. Williams, telephone interview with the author, September 22, 2011.

14. Nicole Brouillard, telephone interview with the author, July 27, 2011.

15. Rotem Perelmuter, telephone interview with the author, July 27, 2011.

16. Rick Marini, telephone interview with the author, August 16, 2011.

Chapter 3

1. Danielle Schaeffer, telephone interview with the author, January 27, 2012.

2. Nancy M. Carter and Christine Silva, *Opportunity or Setback? High Potential Women and Men During Economic Crisis* (New York: Catalyst, 2010).

3. Society for Human Resource Management, "Compensation and Benefits as Recruitment and Retention Tools: The Impact of the Downturn"

(Washington, DC: SHRM, 2009).

4. Council on Adult & Experiential Education, *How Career Lattices Help Solve Nursing and Other Workforce Shortages in Healthcare* (Chicago: CAEL, 2005).

5. Pamela Tate, telephone interview with the author, August 17, 2010.

6. Shawn Hulsizer, multiple telephone interviews with the author, August 2011.

7. Adapted by the author from CAEL, *How Career Lattices Help*.

8. CAEL, "The Map to Your Map," 2007.

9. Jon Nelson, telephone interview with the author, September 7, 2011.

10. Richard Hake, telephone interview with the author, August 22, 2011.

11. Lori K. Long, telephone interview with the author, September 1, 2011.

12. Jill Smart, telephone interview with the author, July 30, 2011.

13. Robert J. Vance, "Employee Engagement and Commitment," (Washington, DC: SHRM, 2006).

14. Long, telephone interview.

15. Nancy Chagares, telephone interview with the author, July 29, 2011.

16. Neal Eddy, telephone interview with the author, August 18, 2011.

17. CAEL, *How Career Lattices Help*.

18. Sonia Bury, telephone interview with the author, August 18, 2011.

19. Kelly Vig, telephone interview with the author, August 24, 2011.

20. Chagares, telephone interview.

21. Tricia Duncan, telephone interviews with the author, March 14, 2009 and February 17, 2010.

22. Doug Griesel, telephone interview with the author, March 14, 2009.

23. Tricia Duncan, telephone interview with Kristen McGuire, March 10, 2011.

24. CAEL, team lattice worksheet, internal document.

Chapter 4

1. Alison Hashimoto, telephone interview with the author, July 21, 2009.

2. Council on Adult & Experiential Learning, *Fueling the Race for Postsecondary Success* (Chicago: CAEL, February 2010), p. 3.

3. Ibid., p. 2.

4. Deborah Dimon Davis, e-mail interview with the author, October 9, 2011.

5. Garriy Shteynberg and Adam D. Galinsky, "Implicit Coordination: Sharing Goals with Similar Others Intensifies Goal Pursuit," *Journal of Experimental Social Psychology*, vol. 47, no. 6 (2011), pp. 1291–1294.

6. Steve Dougherty, *Hopes and Dreams: The Story of Barack Obama* (New York: Tess Press, 2007).

7. Loren Rogers, e-mail interview with the author, October 9, 2011.

8. Myrle Croasdale, telephone interview with the author, October 8, 2011.

9. Marcia Conner, "May I Borrow Your Job?," *Fast Company*, October 3, 2006.

10. Women in Cable and Telecommunications, "The Business Impact of Gender Diversity and Related Best Practices," Path to PAR Report, Part One, December 2010, p. 12.
11. Hashimoto, telephone interview.
12. Ben Kaiser, telephone interview with the author, July 21, 2009.
13. Michele Golden, telephone interview with the author, October 10, 2011.
14. Adapted by the author from Kenneth R. Brousseau and Michael J. Driver, "Career View Concepts: Roadmaps for Career Success" (Stockholm: Decision Dynamics Group, 1998); www.decisiondynamics.us.

Chapter 5

1. Jason Smith is a pseudonym for an anonymous source, interviewed by the author on September 15, 2011.
2. Lisa B. Kahn, "The Long-Term Labor Market Consequences of Graduating from College in a Bad Economy," *Labour Economics*, vol. 17, no. 2 (2010), pp. 303–316.
3. Yahoo! HotJobs and Robert Half International, "What Millennial Workers Want: How to Attract and Retain Gen Y Employees," December 2010, p. 6.
4. CareerBuilder and Harris Interactive, October 2010; www.careerbuilder.com.
5. Johnson Controls, "Generation Y and the Workplace," Annual Report, 2010, p. 34.
6. Dale Kalika, quoted in "Not a Lost Generation, but a 'Disappointed' One: The Job Market's Impact on Millennials," January 2011; http://knowledge.wpcarey.asu.edu/article.cfm?articleid=1960.
7. Johnson Controls, p. 48.
8. Corporate Voices for Working Families, "Business Leadership: Supporting Youth Development and the Talent Pipeline" (Washington, DC: CVWF, February 2007), p. 6.
9. Council on Adult & Experiential Learning, "Moving the Starting Line through Prior Learning Assessment (PLA)" (Chicago: CAEL, 2011).
10. Accenture, "Millennial Women in the Workplace Success Index" (Dublin: Accenture, January 2010), pp. 5–7.
11. Marianne Bertrand, Claudia Goldin, and Lawrence Katz, "Dynamics of the Gender Gap for Young Professionals in the Financial and Corporate Sectors," National Bureau of Economic Research, January 2009, NBER Working Paper No. 14681.
12. Wilson-Taylor Associates, "2011 Accounting MOVE Project Executive Report" (Chicago: American Society of Women Accountants, March 2011), p. 14.
13. Tammy Young, telephone interview with the author, March 20, 2011.
14. Joe Walker, "PwC Pays for Priority on LinkedIn," *Wall Street Journal*, October 4, 2010.

15. CVWF, "Business Leadership," pp. 9–12.
16. Ibid., pp. 13–15.
17. Wallace Immen, "Generation Y: In It for the Long Haul," *Toronto Globe and Mail*, September 21, 2010.
18. Lindsey Pollak et al., *Shaping a New Future: Women Navigating Adulthood in the New Millennium*, A Report on Behalf of Levi Strauss & Co. (StrategyOne, 2011), p. 22.
19. Accenture, "Millennials at the Gates," (2008) p. 6, http://www.scribd.com/doc/12707647/New-Generation-Workers-Accenture-Research-Report-Millennials-at-the-Gates.
20. Vanessa Wilczewski, telephone interview with the author, August 9, 2011.
21. Women in Cable Telecommunications, "The Business Impact of Gender Diversity and Related Best Practices," Path to PAR Report, Part Two (Chantilly, VA: WICT, December 2010), p. 7.
22. Pamela O'Leary, telephone interview with the author, July 23, 2011.

Chapter 6

1. Jill Kaplan, telephone interview with the author, August 10, 2011.
2. Alexandra Kalev, "Cracking the Glass Cages? Restructuring and Ascriptive Inequality at Work," *American Journal of Sociology*, vol. 114, no. 6 (May 2009), p. 1592.
3. Alexandra Kalev, Frank Dobbin, and Erin Kelly, "Diversity Workforce Management Practices," *Contexts* (Fall 2007), pp. 21–27.
4. Women in Cable Telecommunications, "The Business Impact of Gender Diversity and Related Best Practices," Path to PAR Report, Part Two (Chantilly, VA: WICT, December 2010), p. 4.
5. Deborah Westfall, telephone interview with the author, September 26, 2011.
6. Barbara Foote, telephone interview with the author, July 22, 2011.
7. Dianne Blackwood, telephone interview with the author, July 29, 2009.
8. WICT, PAR Initiative Executive Report (2007), p. 10.
9. WICT, "The Business Impact," Part One, p. 8.
10. Phyllis Snyder, telephone interview with the author, August 23, 2011.

Chapter 7

1. Shellye Archambeau, telephone interview with the author, September 23, 2011.
2. Association of Executive Search Consultants, "BlueSteps 2011 Executive Mobility Report," April 2011.

3. Elizabeth Craig, John R. Kimberly, and Peter Cheese, "How to Keep Your Best Executives," *Wall Street Journal*, October 26, 2009.
4. Joann S. Lublin, "Executives Try Out Unfamiliar Roles," *Wall Street Journal*, February 22, 2011.
5. Yolande Piazza, telephone conversation with the author, October 6, 2011.
6. Corey Woods, telephone interview with the author, October 6, 2011.
7. Laure Nordholt, telephone interview with the author, October 11, 2011.
8. Kerry Hester, telephone interview with the author, October 11, 2011.
9. Alison Smith, telephone interview with the author, October 4, 2011.
10. Elise Eberwein, telephone interview with the author, October 4, 2011.
11. Erin Hand, telephone interviews with the author, July 21, 2009, and October 29, 2011.
12. Towers Watson with WorldatWork, *Leading Through Uncertain Times*, 2011 Annual Talent Management and Employee Rewards Survey, p. 2.
13. Woods, telephone interview.
14. Dan Schawbel, interview with Doug Conant, *Personal Branding*, April 2011.
15. Anonymous, interview with the author.
16. Nat Worden and Ethan Smith, "Cable, ABC Help Disney Profit Rise 18%; Two Executives Switch Jobs," *Wall Street Journal*, November 13, 2009.
17. Woods, telephone interview.
18. Nordholt, telephone interview.
19. Hester, telephone interview.
20. Woods, telephone interview.
21. Mercer, "ERGs Come of Age: The Evolution of Employee Resource Groups," A study by Mercer's Global Equality, Diversity, and Inclusion Practice, January 2011, p. 1.
22. Booz Allen Hamilton, *Keeping Talent: Strategies for Retaining Valued Federal Employees* (McLean, VA: Booz Allen Hamilton, January 2011), p. 7.
23. Joanna Barsh and Lareina Yee, "Unlocking the Full Potential of Women in the U.S. Economy," *Wall Street Journal*, April 2011.
24. Marti Barletta, Presentation at PINK Conference (Chicago, IL: October 13, 2009).
25. Benita Fitzgerald Mosley, telephone interview with the author, October 13, 2011.

Chapter 8

1. Melissa Randall, interview with the author, July 29, 2011.
2. Cali Yost et al., "Changing the Career Ladder: Paving Flexible Pathways for Today's Talent" (Aquent, Tuck School of Business, and Work + Life Fit, May 2007), p. 4.
3. Ibid., p. 5.
4. Cathy Benko and Molly Anderson, *The Corporate Lattice* (Boston: Harvard Business Review Press, 2010), p. 136.

5. Sylvia Ann Hewlett, Lauren Leader-Chivee et al., *The X Factor: Tapping into the Strengths of the 33- to 46-Year-Old Generation* (New York: Center for Work-Life Policy, September 2011), p. 8.

6. Till von Wachter, Jae Song, and Joyce Manchester, "Long-Term Earnings Losses due to Mass Layoffs During the 1982 Recession: An Analysis Using U.S. Administrative Data from 1974 to 2004," *American Economic Review*

7. ManpowerGroup, "'Manufacturing' Talent for the Human Age 2011 Talent Shortage Survey" (Milwaukee, WI: ManpowerGroup, 2011), p. 1.

8. Hewlett, Leader-Chivee et al., *The X Factor*, p. 10.

9. Ibid., p. 2.

10. Society for Human Resources Management, 2011 Employee Benefits Study (Washington, DC: SHRM, 2011), p. 5.

11. Maria Wolff, telephone interview with the author, August 18, 2011.

12. Lois Joy et al., *The Bottom Line: Corporate Performance and Women's Representation on Boards* (New York: Catalyst, October 2007), p. 6.

13. Corporate Leadership Council, *Fostering Women's Leadership* (February 2004).

14. http://www.youtube.com/watch?v=18uDutylDa4.

15. Wilson-Taylor Associates, American Society of Women Accountants and the American Woman's Society of Certified Public Accountants, "2011 Accounting MOVE Project Executive Report" (Chicago:Wilson-Taylor Associates, March 2011), p. 13.

16. Sylvia Ann Hewlett et al., "Off-Ramps and On-Ramps Revisited," *Harvard Business Review*, June 1, 2010, p. 2.

17. http://www.catalyst.org/publication/132/us-women-in-business.

18. Wilson-Taylor Associates, "2011 Accounting MOVE Project," p. 8.

19. Sue Shellenbarger, "Why Women Rarely Leave Middle Management," *Wall Street Journal*, April 10, 2011.

20. Teresa Amabile and Steven J. Kramer, "The Power of Small Wins," *Harvard Business Review*, May 2011.

21. Evelyne Steward, telephone interview with the author, October 24, 2011.

22. Jessica Banks Poawui, telephone interview with the author, September 2011.

23. American Business Collaboration for Quality Dependent Care, "New Career Paradigm: Flexibility Briefing" (Newton, MA: WFD Consulting, 2007), p. 2.

24. Julie Levine and Julie Rocco, telephone interview with the author, September 10, 2010.

25. Dawn S. Carlson et al., "Health and Turnover of Working Mothers After Childbirth via the Work–Family Interface: An Analysis Across Time," *Journal of Applied Psychology*, vol. 96, no. 5 (September 2011), pp. 1045–1054.

26. Wilson-Taylor Associates, "2011 Accounting MOVE Project," p. 14.

Chapter 9

1. Sari Crevin, telephone interview with the author, October 20, 2011 and e-mail December 19, 2011.
2. Sylvia Ann Hewlett, *Off-Ramps and On-Ramps: Keeping Talented Women on the Road to Success* (New York: Center for Work-Life Policy, March 2005).
3. Sylvia Ann Hewlett et al., "Off-Ramps and On-Ramps Revisited," *Harvard Business Review*, June 1, 2010.
4. Ibid.
5. Nancy M. Carter and Christine Silva, *Opportunity or Setback? High Potential Women and Men During Economic Crisis* (New York: Catalyst, 2010), p. 3.
6. Monica McGrath, Marla Driscoll, and Mary Gross, *Back in the Game: Returning to Business After a Hiatus* (Philadelphia: Wharton Center for Leadership and Change, June 2005), p. 9.
7. Cali Yost et al., "Changing the Career Ladder: Paving Flexible Pathways for Today's Talent" (Aquent, Tuck School of Business, and Work + Life Fit, May 2007), p. 4.
8. Brian Leleux, telephone interview with the author, October 5, 2011.
9. Gallup-Healthways Well-Being Index, http://www.well-beingindex.com/.
10. Yost et al., "Changing the Career Ladder," p. 5.
11. Scott Shane, *Illusions of Entrepreneurship: The Costly Myths that Entrepreneurs, Investors and Policymakers Live By*, (New Haven, CT: Yale University Press, 2008), p. 99.
12. Marilyn Lunnemann, telephone interview with the author, August 22, 2011.
13. Brian Kurth, telephone interview with the author, August 19, 2011.
14. Dermot Berkery, *Raising Venture Capital for the Serious Entrepreneur* (New York: McGraw-Hill, 2007), pp. 135–136.
15. Gavin Cassar, "The Roles of Industry and Startup Experience on Entrepreneur Forecast Performance at New Business Entry" (December 23, 2010); http://ssrn.com/abstract=1730318.
16. Jennifer Soltesz, telephone interview with the author, August 20, 2011.
17. Melissa Korn, "Boomerang Employees," *Wall Street Journal*, October 24, 2011.

Chapter 10

1. Elisabeth Schuler Russell, telephone interview with the author, August 3, 2011.
2. E. S. Browning, "Debt Hobbles Older Americans," *Wall Street Journal*, September 7, 2011.
3. *Advertising Age* (in conjunction with AARP), *50 and Over: What's Next?* (New York: Crain Communications, April 4, 2011).

4. David Rosnick and Dean Baker, "The Wealth of the Baby Boom Cohorts After the Collapse of the Housing Bubble" (Washington, DC: Center for Economic and Policy Research, February 2009), p. 1.

5. Richard W. Johnson and Corina Mommaerts, *Age Difference in Job Loss, Job Search, and Reemployment* (Washington, DC: Urban Institute, January 2011), p. 22.

6. American Institute of Certified Public Accountants, "Survey of Member CPA Financial Planners" (New York: AICPA, February 2010).

7. TNS Global, "Affluent Market Research Program" (July 2011) http://www.tnsglobal.com/news/news-39850331EAB44715960D1881A1D 1DB47.aspx.

8. Paul Taylor, Cary Funk, and Peyton Craighill, "Working After Retirement: The Gap Between Expectations and Reality" (Washington, DC: Pew Research Center, 2010), p. 1.

9. Maria Heidkamp, Nicole Corre, and Carl E. Van Horn, "The New Unemployables: Older Job Seekers Struggle to Find Work During the Great Recession" (Boston: Sloan Center on Aging and Work at Boston College, Issue Brief 25, November 2010), p. 19.

10. Barry Bluestone and Mike Melnick, "After the Recovery: Help Needed" (Boston: Michael and Kitty Dukakis Center on Urban and Regional Policy at Northeastern University, 2010), p. 5.

11. *Advertising Age, 50 and Over*, p. 7.

12. Sloan Center on Aging and Work, "Entrepreneurship and the Older Worker" (Boston: Sloan Center on Aging and Work at Boston College, Fact Sheet 26, February 2010), p. 2.

13. Bluestone and Melnick, "After the Recovery," p. 18.

14. Penn Schoen Berland, "Encore Career Choices: Purpose, Passion and a Paycheck in a Tough Economy," (San Francisco: Civic Ventures/Met Life Foundation, 2011), 3.

15. Kevin E. Cahill, Michael D. Giandrea, and Joseph F. Quinn, "Down Shifting: The Role of Bridge Jobs After Career Employment" (Boston: Sloan Center on Aging and Work at Boston College, Issue Brief 6, April 2007), p. 3.

16. Council on Adult and Experiential Learning with the Council on Competitiveness, *Developing the Workforce as It Matures* (Chicago: CAEL, 2011), p. 4.

17. Ibid., p. 7.

18. Erin Hand, telephone interview with the author, July 14, 2009.

19. Sloan Center on Aging Work at Boston College, "Talent Management and the Prism of Age" (March 2010), p. 5.

20. http://info.cvscaremark.com/careers/seniors.

21. http://www.ey.com/US/en/About-us/Corporate-Responsibility/CR---Entrepreneurs-create-jobs-and-build-communities.

22. Peggy Wolf, "Generations in the Workplace; Baby Boomers in Action" (Cisco, Lunch & Learn Webinar, April 8, 2010); www.people-on-the-go.com.

23. CAEL with The Conference Board, *Baby Boomers & the Bottom Line: How to Leverage Your Mature Workforce for Business Success* (Chicago: CAEL, 2007), p. 3.

24. Ibid., p. 4.

25. Taylor et al., "Working After Retirement," p. 8.

26. Mariko L. Chang, *Shortchanged: Why Women Have Less Wealth and What Can Be Done About It* (London: Oxford University Press, 2010), p. 10.

27. Laurie Orlov, telephone interview with the author, August 15, 2011.

28. Robert W. Fairlie, "Kauffman Index of Entrepreneurial Activity" (Kansas City, MO: Ewing Marion Kauffman Foundation, March 2011), p. 9.

29. CAEL, *Baby Boomers and the Bottom Line*, p. 6.

Index

ABOUT THE AUTHOR

Joanne Y. Cleaver has been a business journalist and communication consultant since 1981. Since 1998, her firm, Wilson-Taylor Associates, Inc., has designed and managed national research projects that measure the progress of women in the workplace. The Wilson-Taylor MOVE methodology pivots on factors proven to remove barriers so that women can fully participate in driving business results. Current and past clients include the American Society of Women Accountants/American Women's Society of CPA's, Women in Cable Telecommunications, *Pink* magazine, the Alliance for Workplace Excellence, *Working Woman* magazine, and others. Learn more about Wilson-Taylor at www.wilson-taylorassoc.com.

As a strategic communication consultant and media trainer, Cleaver is certified through MediaSkills USA, which formulated the first and only standards and credentials for this profession. Corporate clients include Rothstein Kass, Ebyline.com, and others.

A widely published writer, Cleaver's articles, essays, blog posts, and interactive features have been published by the Chicago *Tribune*, Crain's *Chicago Business*, Crain's *New York Business*, *Good Housekeeping*,

Parents, Parenting, Inc., the *Los Angeles Times,* the Chicago *Sun-Times,* Moneywatch, CBS Interactive, *Working Woman, Working Mother,* and many other publications and websites. Cleaver has been a deputy business/real estate editor at the Milwaukee *Journal Sentinel* and a senior content producer at Tribune Digital. Her six prior books focus on entrepreneurship and family travel. Read more of her work at www.jycleaver.com.